CORK HARBOUR

THROUGH TIME

Kieran McCarthy &
Daniel Breen

AMBERLEY PUBLISHING

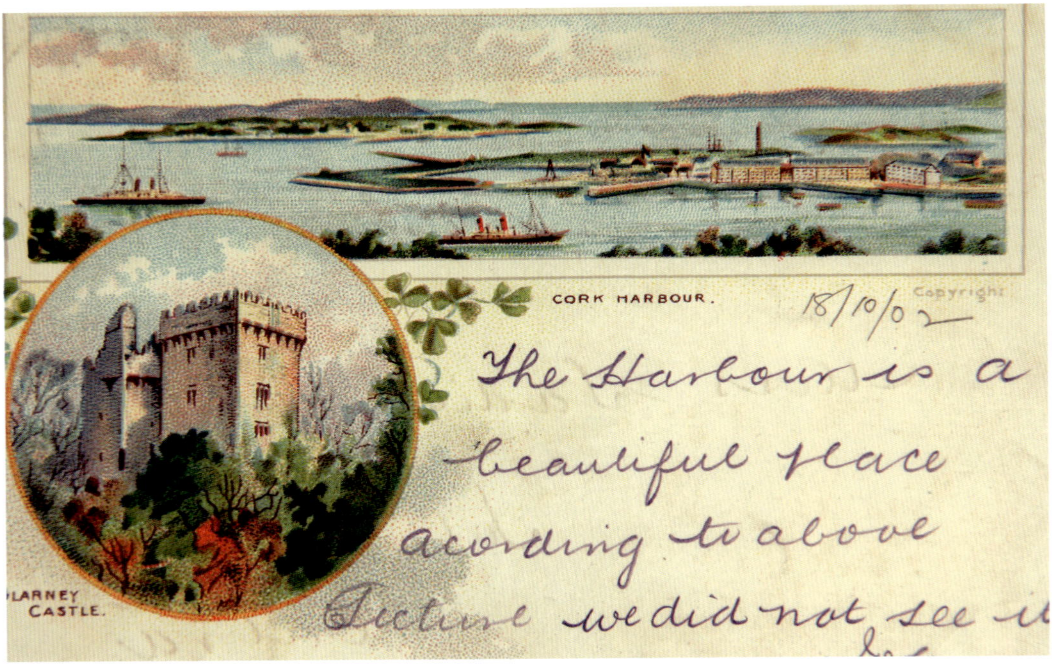

Photographed and painted in detail, Cork Harbour has been the muse of people over several centuries. At times, its heritage is like a hidden treasure trove awaiting rediscovery. This book shines a light on some of its multiple gems.

Dedicated to all those guardians of the heritage of Cork Harbour

First published 2014

Amberley Publishing
The Hill, Stroud, Gloucestershire, GL5 4EP
www.amberley-books.com

ISBN 978 1 4456 3419 7 (print)
ISBN 978 1 4456 3426 5 (ebook)

British Library Cataloguing in Publication Data.
A catalogue record for this book is available from the British Library.

Typesetting by Amberley Publishing.
Printed in the UK.

Introduction

The Edge of Memory

How do you capture a harbour in all its beauty? Being the second largest natural harbour in the world brings a focus and energy that Cork Harbour has always been open to. The ebb and flow of the tide through the ages has carved a unique landscape of cliffs, sand and gravel beaches that expose an underlining geology of limestone and sandstone. Invigorating this landscape are multiple monuments from different ages, many of which the postcards in this book seek to capture. Colourful villages provide different textures and cultural landscapes in a sort of cul-de-sac environment, with roads ending at harbours and car parks near coastal cliff faces and quaysides. The villages are scattered around the edges of the harbour, each with their own unique history, all connecting in someway to the greatness of this harbour.

Walking along several junctures of fields, one can get the feeling you are at the 'edge of memory'. There are the ruins of old structures that the tide erodes away. One gets the sense that a memory is about to get swept away by the sea, or that by walking in the footsteps trodden by photographers 100 years ago, one could get carried away by their curiosity. This book tracks the space and historical context of 100 postcards in Cork Harbour, many of which were taken *c.* 1900–20. Many of the sites have been written extensively on over centuries, while others await proper exploration and critique.

Chapter 1 begins in the city and takes the reader from Ireland's southern capital of Cork City eastwards into the River Lee's tidal estuary. This city is built on a shifting landscape of sand, gravel, rushes and reeds, a wetland knitted together to form a working port through the ages. In *Cork City Through Time* (2012), we showcased the old postcards of Cork City. Moving eastwards past the port, the river begins to spread in width, creating vast scenic vistas along areas like the Marina, extending to the late seventeenth-century structure of Blackrock Castle and beyond, to the reed beds of Lough Mahon and Douglas Estuary. All are hidden places of beauty, much of which may be explored by the amenity walk along the old Blackrock & Passage Railway Line. When the line opened in 1850, it hosted 200,000 people in the first six months. In 1903, this line was later extended to Crosshaven. The resonances of such a venture are echoed along the walkway as old platforms, ivy clad stone-arch bridges provide legacies to admire. Passage, the first terminus for the railway, was once a shipbuilding centre of the south of Ireland. Nowadays, old quaysides and eerie, abandoned warehouses haunt the area. One can almost hear the hammers and whispers of workers' repairing and patching together ocean-going ships. Further along the river, Monkstown provides insight into the past with its colourful Victorian mansions. The same can be said about the scenic wooded village of Glanmire, the iconic Father Mathew Tower and Fota House. All exist as rich storehouses of memory and are awe-inspiring to walk around at any time of the year.

Chapter 2 takes the reader on a journey through some of the landscapes on Great Island, and naturally Cobh is a central focus. Drawn through several centuries and photographed since the invention of the camera, it is difficult not to be drawn to the town's rich architectural steeple and exterior artwork on the late nineteenth-century construct of St Colman's Cathedral. Cobh has stunning scenic quay vistas and a colourful selection of buildings. The town is also known for its stories of emigration and the legendary *Titanic*. One can feel its journey across the ocean and the role the town played in its part in the North Atlantic's human history.

The sites and spaces seen from Cobh's specifically constructed building parapets are explored in Chapter 3. The harbour islands, such as Spike Island and Haulbowline, have histories dating back over 400 years. They were first fortified by star-shaped forts and secured for the expanding British Empire. Two more forts exist near the entrance to the harbour, Camden Fort Meagher and Fort Davis. Originally built in the 1780s, one can explore the town's military history and connections to a far-flung British empire through the harbour's role in securing its might and power. However, one is humbled by stories of the Irish War of Independence, and how these forts in time were secured by the Irish Government as Ireland's last lines of defence. Today, these represent large community-based tourism projects.

Chapter 4 explores the eastern shores of Cork Harbour. Here lies the great market town of Midleton, the old large malthouses of Ballincurra, the ancient tower at Cloyne, the quaint spaces within villages at Rostellan and Whitegate, and the ruins of old houses. Connect these with industrial projects such as Whitegate Oil Refinery, and family holiday centres such as Trabolgan, and all reveal rich stories. However, standing overlooking all within the harbour is the great lighthouse at Roches Point, warning ships of imposing rocks and providing a grand entrance gateway to the harbour. On a clear day, the views show a canvass of stories and memories. Together they create a diverse, rich sense of place and identity in the second largest natural harbour in the world. Enjoy!

Kieran McCarthy & Daniel Breen

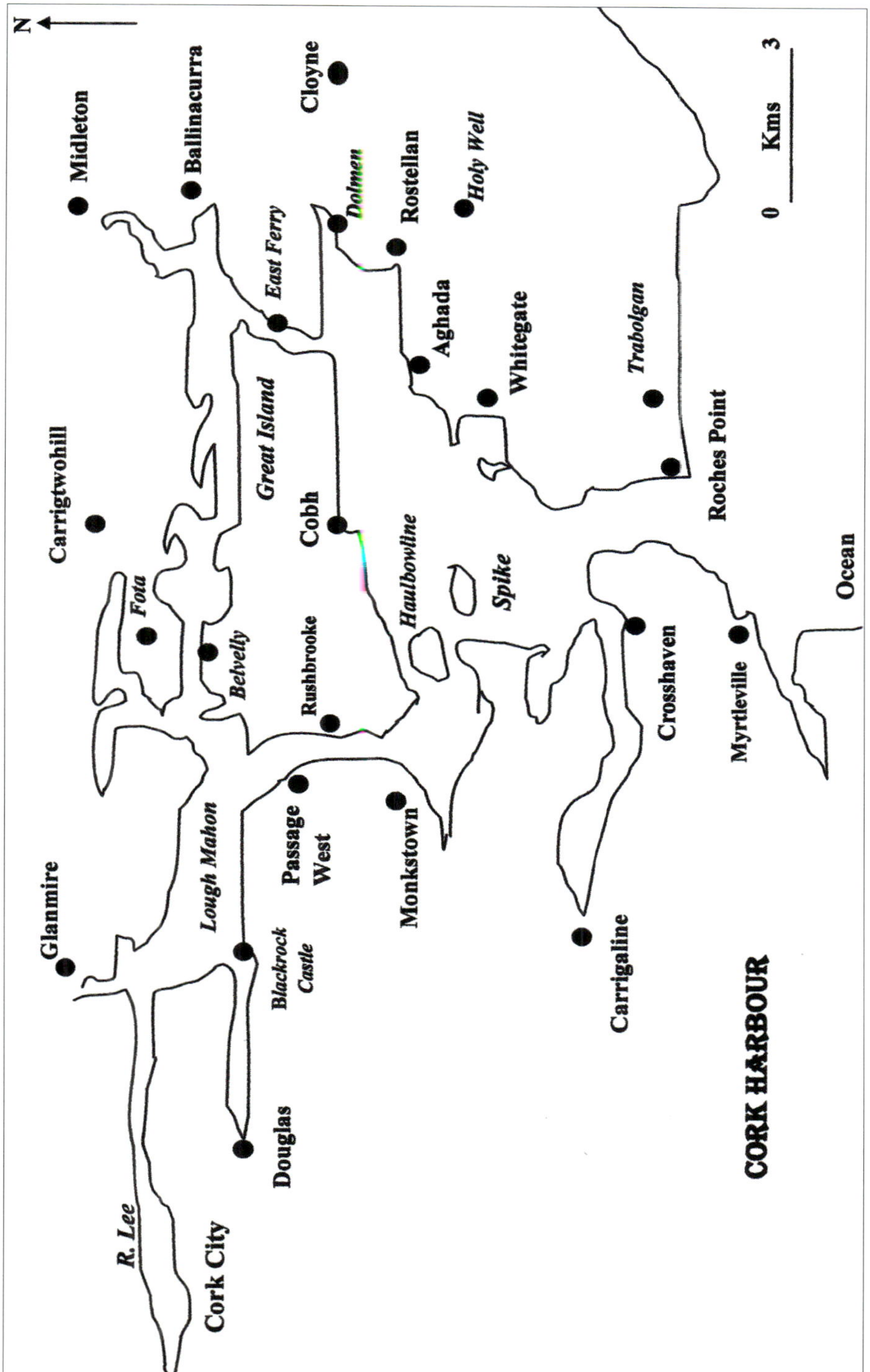
N
Midleton
Ballinacurra
Cloyne
Dolmen
Rostellan
Holy Well
East Ferry
Aghada
Whitegate
Trabolgan
Roches Point
Great Island
Cobh
Carrigtwohill
Fota
Belvelly
Rushbrooke
Haulbowline
Spike
Ocean
Crosshaven
Myrtleville
Passage West
Monkstown
Lough Mahon
Glanmire
Blackrock Castle
Carrigaline
Douglas
R. Lee
Cork City
CORK HARBOUR
0 Kms 3

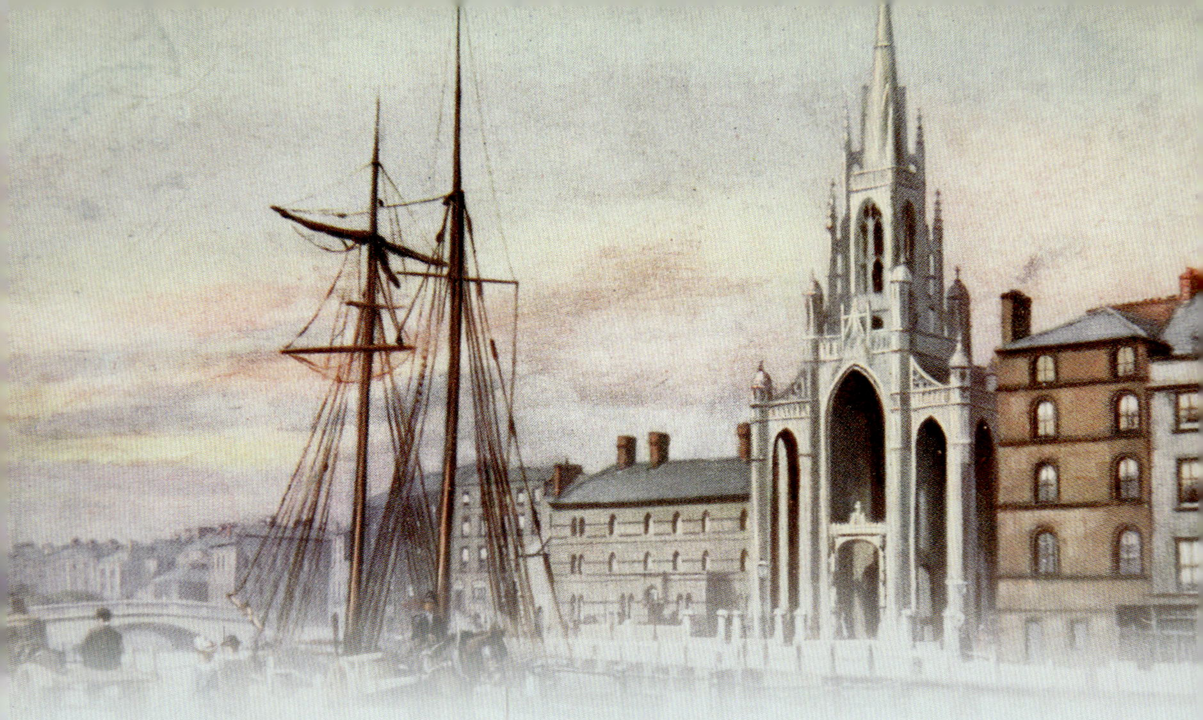

CHAPTER 1

The Inner Harbour, The Lee Estuary

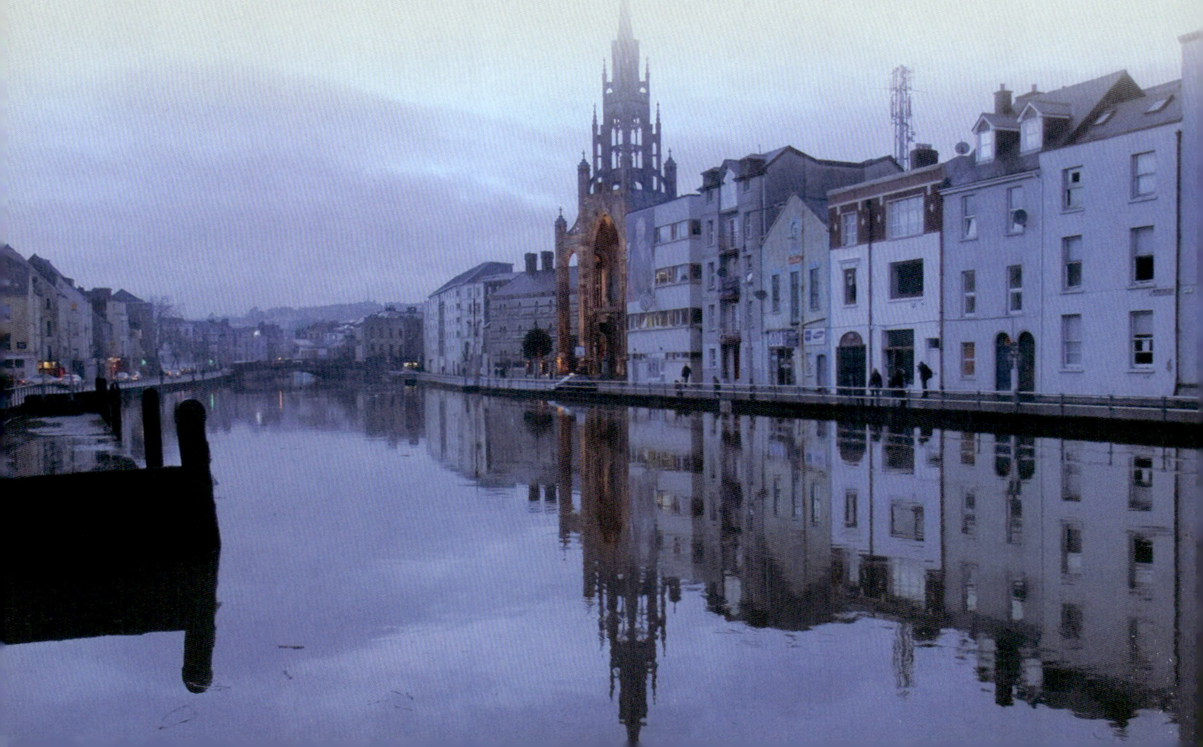

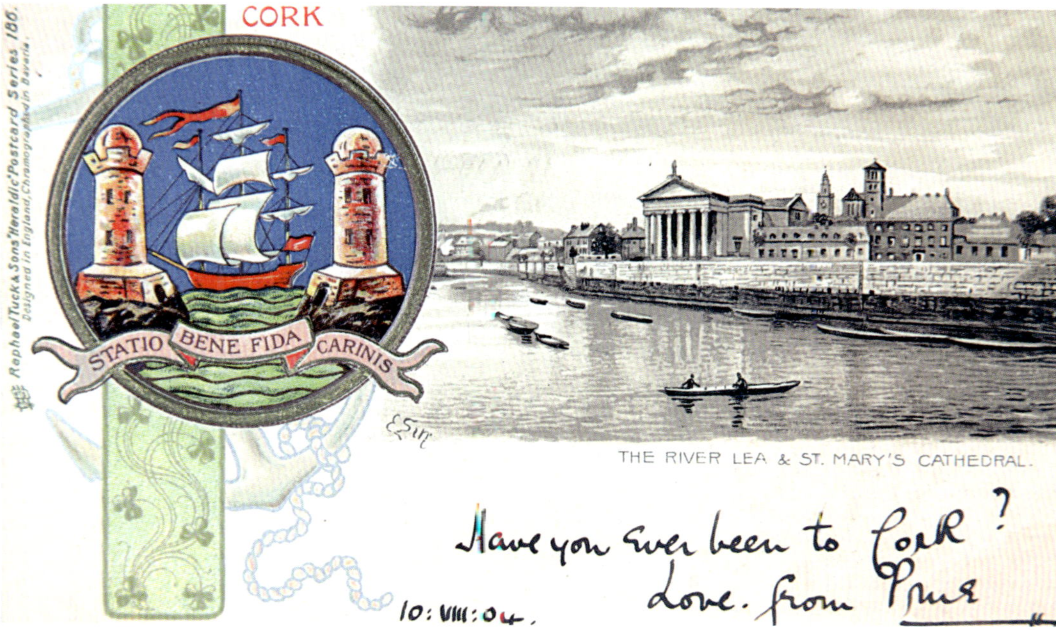

A City on a Marsh

As a city that is built at the lowest crossing point with the river Lee and the tide (a swamp to be exact), water defines the topographic character of Cork. Once an area of multiple river channels, just two survive. The north channel of the Lee boasts an abundance of beautiful scenery. As a port through the ages, the city has a myriad of architectural styles, as revealed in the two pictures above and below – St Mary's Dominican church, a neoclassical monument built in 1832. At any time of year it is impressive, but add in the changing seasons and the late nineteenth-century quay wall, and further character is added to this part of the city.

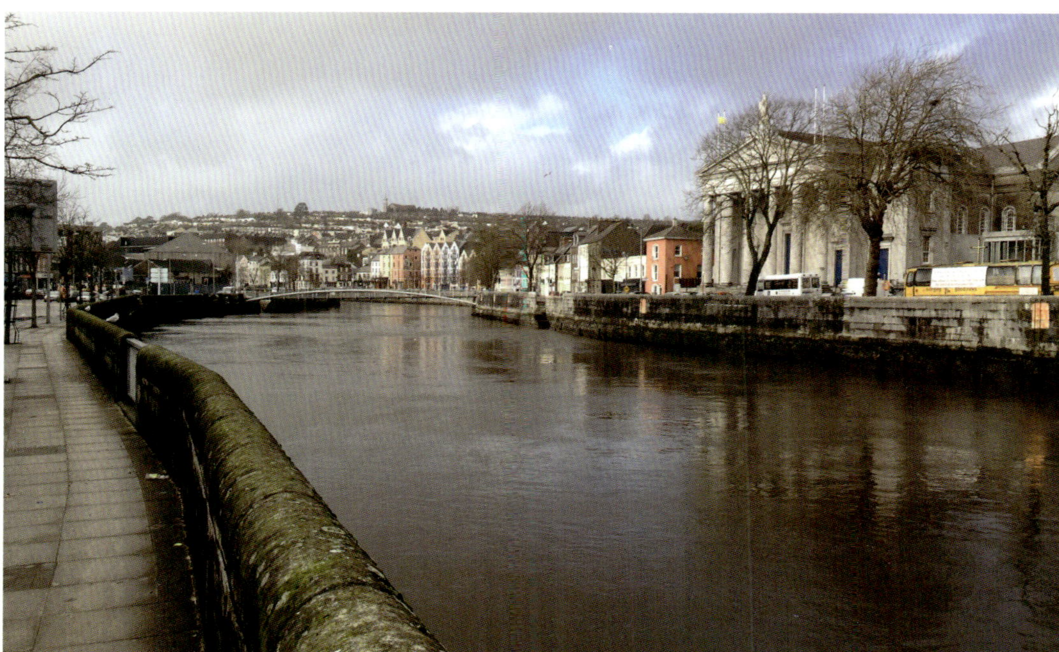

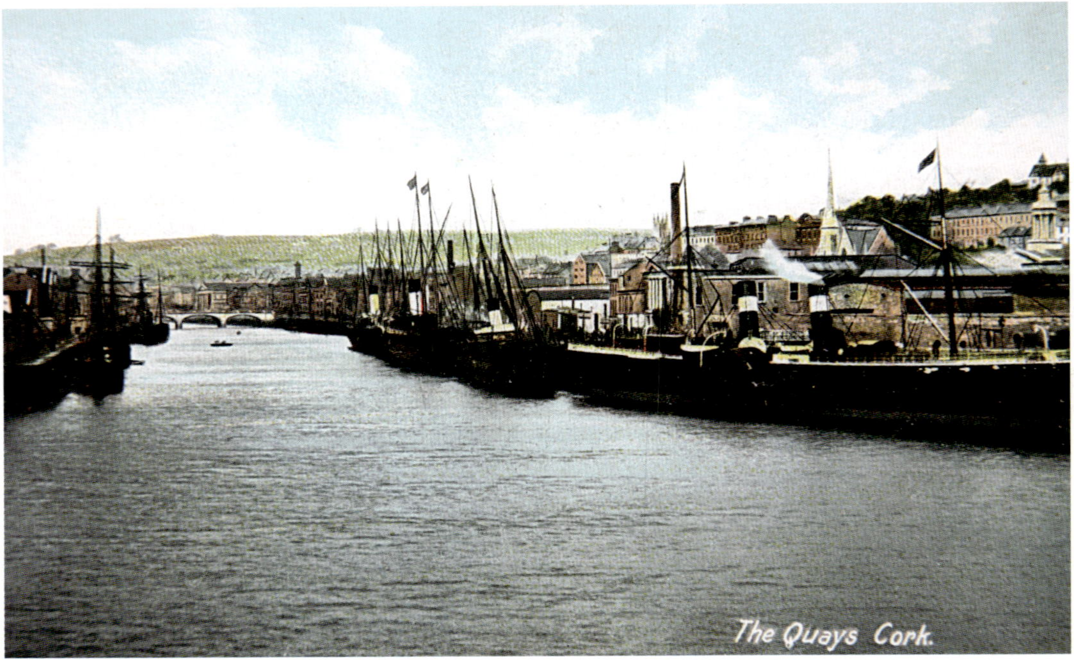

City of Trade and Experience

Dating back over 1,000 years to Viking times, from the Anglo-Norman time of a walled town to the present day, boats of all dimensions have been travelling through Cork's riverine and harbour region, continuing a legacy of trade. Port trade was the engine in Cork's development. On the right of the postcard is Penrose Quay. The quay is named after the Quaker family of Penroses, who owned manufacturing enterprises in both Waterford and Cork. These factories comprised skilled craftsmen who created fine cut-glass decanters, chandeliers and drinking glasses. The Penroses also imported timber and were involved in property development in both cities.

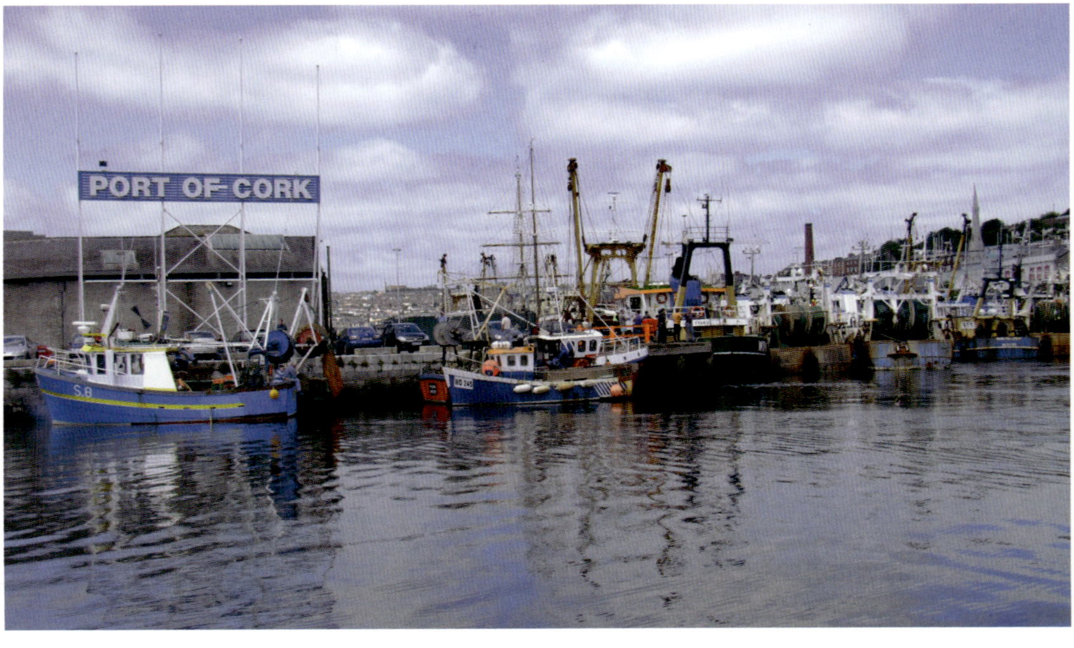

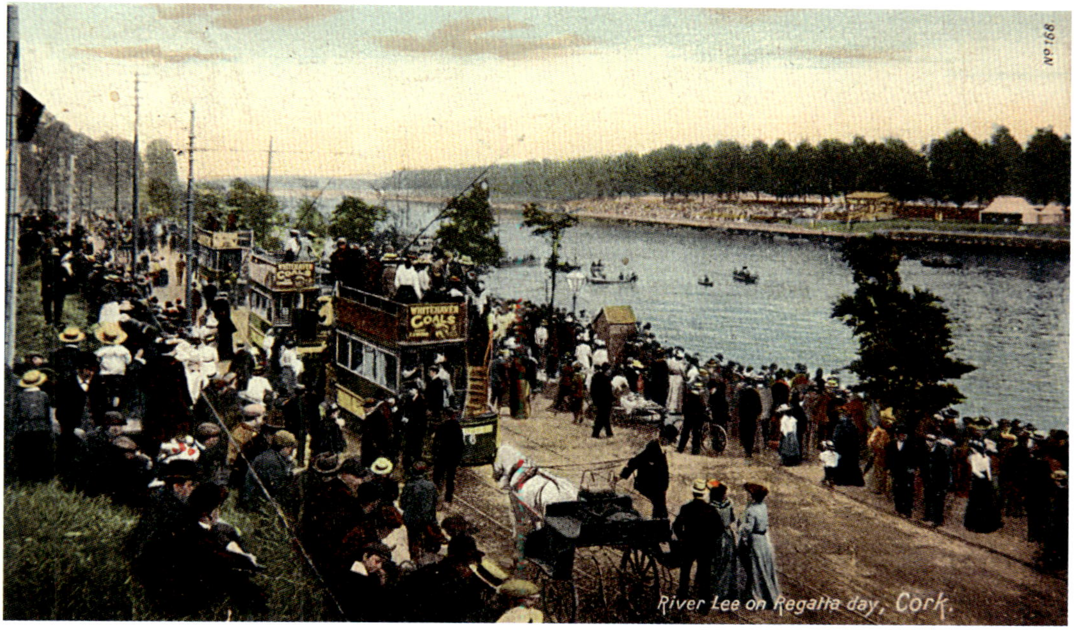

The Recreational River

Cork's marina, originally called the Navigation Wall, was completed in 1761. In 1820, Cork Harbour Commissioners formed and purchased a locally built dredger. The dredger deposited the silt from the river into wooden barges, which were then towed ashore. The silt was re-deposited behind the Navigation Wall. During the Great Famine, deepening of the river created jobs for 1,000 men who worked on creating the Navigation Wall's road – the Marina. The environs are also home to three rowing clubs – the Lee Rowing Club, founded in 1850 and the second oldest club in the country; Shandon Boat Club, founded in 1875, and Cork Boat Club, founded in 1899 by members of Dolphin Swimming Club – all of which ply the waters of the river regularly and hold annual regattas.

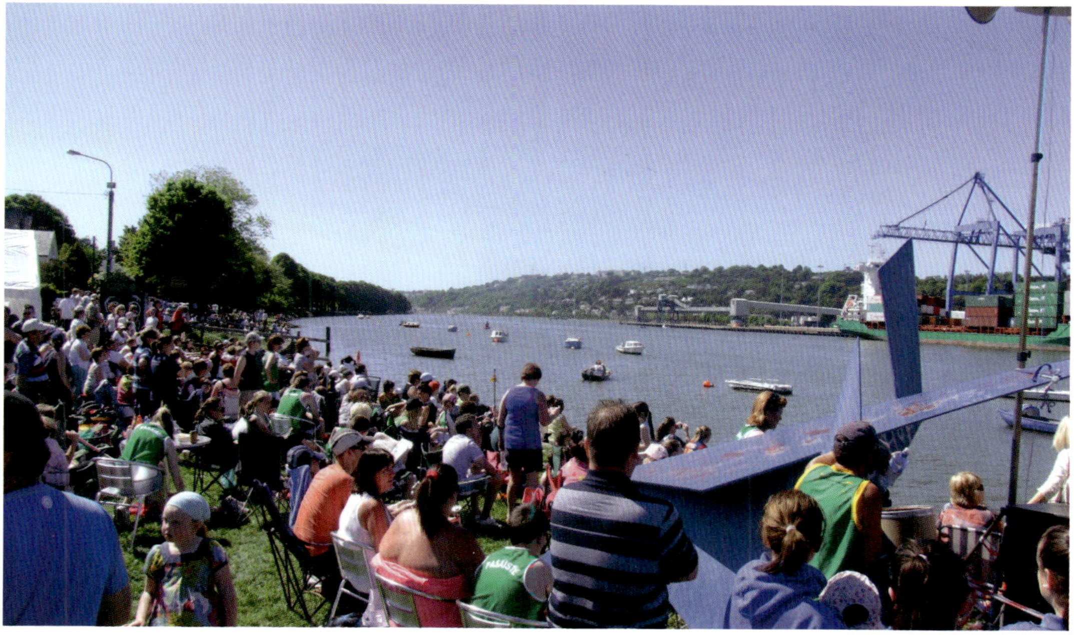

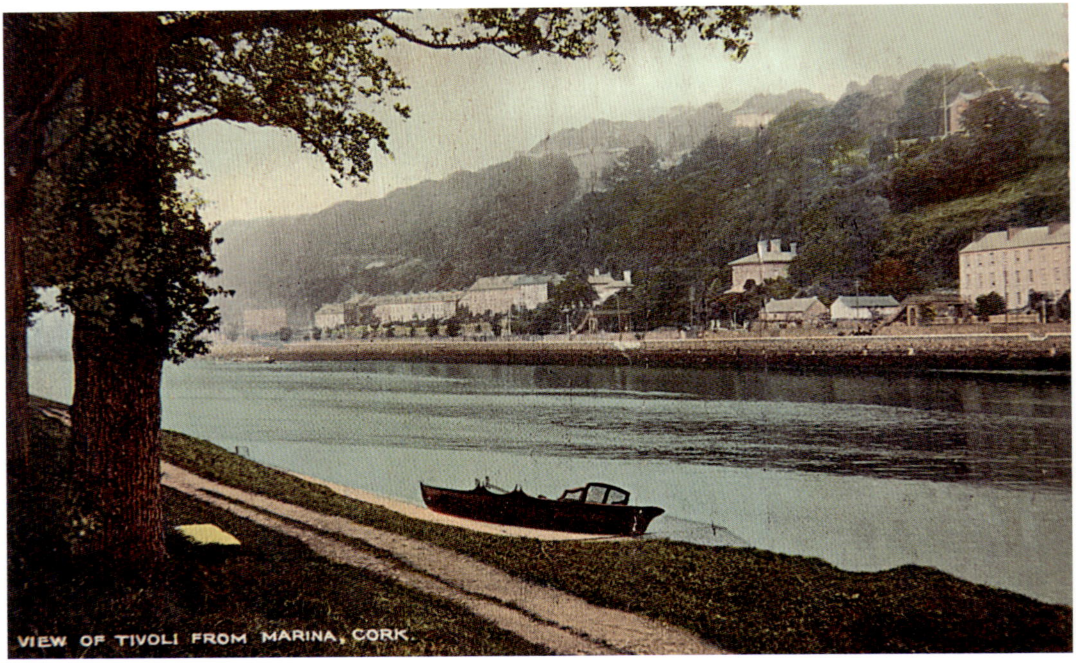

Riverine Vistas

A study of the suburban development of Cork from the eighteenth and nineteenth centuries reveals an abiding interest by the middle and upper classses to live by the river and the harbour. From a status point of view, many of the houses, even where they didn't have famous Cork merchants living in them, still have striking architecture. A large proportion of the riverfront in this vicinity is occupied by houses and detached mansions that command extensive views of the beautiful scenery.

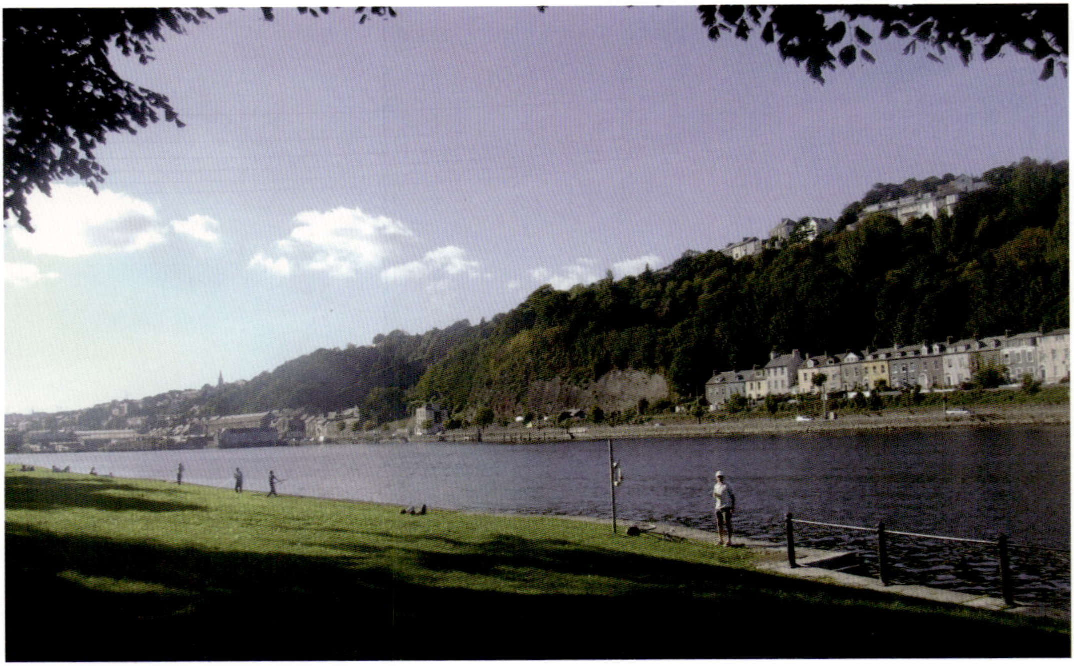

Lakelands, Mahon

At one time, approximately fifty mansions in the south-eastern suburbs of Cork City overlooked Cork Harbour. One of the largest was that of Lakelands, owned by the Crawford family. By 1792, William Crawford Snr had moved from County Down to Cork, where he co-founded the successful Beamish and Crawford brewery. He occupied a fine residence – Lakelands at Blackrock – to the east of the city, overlooking the widening River Lee. His son, William Crawford Jnr, as depicted sitting in the silhouetted picture (by Edourt), continued his involvement with the brewery, but was also active in the cultural life of Cork City. He was one of the founders of the Crawford School of Art, of which his son, William Horatio, was a generous benefactor. Lakelands was demolished by 1890 and is now occupied by a regional road and apartment complex, while the core of the former estate is marked by Mahon Point Shopping Centre.

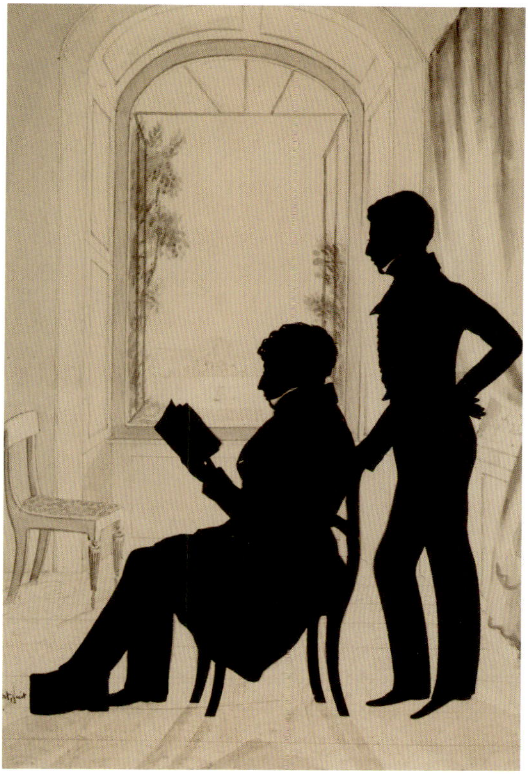

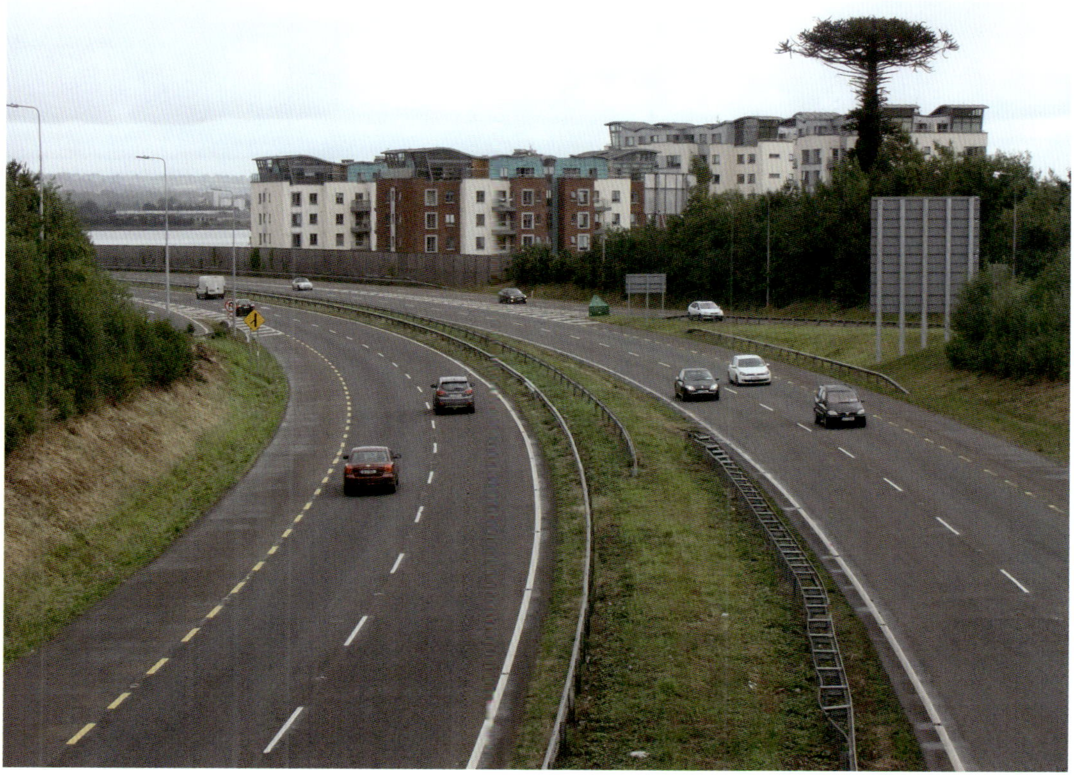

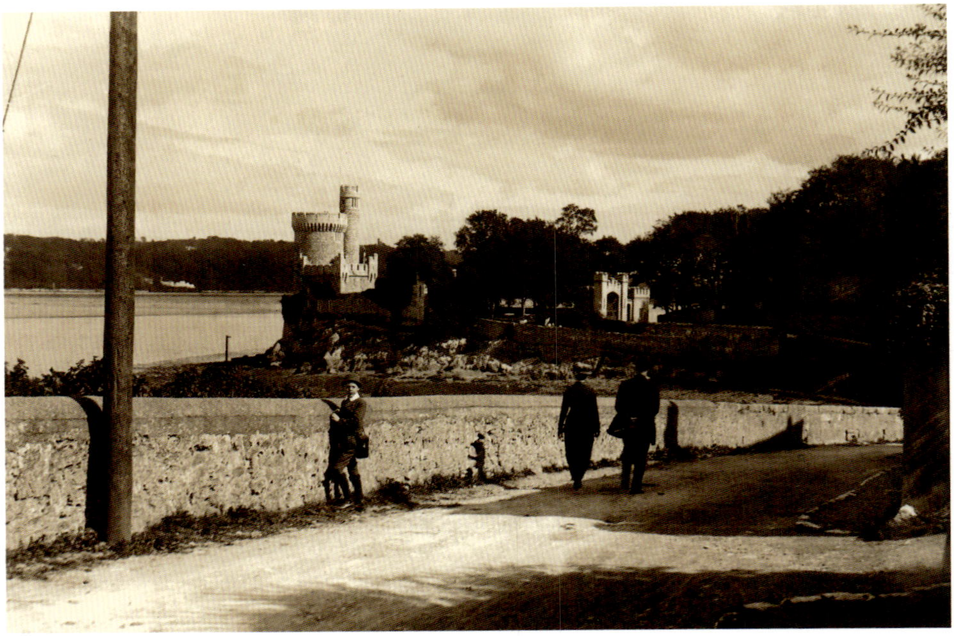

Etched in the Skyline, Blackrock Castle

The imposing Blackrock Castle is the third structure on the site. The original fort (or castle) was built in 1582 by the citizens of Cork to safeguard ships against pirates, who would come into the harbour and steal away the vessels entering the harbour. In 1722 and 1827, the old tower was destroyed by a fire and a new one built. Admiralty courts were held at the castle in the eighteenth century to legislate over the fishing rights of the citizens. CIT Blackrock Castle Observatory is now home to Cosmos at the Castle, Cork's fun and exciting location to learn about the universe.

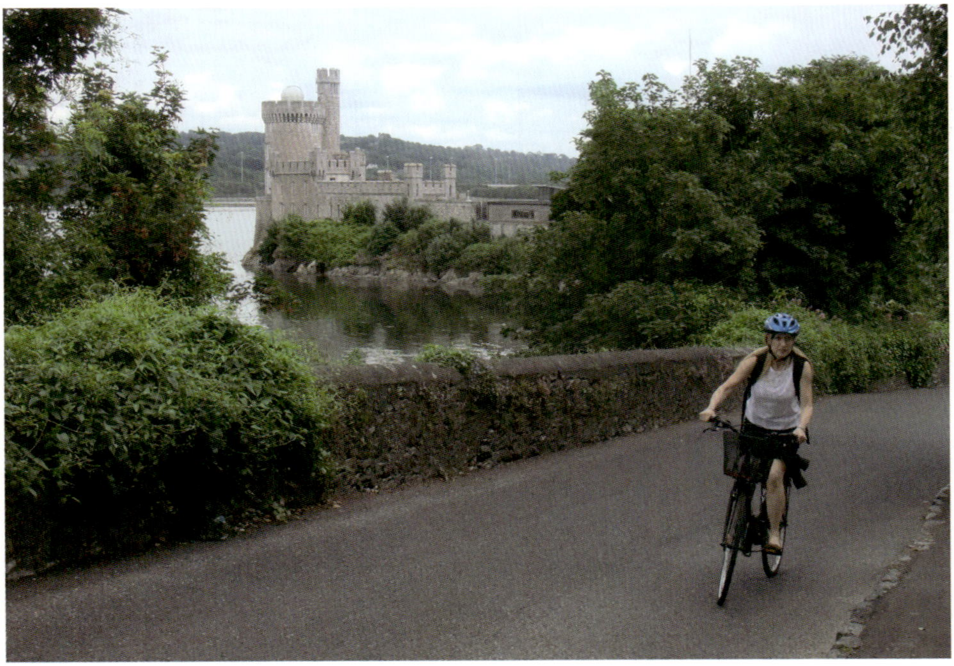

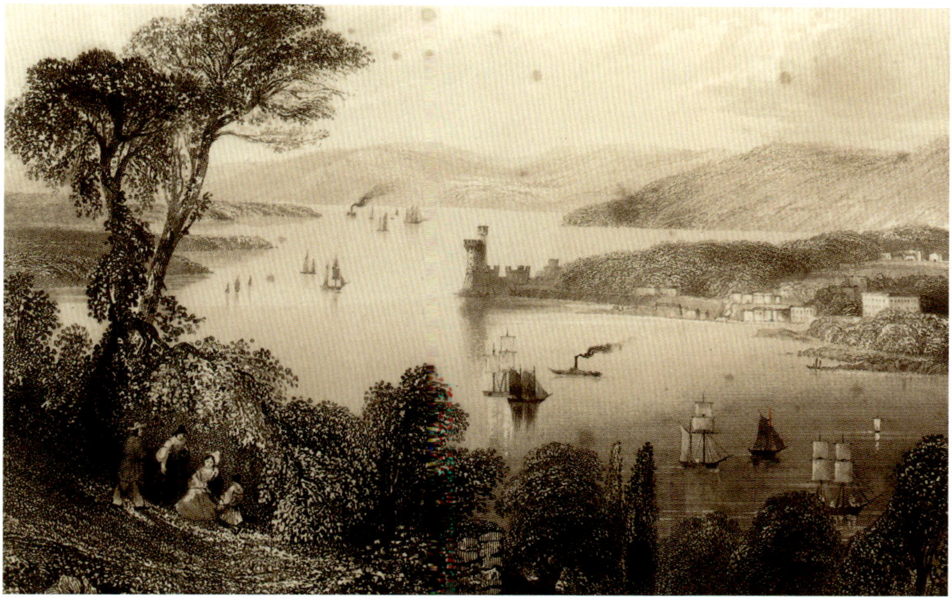

Lough Mahon Bound

Under various charters granted many centuries ago, the Mayor of Cork enjoyed admiralty jurisdiction to the mouth of Cork harbour. The history of fishing and fishermen in Blackrock dates back to the early 1600s. In 1911, sixty-four fishermen, ranging in age from fourteen to seventy, are listed in the census as living in Blackrock village and operating in and around the castle, Lough Mahon and harbour area. The black-and-white engraving shows a view across the estuary from the city's northern suburbs. It was produced by George K. Richardson (*fl.* 1833–46) for *The Scenery and Antiquities of Ireland* (1840–42). The location of ships at the base of the engraving is now the site of Tivoli container docks, a space created in the late 1920s and enlarged in the 1950s.

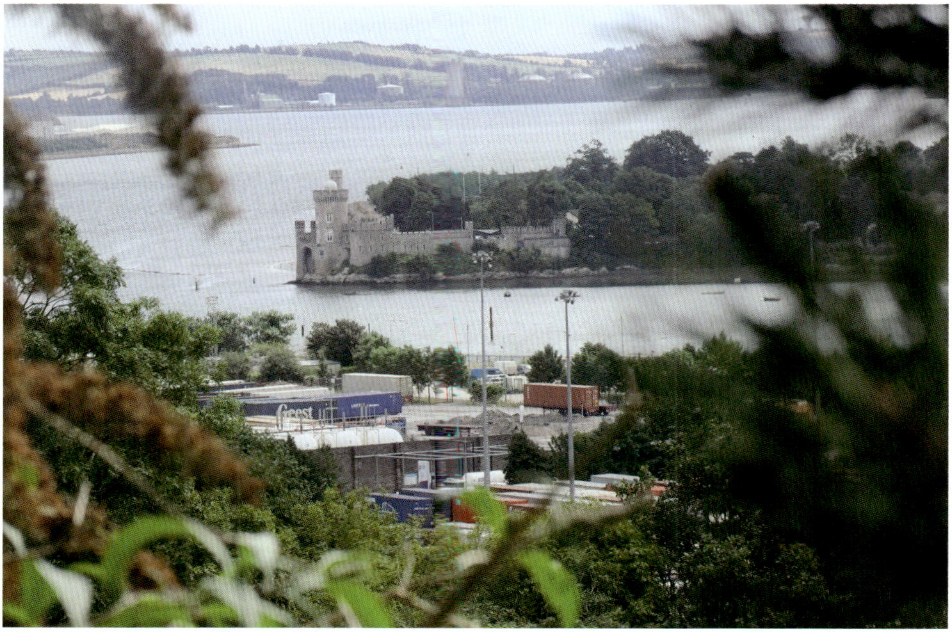

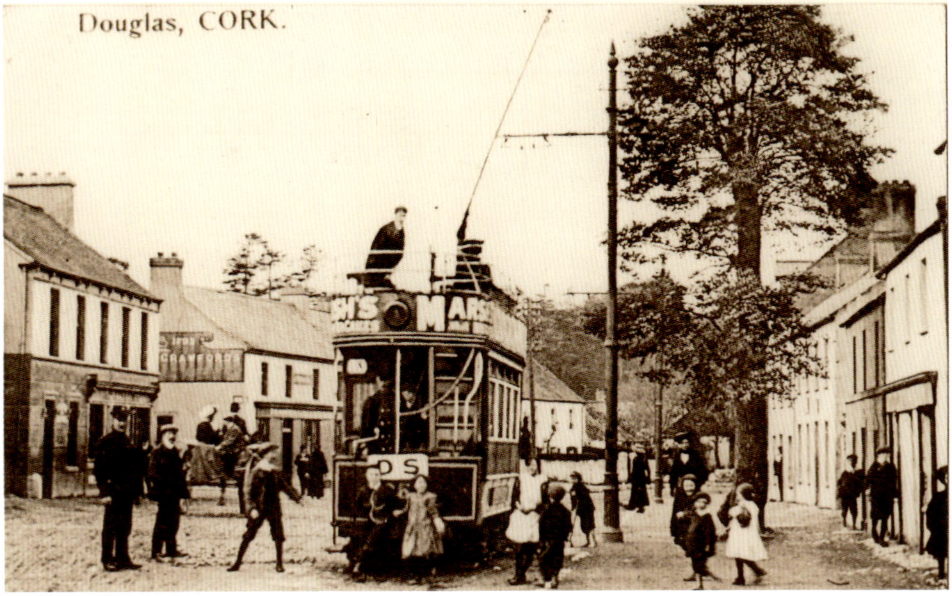

Sailcloths and Woollens, Douglas

The District of Douglas village takes its names from the river or rivulet bearing the Gaelic word *Dubhghlas* or 'dark stream', which enters the tidal area nearby. As early as the late thirteenth century, King John of England made a grant of land to Philip de Prendergast near the city of Cork. On 1 June 1726, the building of the Douglas Factory commenced. Samuel Perry & Francis Carleton became the first proprietors. The Douglas Sailcloth Factory is said to have been founded by a colony of weavers from Fermanagh. The eighteenth century was a golden age for wooden sailing ships, which made steam and iron prerequisites for modern navies and trading fleets. Today, the suburban village of Douglas boasts two suburban shopping centres and still has a bustling heart.

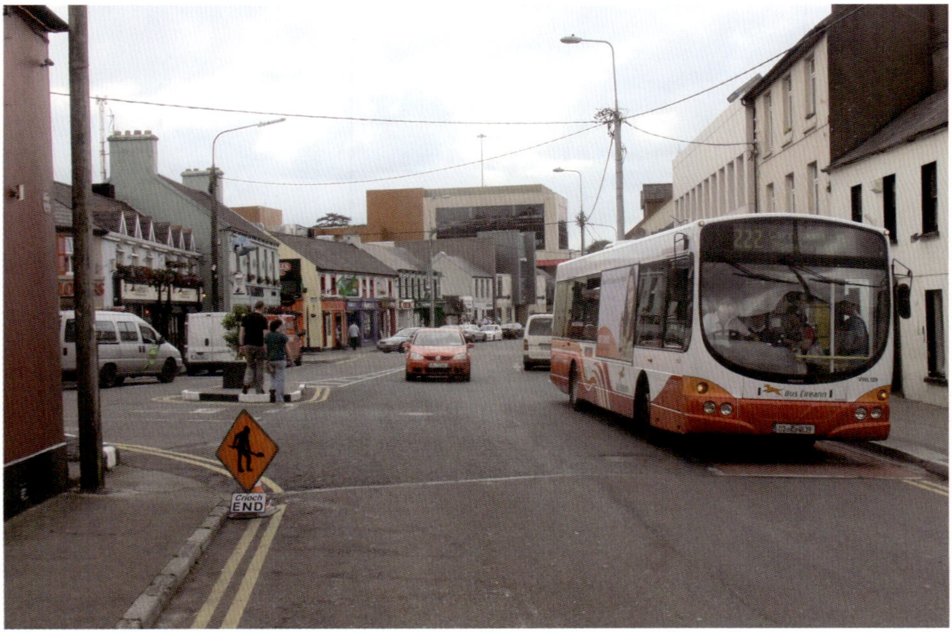

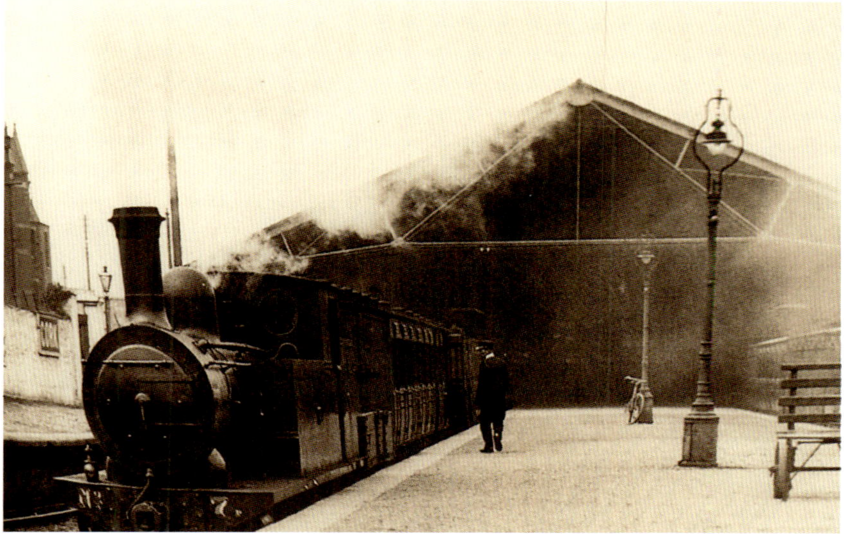

Cork, Blackrock & Passage Railway Line

The Cork, Blackrock & Passage Railway opened in 1850, and was among the first of the Irish suburban railway projects. The original terminus, designed by Sir John Benson, was based on Victoria Road, but moved in 1873 to Hibernian Road (as shown above and now built upon). The entire length of track between Cork and Passage was in place by April 1850 and, within two months, the line was open for passenger traffic. In 1904, the line was extended from Passage to Crosshaven through tunnels in the coastline. The line, as marked on the left of the map, shows the full train line *c.* 1910, and the steamer connections to different parts of the harbour that the rail line also operated.

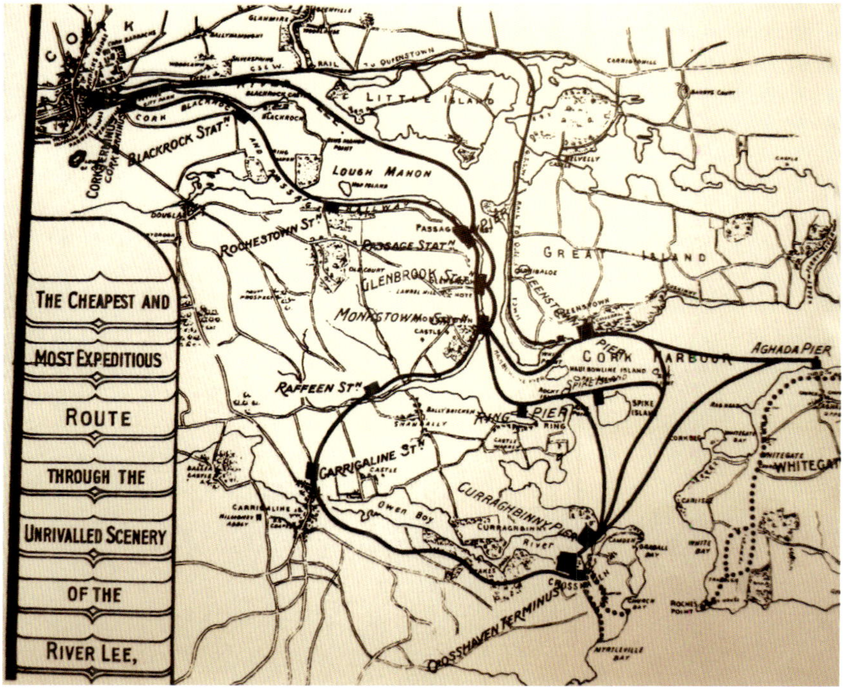

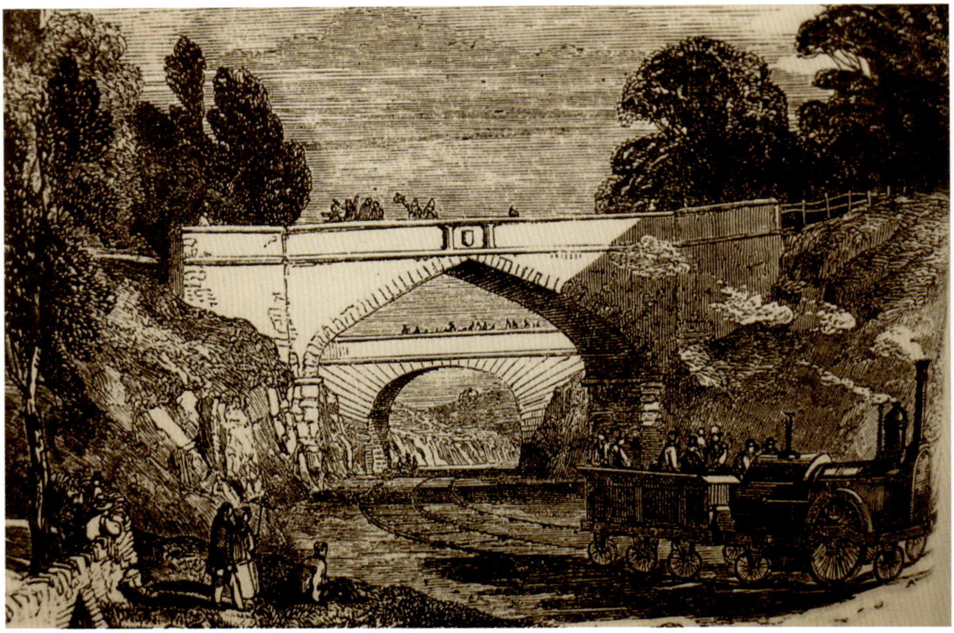

The Blackrock Railway Cutting

In May 1847, low embankments were constructed to carry the railway over Monarea Marshes (Albert Road to the marina area). In Blackrock, large amounts of material were removed and cut at Dundanion to create part of the trackway there. Due to the fact that construction was taking place during the Great Famine, there was no shortage of labour. A total of 450 men were taken on for the erection of the embankments at the Cork end of the line. Another eighty were employed in digging the cutting beyond Blackrock. The test run shown took place on Tuesday 14 May 1850. The train left Passage at around 3 p.m. and reached the terminus at Cork in 18 minutes.

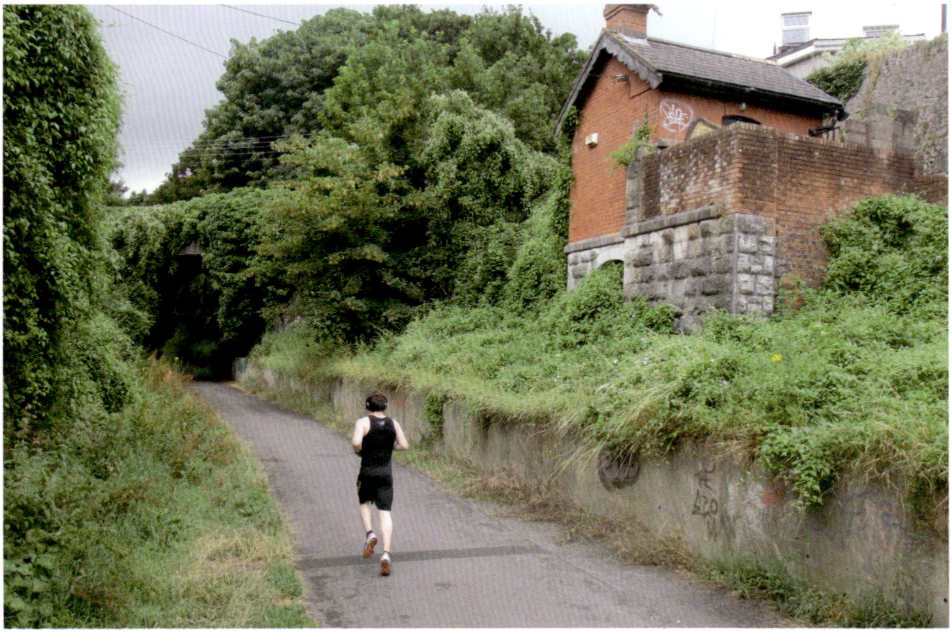

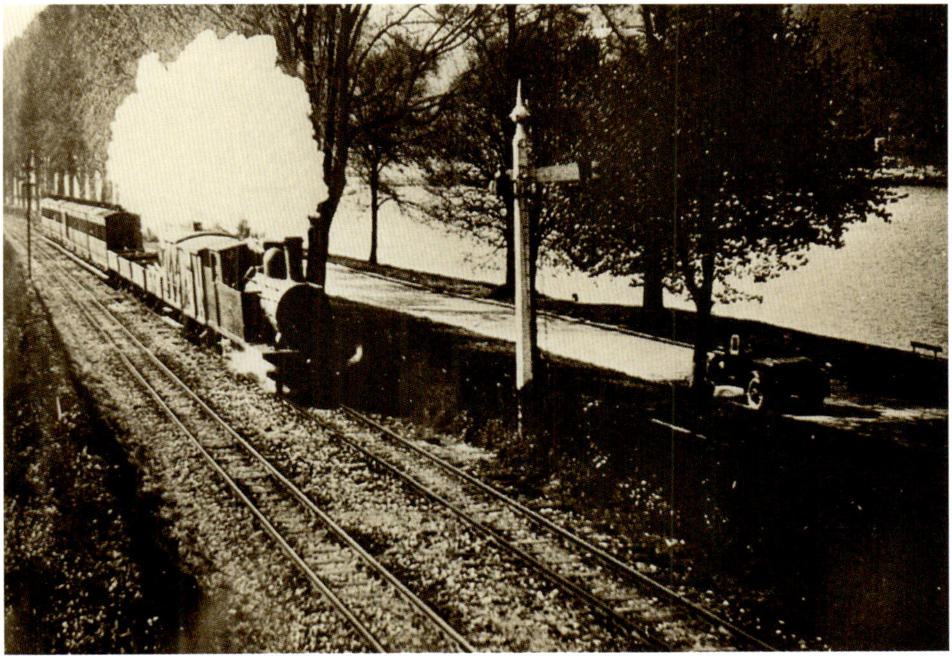

Along the Marina

In 1850, the train service consisted of ten trains each way on Saturdays, eight each way on weekdays and nine on Sundays. Trains from Cork left on the hour, while the corresponding workings departed Passage at half past the hour. The first fare was 6*d* and second class was 4*d*. Later, a third-class fare was introduced. Third-class carriages were little better than cattle trucks. The line was served by three small 2-2-2 well tanks, which remained in service for fifty years. Built by the Sharp brothers, they were delivered in 1850 and were named 1, 2 and 3.

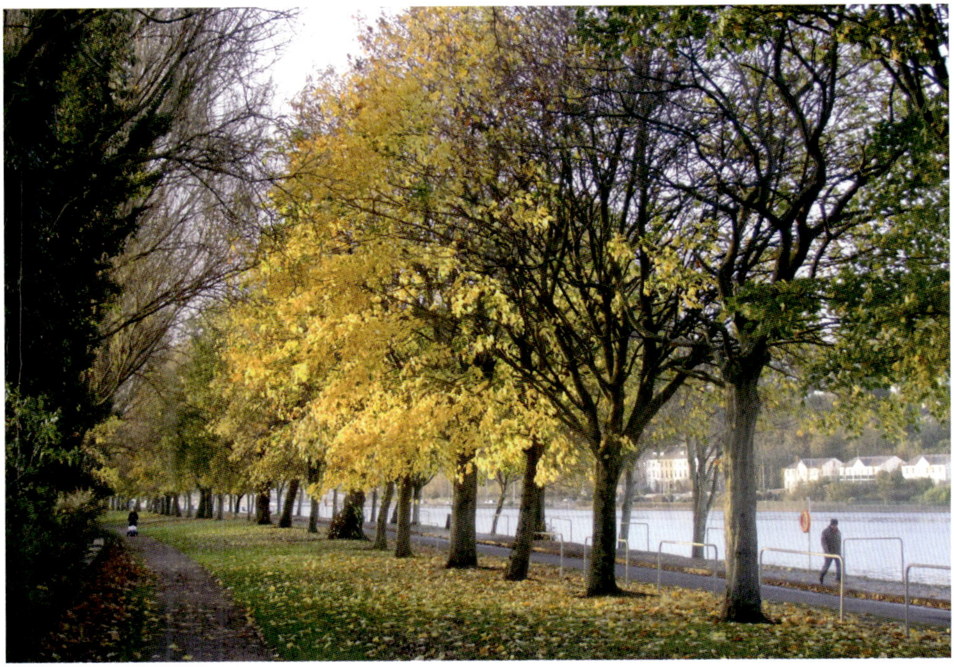

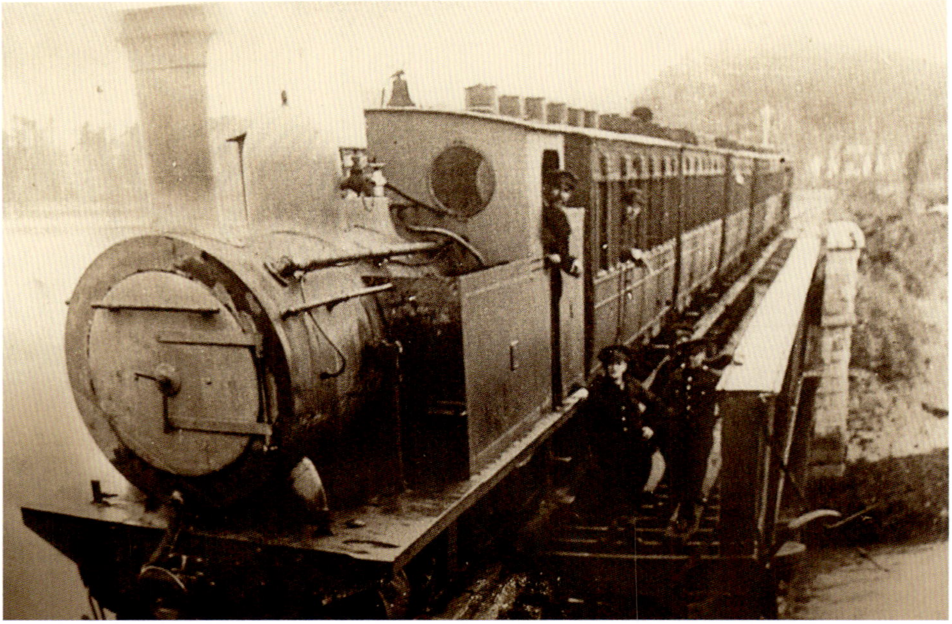

Across the Douglas Viaduct

In 1886, a contract was given by the railway company to build an iron viaduct across Douglas Estuary. On 8 August 1922, the Irish Free Army blew up a part of this bridge, which was duly replaced. Due to competition from buses and financial losses, the eight-two-year-old line closed on 10 December 1932. Today, the majority of the elaborate railway line is an amenity walk being maintained by Cork City and Cork County Councils, where old bridges, embankments, cuttings and tunnels can be explored at ease, and the achievements of the railway line truly appreciated.

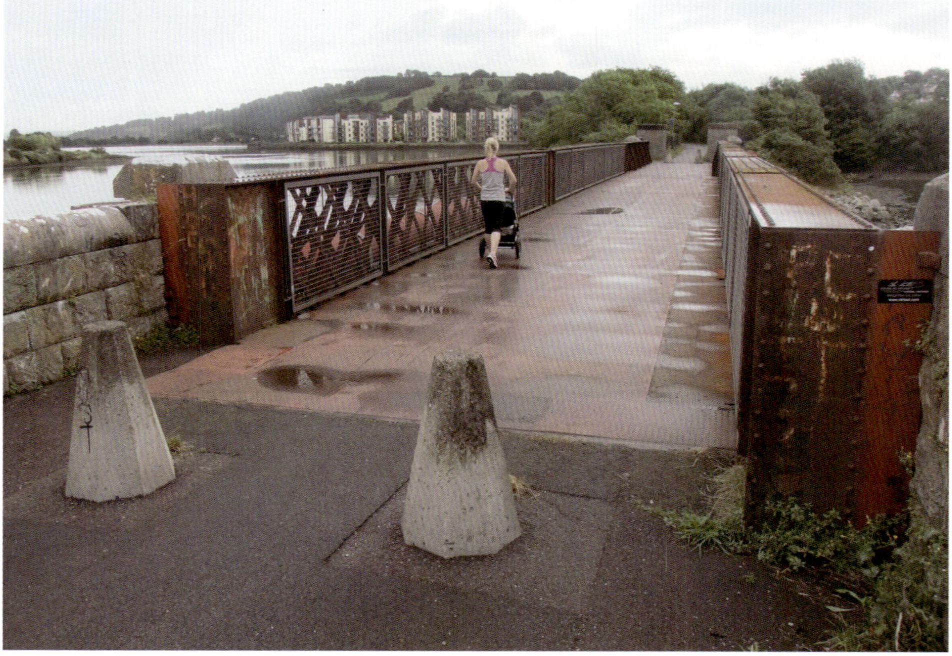

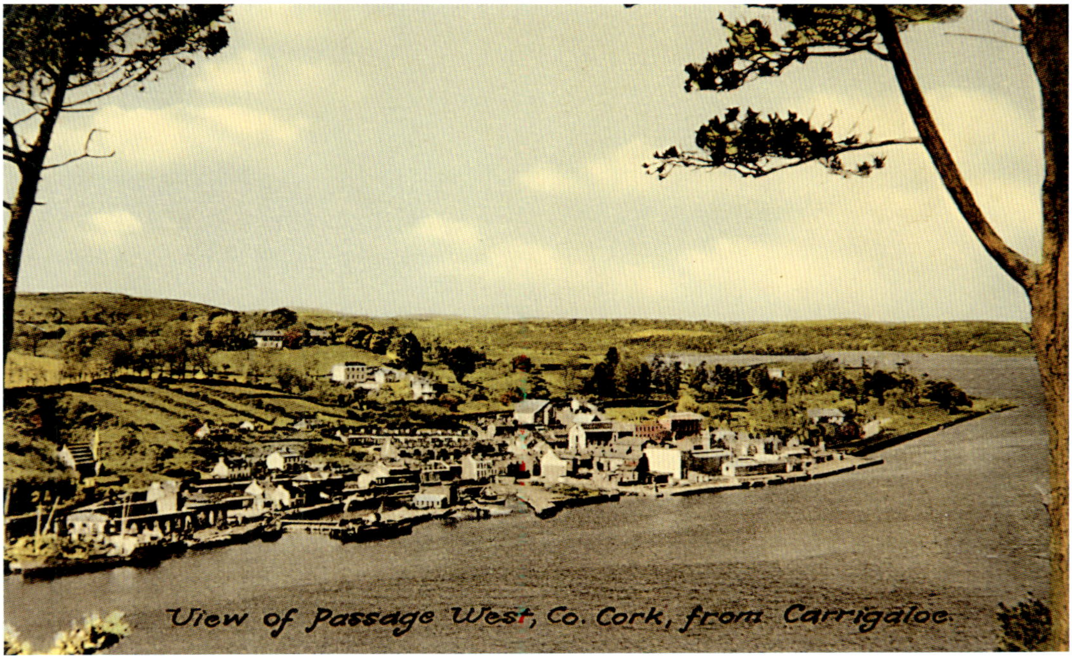

Town of Enterprise, Passage West

With the establishment of a dock and shipyard in Passage West in the nineteenth century, many merchants became shipowners, and carried on an extensive trade in their own vessels. Three of these individuals were well-known entrepreneurs – William Parker (who engaged in foreign speculations in shipping), Thomas Parsons Boland and the Brown family. A large, dry dock was constructed by Mr Brown in the 1830s for the purpose of shipbuilding. Much employment was also afforded to labourers involved in discharging cargoes of all large vessels bound for Cork, as the river up to Cork was not navigable for those above 400 or 500 tons. The ferry to Great Island and Cobh was, and still is, at the eastern extremity of the town.

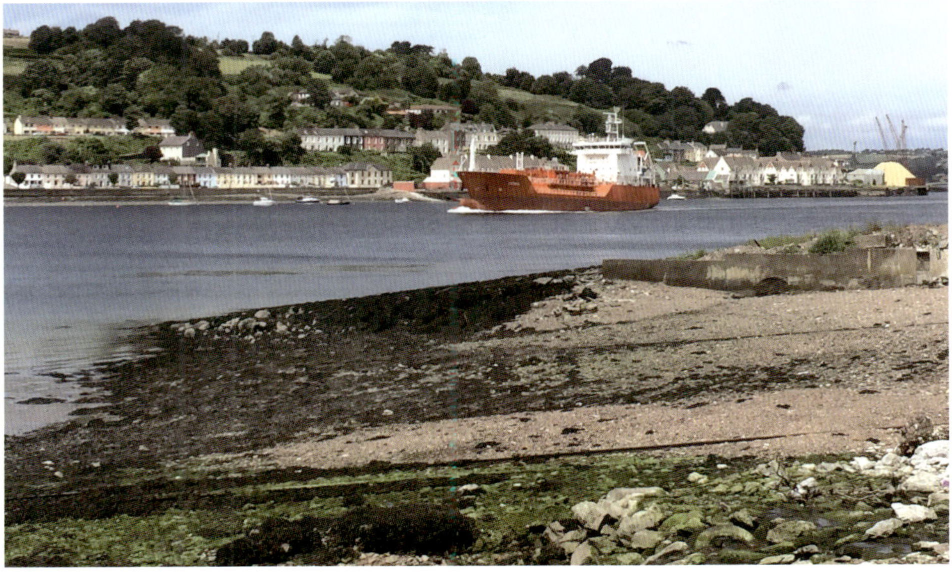

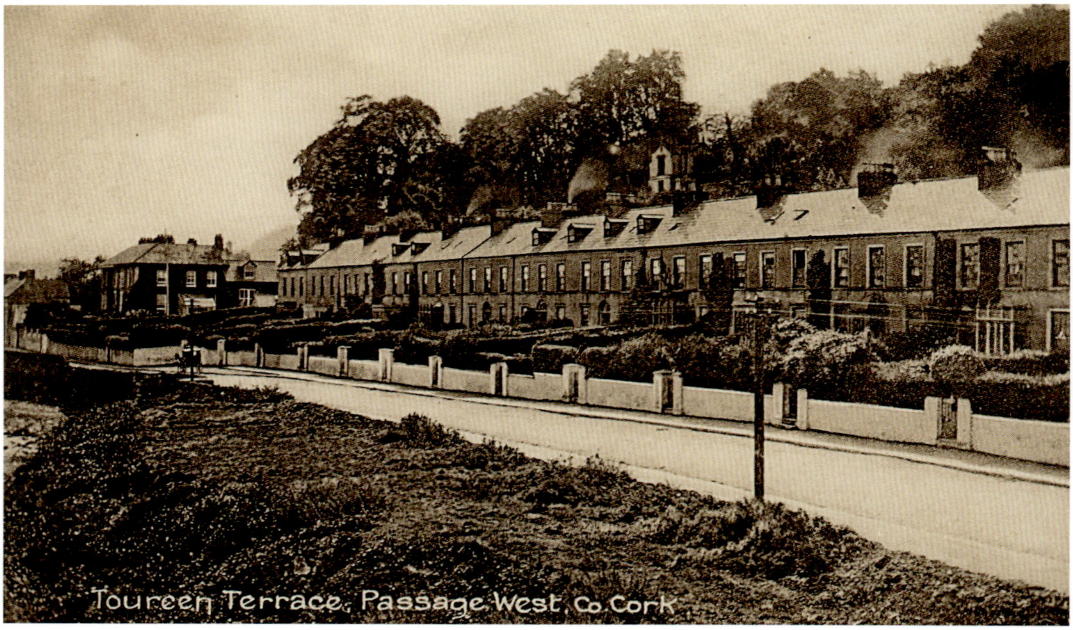

Toureen Terrace, Passage West

During the nineteenth century, many merchants in Passage West built their own big houses and terraces. This town recorded upwards of 100 covered cars called jingles engaged almost daily in the transport of people between Passage and Cork. Steamboats and several small boats also ploughed the waters between Cork and Passage several times daily. Before the Terrace (formerly known as Mariner's Row) was built, in the early nineteenth century the site was a fair field. Every summer a popular event called The Donnybrook of Cork was held, at which horse racing and boat races took place. The town was also much frequented during the summer for its 'fine air and sea-bathing', with saltwater baths open in the nearby Glenbrook.

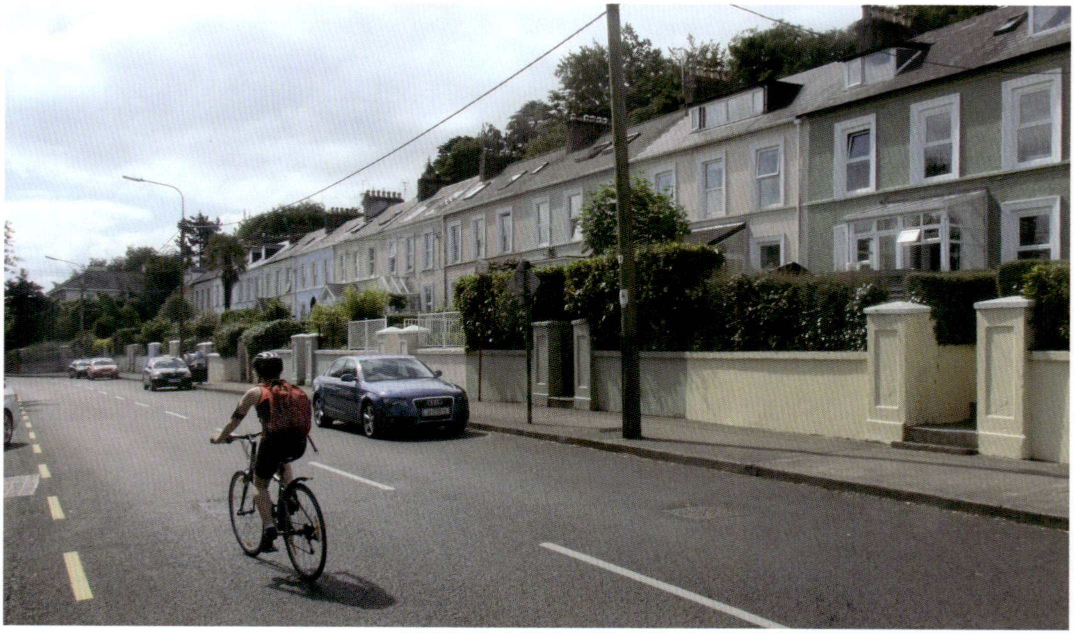

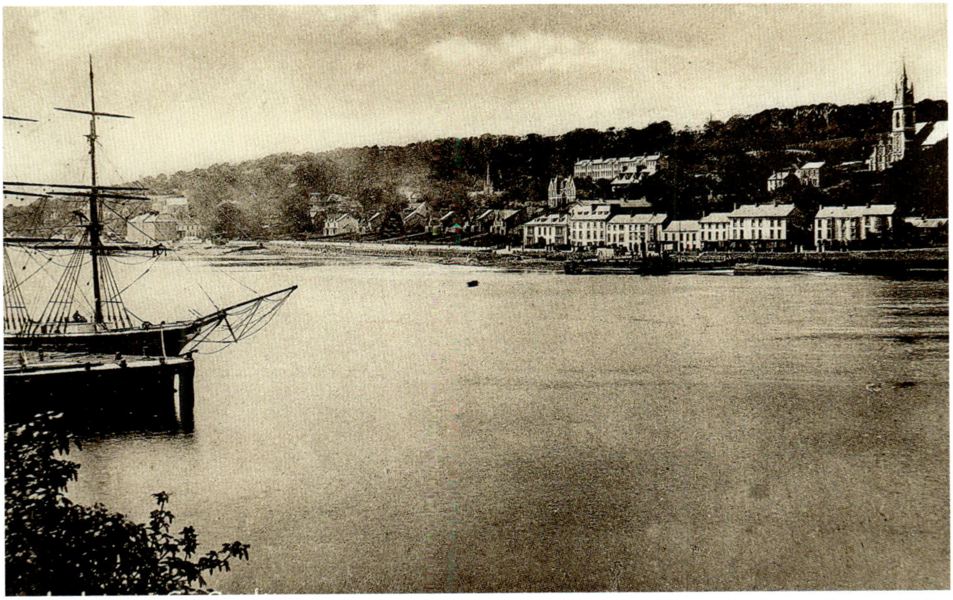

Anchorage at Monkstown

Monkstown derives its name from a small establishment of Benedictine monks, called Legan Abbey, belonging to the priory of St. John's, Waterford. They formed a branch there in the fourteenth century, on a grant of land made to the original establishment by the family of McCarthy. In 1636, a house in the Elizabethan style was built on the side of a glen by Eustace Gould, called Monkstown castle. Nearby, there were several quarries of a red and brown stone, useful for many purposes, but being chiefly used for lining lime kilns. One hundred years ago, the river Lee afforded every facility for water carriage, and here there was excellent anchorage for vessels of all sizes as well as one of the connecting steamers to Cobh from the Cork Blackrock and Passage Railway Line.

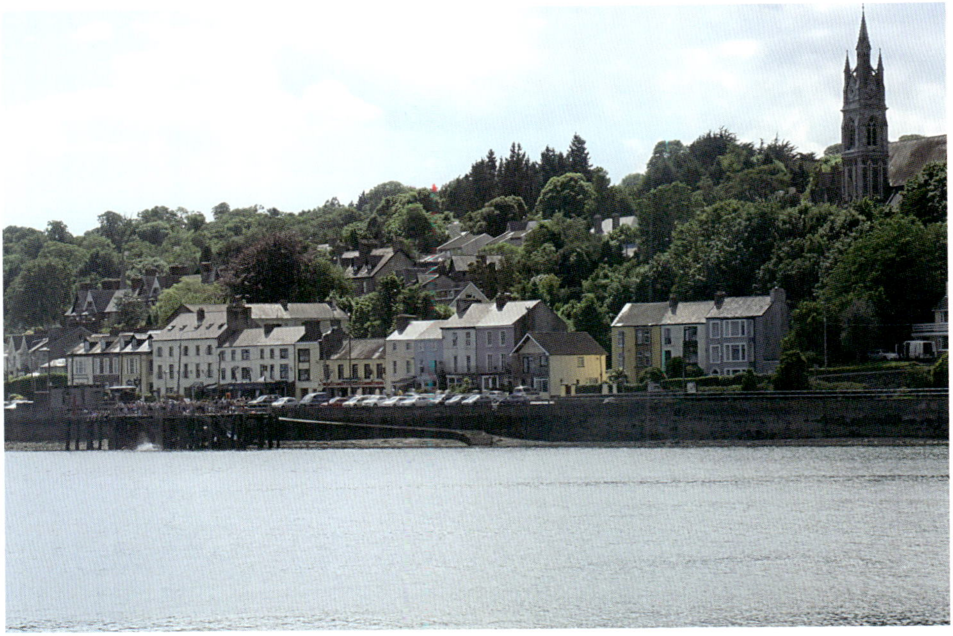

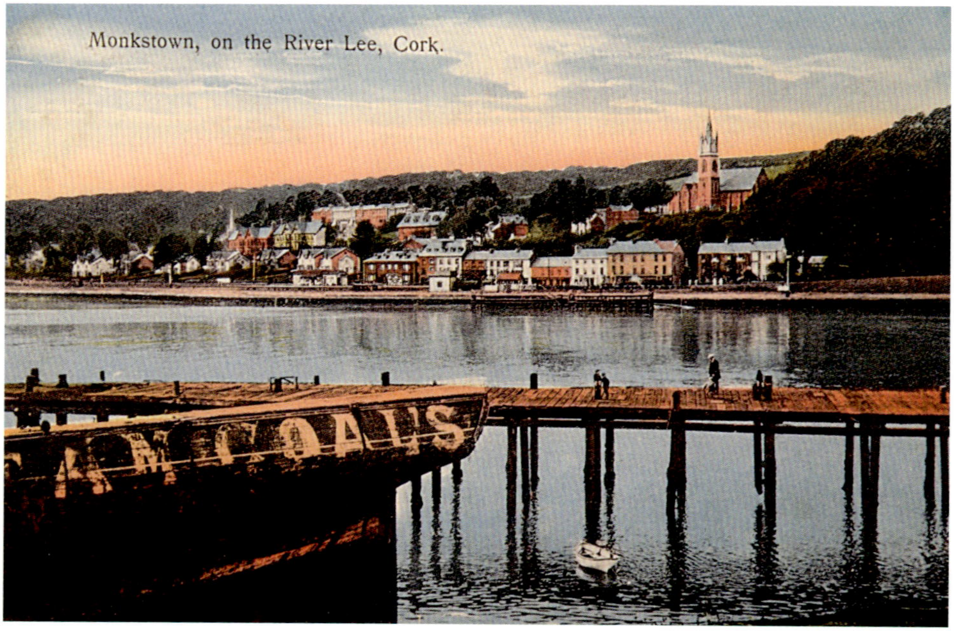

A Community Bell, Monkstown

The church, which stands on a picturesque elevation, is a cruciform edifice in the early English style, with a 70-foot high tower and spire at the east end. In 1832, it was built of hewn limestone at an expense of £950, raised by subscriptions from the patrons and others. The west window is stained glass, exhibiting the armorial bearings of the principal subscribers. The bell has on it this inscription: 'Monkstown Protestant church, erected by voluntary contributions, collected in Ireland and England by Gerard Callaghan, Esq., MP for Cork, and the Rev A G H Hollingsworth.'

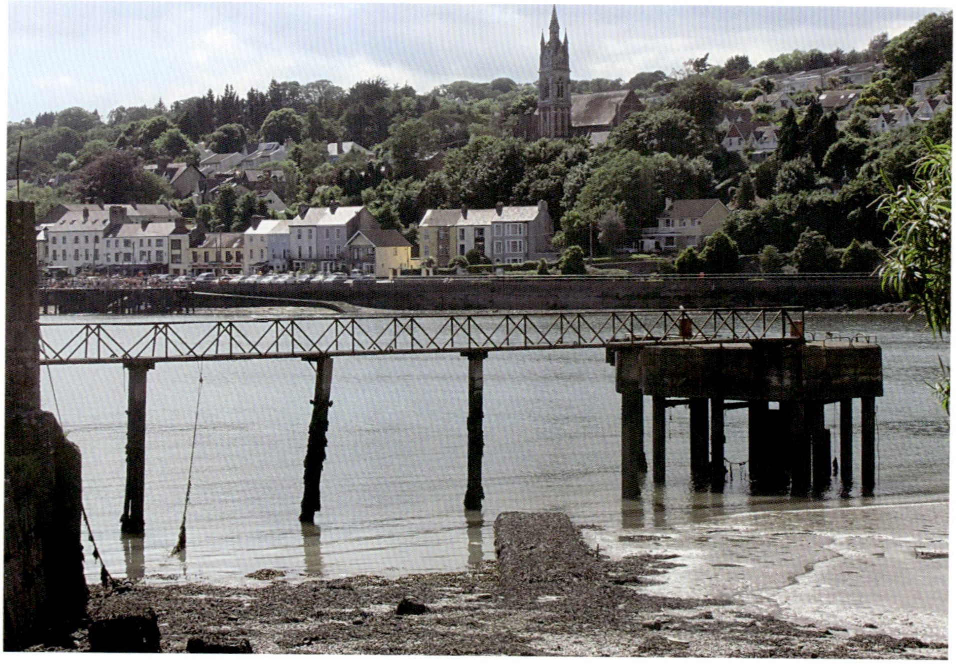

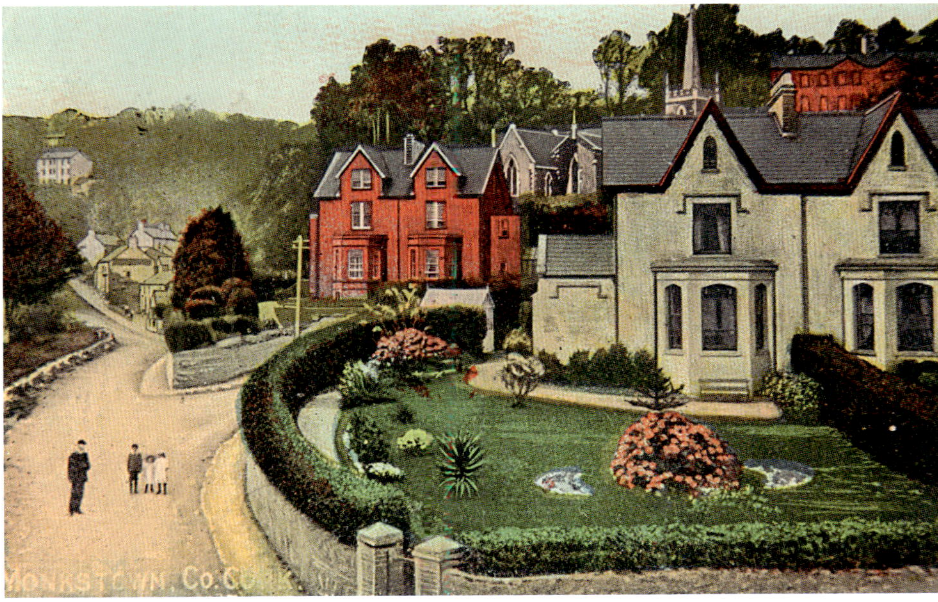

Beautiful Architecture, Monkstown

Colourful Victorian houses add immensely to the sense of place in Monkstown. In 1875, a general depression within the shipping trade hit the local dockyards. In 1900, there was talk of Harland & Wolfe coming to Monkstown and, although there was much enthusiasm for the project, it never materialised. The Royal Victoria Dockyard in Passage West began a policy of salvaging and reconstructing vessels. For a time, this was successful. Monkstown Golf Club was set up in 1908, in attempt to attract some of the railway passengers to the area. By the summer of 1909, thirteen trains were running on weekdays between Cork and Monkstown; however, the train service ran at a loss. Today, Monkstown is now well known for its marina and popular, award-winning restaurants.

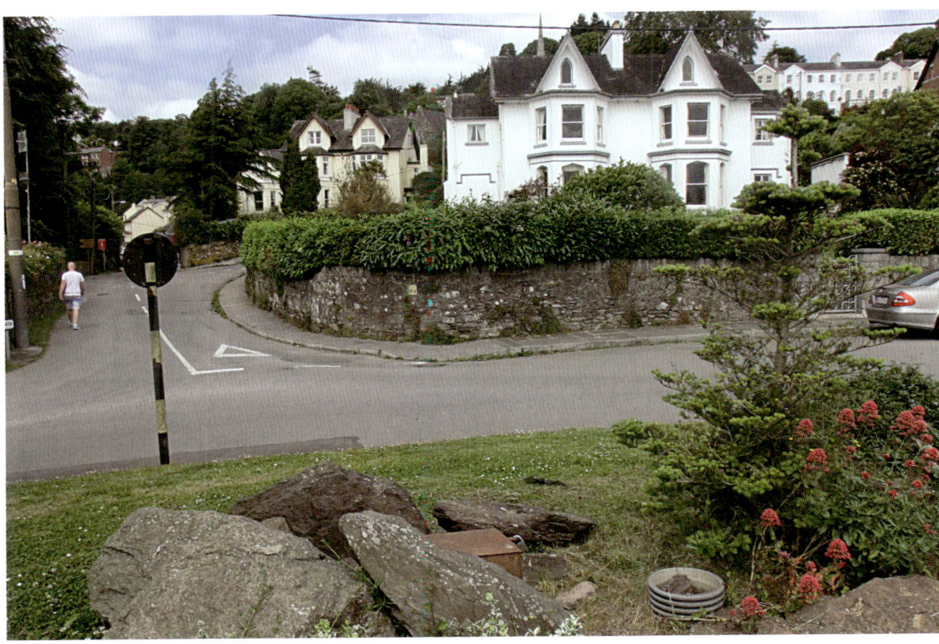

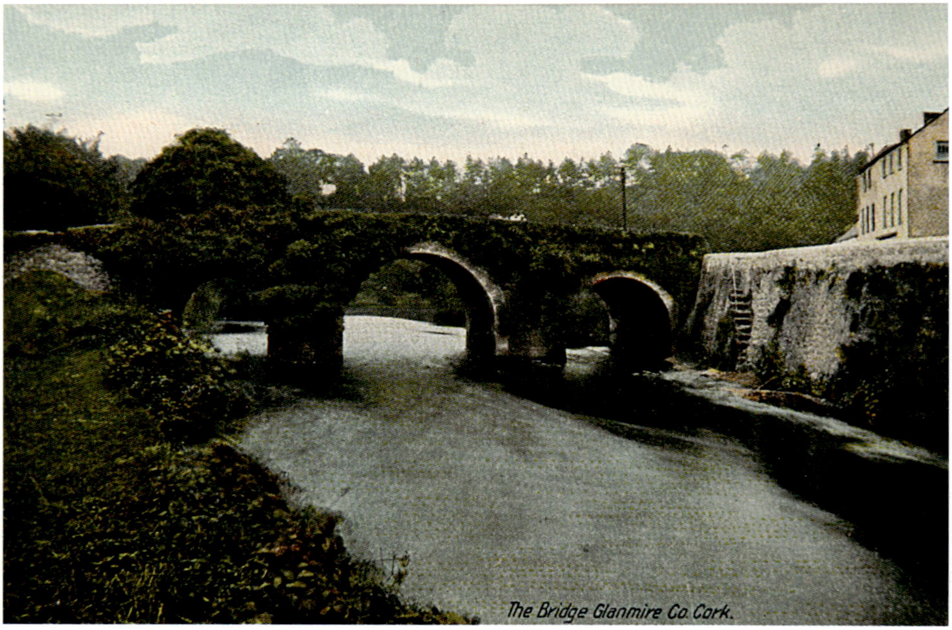

Bridge the Past, Glanmire

The village of Glanmire is situated on both sides of the meandering Glashaboy River. At one time, the vicinity was enlivened with many plantations, hanging woods, and a number of gentlemen's seats and villas. In the village were extensive flour mills belonging to Mr Shaw, and in the surrounding area were those of Messrs Thorley & Son for finishing calico and linen, and Mr Lyons and Hanly's woollen factory. Glanmire (*Gleann Maghair*) literally means 'The valley of the small fish', or the valley of the ploughed land, or the 'still vale' or the 'valley of the young fish'. With a current population of 15,498, Glanmire is used generally by residents of the area to mean the Greater Glanmire area, encompassing the Riverstown, Brooklodge and Sallybrook areas.

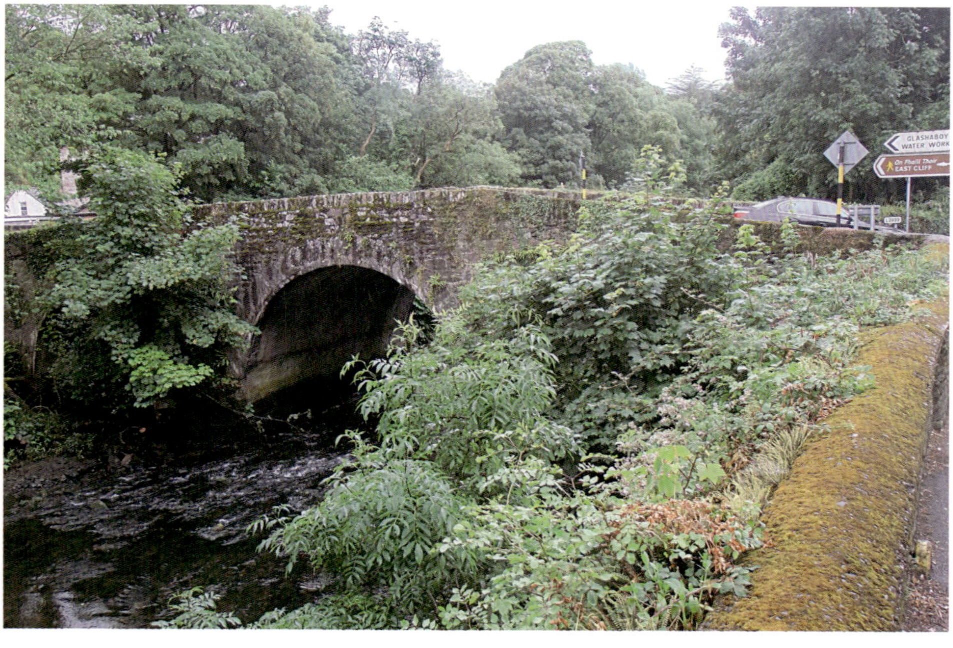

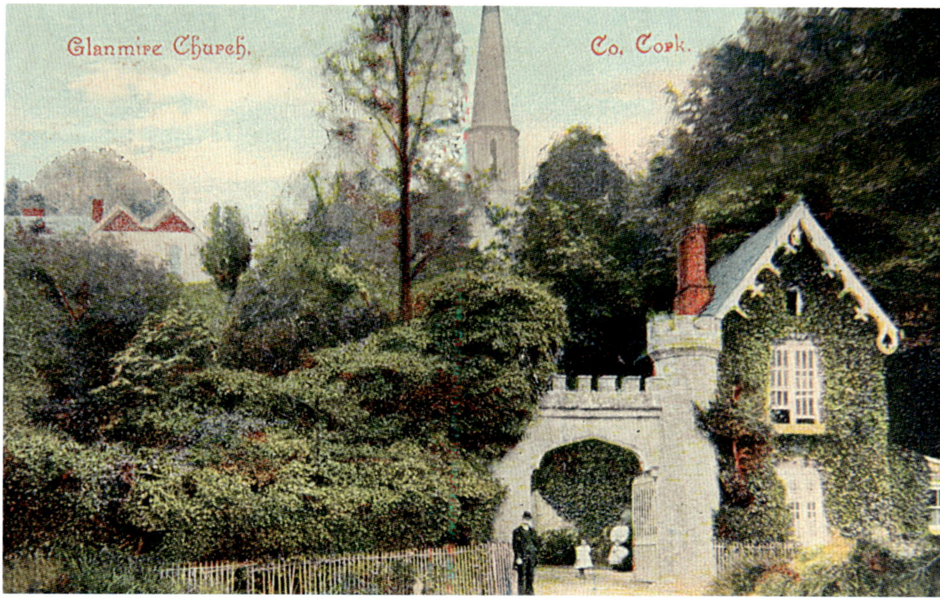

Through the Trees, Glanmire

The Church of Ireland, Saint Mary's & All Saints, Glanmire, is a plain, neat building with a tower and spire. It was erected in 1784 on a site given by R. Rogers. One of its most famous patrons was Sarah Curran (1782–1808). She was born in Newmarket, County Cork, and was the daughter of the prominent lawyer John Philpot Curran. When living in Dublin, she fell in love with the United Irishman Robert Emmet, who was executed in 1803. Disowned by her father, Sarah Curran moved to Cork, where, in 1805, she married Capt. Henry Sturgeon in Glanmire church. St Michael's church in Upper Glanmire was dedicated and reopened for worship in 1808, following major restructuring. Nearby is the beautiful Catholic St Joseph's church in Springhill, which was dedicated in 1837.

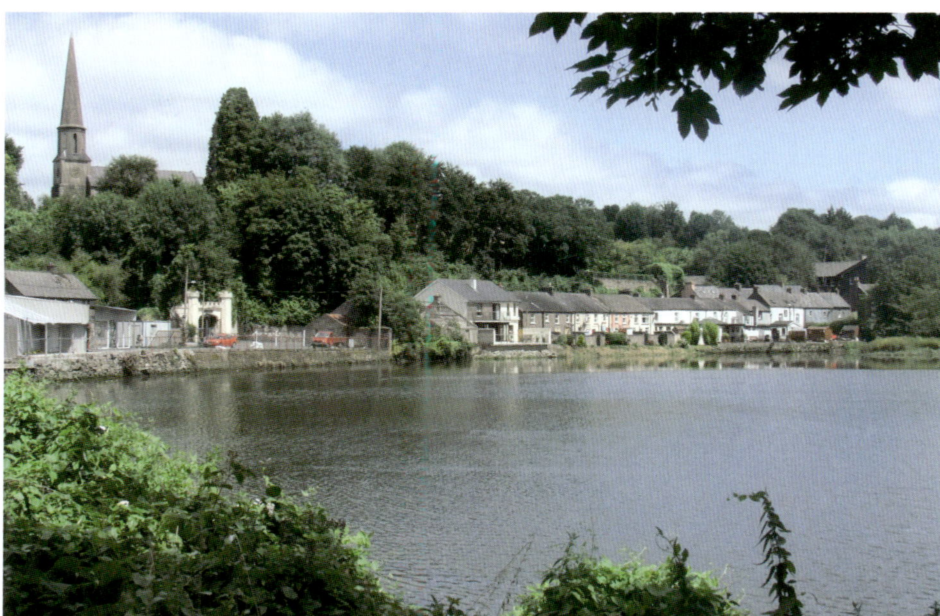

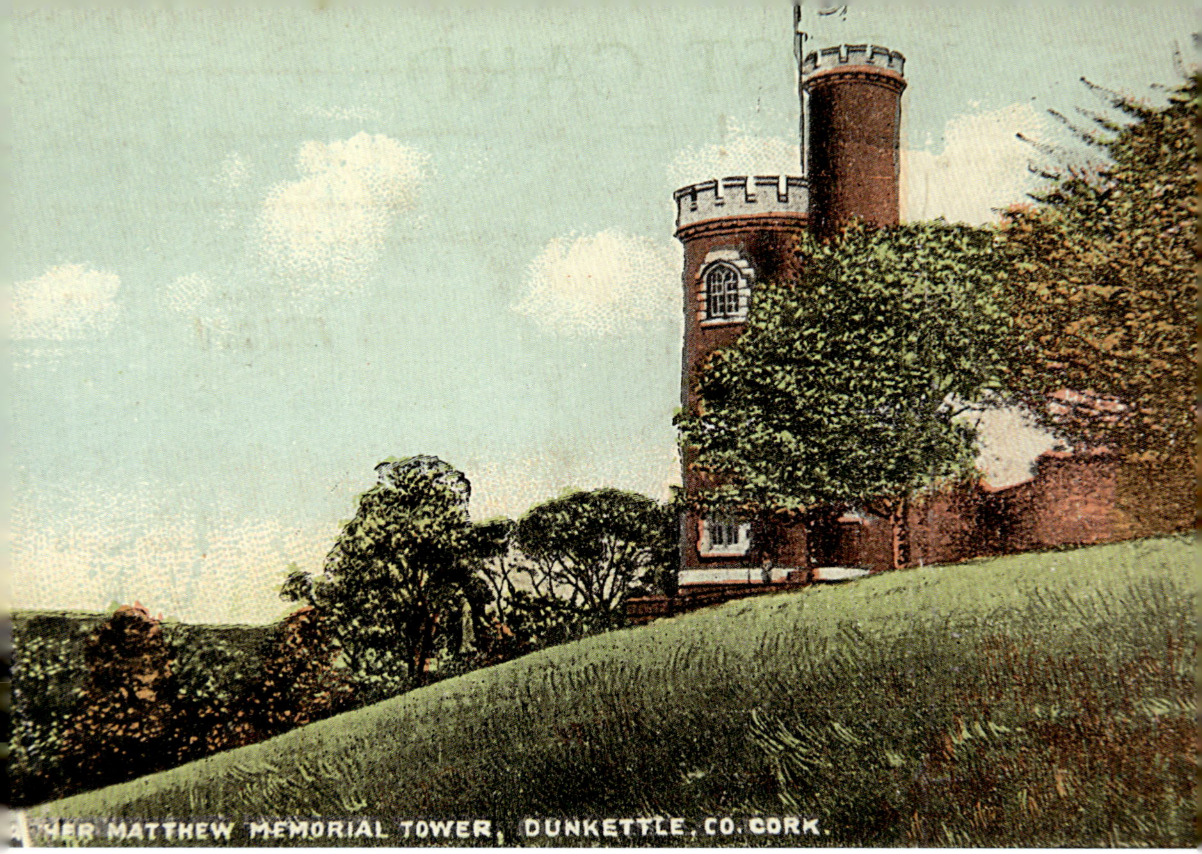

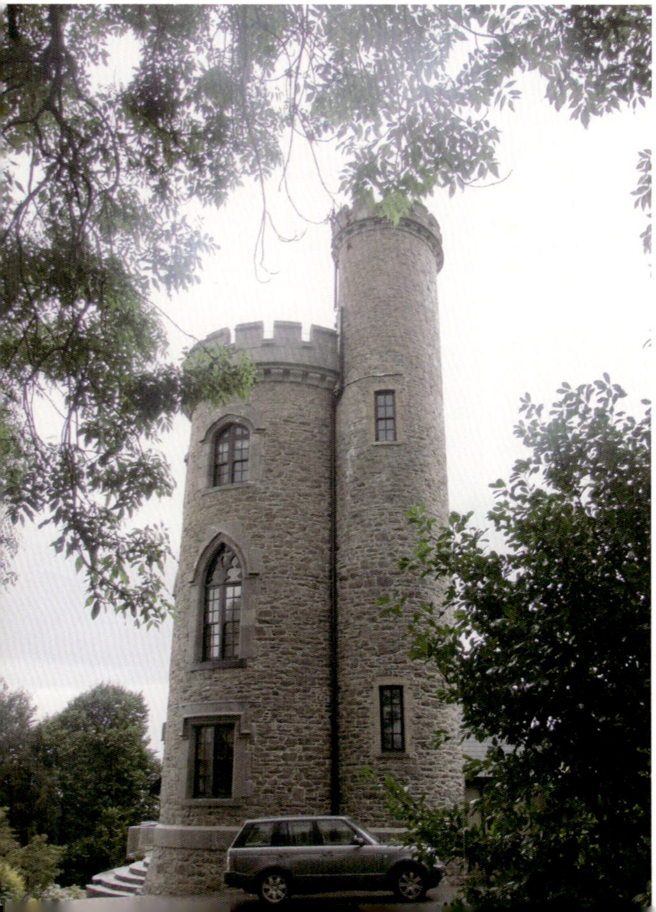

Father Mathew Memorial Tower

The tower was built to commemorate Father Theobald Mathew, the mid-nineteenth-century apostle of temperance. Father Mathew witnessed the tower's completion in 1846. Despite the onset of the Famine, the foundation stone was laid in 1843, and the Gothic structure was finished and officially opened in November 1846. It was built by a local merchant tailor, William O'Connor, who had met with the Tipperary-born Father Mathew in London's Strand, who felt he deserved to be honoured in his home country. The graceful towers, one about 80 feet high and another 100 feet high, were created for sightseeing. The overall structure was designed by George Pain, the architect of Blackrock Castle. It is perhaps appropriate that each of the turrets have views to the castle along the River Lee and Lough Mahon.

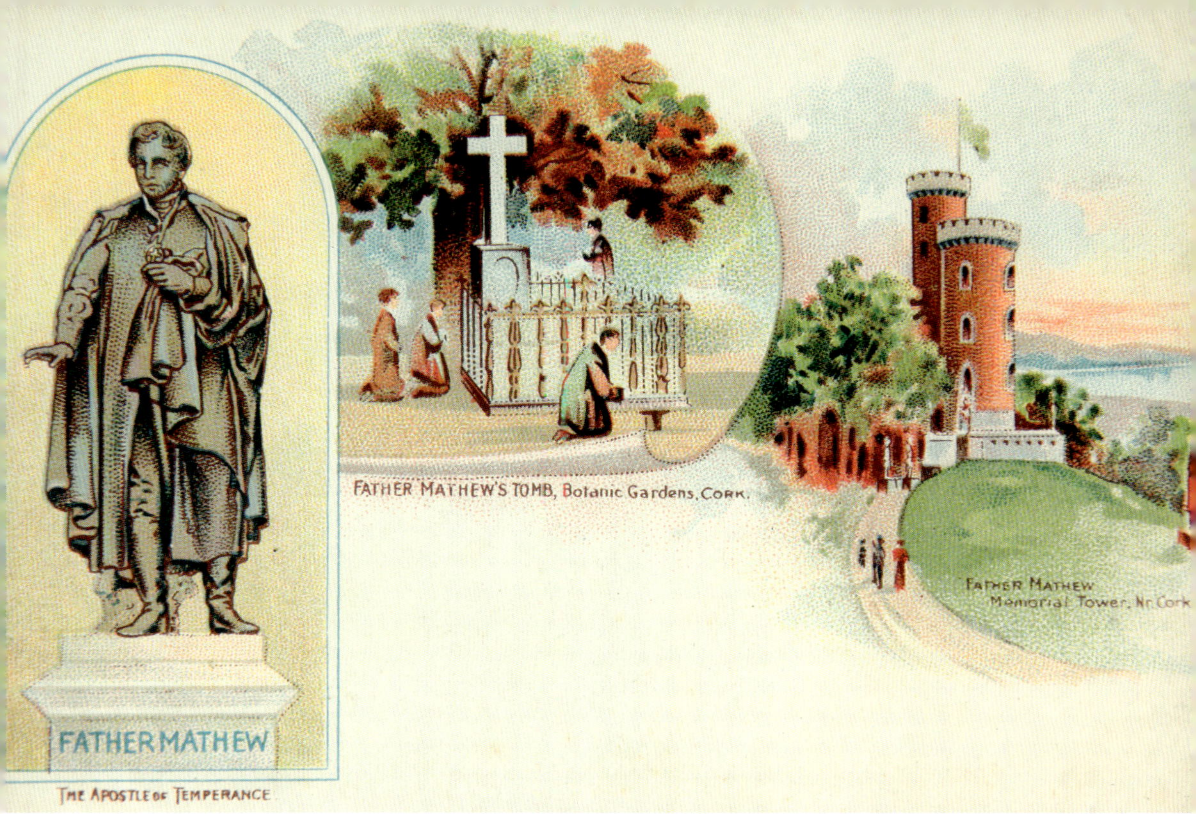

Remembering Cork's Temperance Leader

By the end of 1839, the reputation of the Cork Temperance Society, the first such known effective society in the city, began to spread further into north Munster. It was at this time that Father Mathew began to be acclaimed as the 'Apostle of Temperance'. By the end of 1840, it is recorded that 180,000 to 200,000 had taken the pledge nationwide. In the late 1840s, Father Mathew went to America to rally support for his teetotaller cause and, as a result, the cause in Ireland and England started to suffer by his absence. He died in December 1856 and was buried in St Joseph's cemetery, Cork, his own cemetery that he created for the poor. Father Mathew has left a legacy in this city that has been maintained and respected since his death. Of all his commemorative features in the city, the Father Mathew Statue, erected in 1864 on St Patrick's Street, very much honours the man.

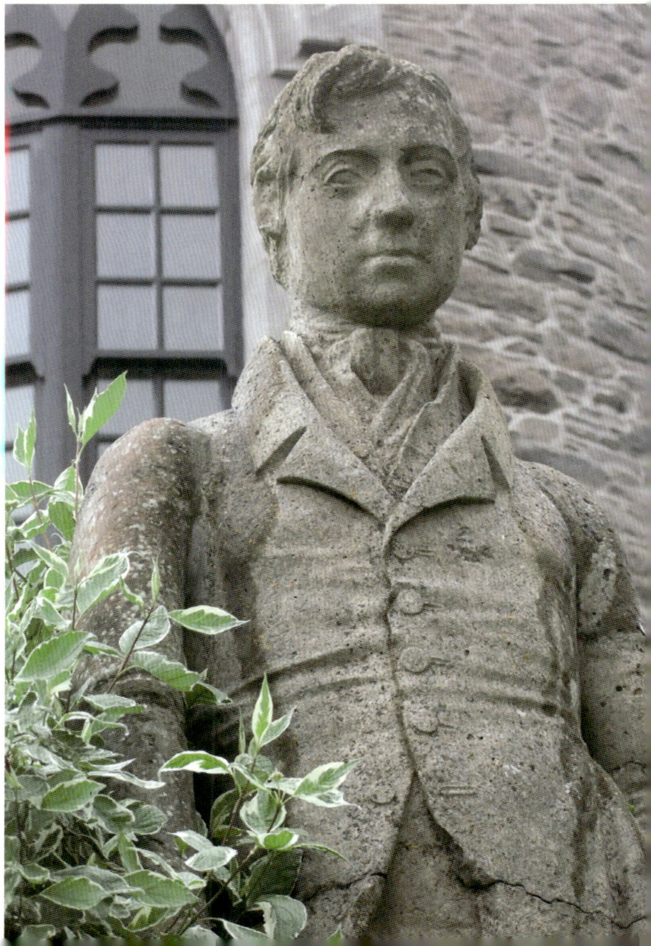

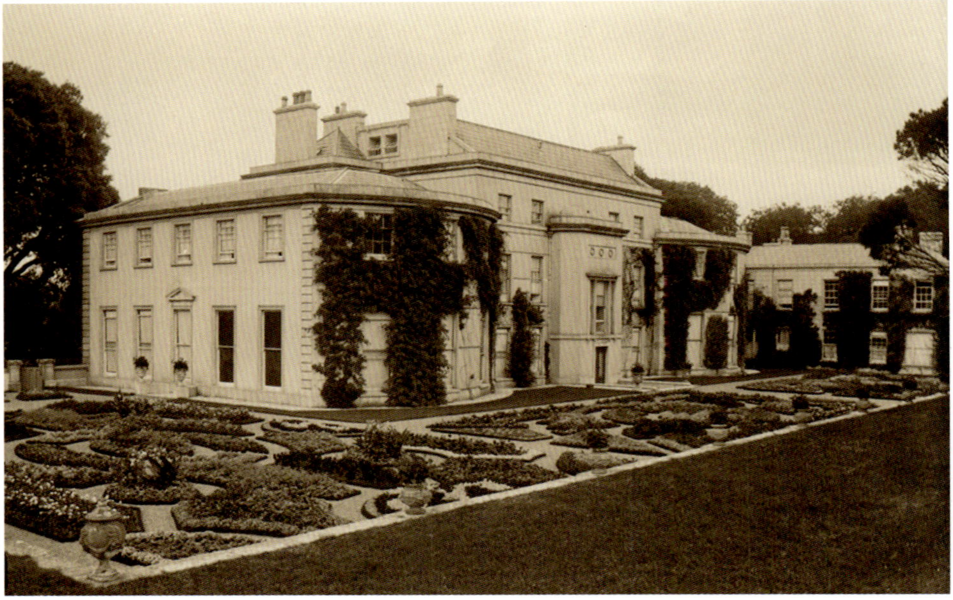

A Parkland of Narratives, Fota House, Foaty Island

Fota House, formerly an eighteenth-century hunting lodge, was the centrepiece of an estate on the 780-acre Fota Island. Early in the nineteenth century, the house was enlarged for John Smith Barry by Richard and William Morrison, architects of some of Ireland's finest buildings. John Smith Barry also embarked on a programme of works to turn the entire island into an estate of parkland, woods and pleasure grounds. The arboretum, with its beautiful orangery, formal walled gardens and 12 acres of parkland, was begun in the mid-nineteenth century. Today, the parkland boasts one of the finest collections of rare and tender trees and shrubs grown outdoors in Ireland and Britain, and open to the public to view. In addition, Fota Wildlife Park and Fota Golf Course are open to the public.

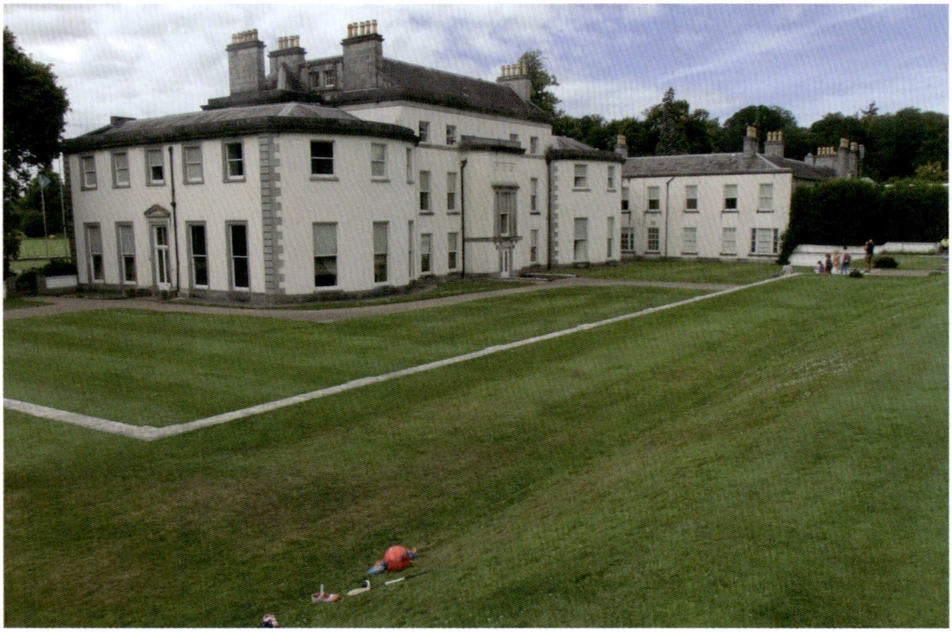

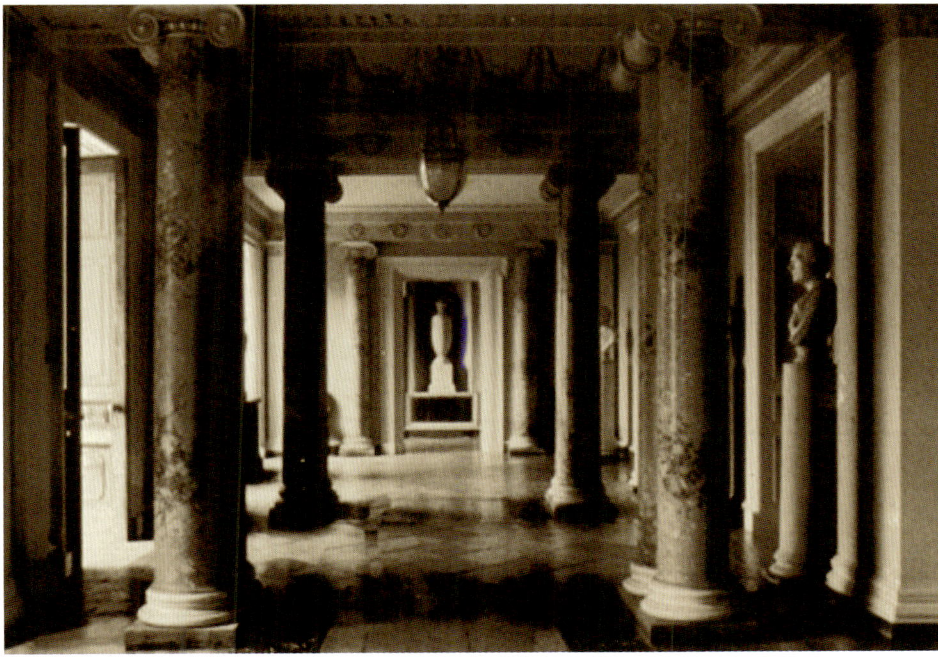

Classical Stories, Fota House

The style of Fota House is classical throughout, and the decor in the principle rooms reflects continental trends in the gilt, marble work, painted ceilings and magnificent plaster details. Guided tours during the year allow the visitor to experience the fine craftsmanship that existed in the eighteenth and nineteenth centuries. It boasts a fully restored kitchen and game larder, as well as one of the most important collections of Irish art and furniture in Ireland.

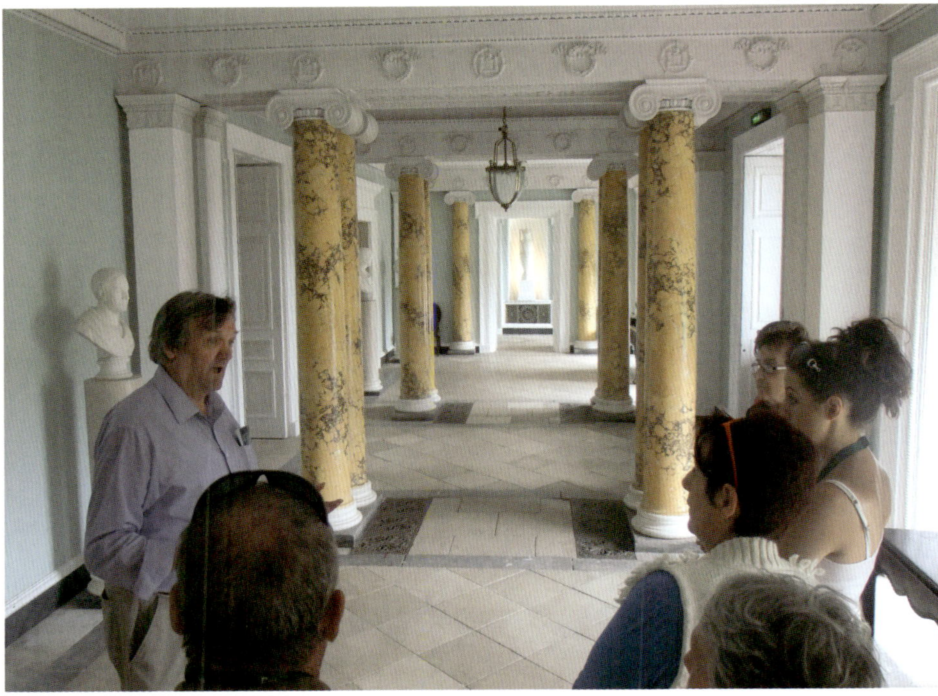

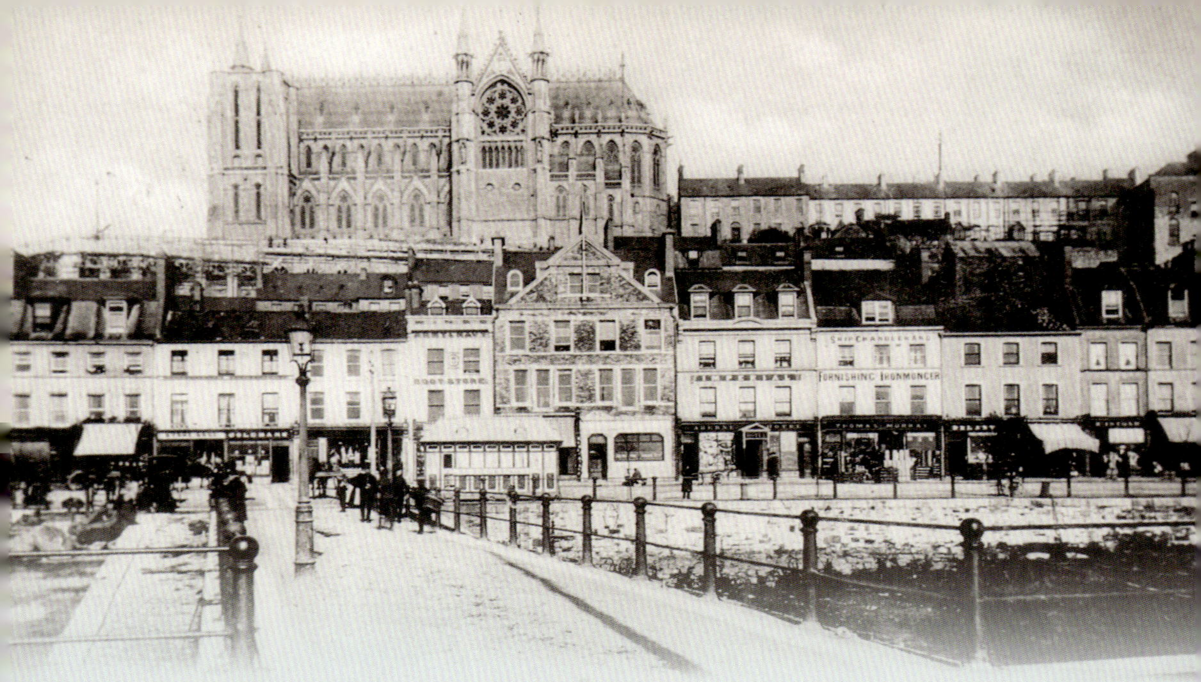

CHAPTER 2

The Great Island

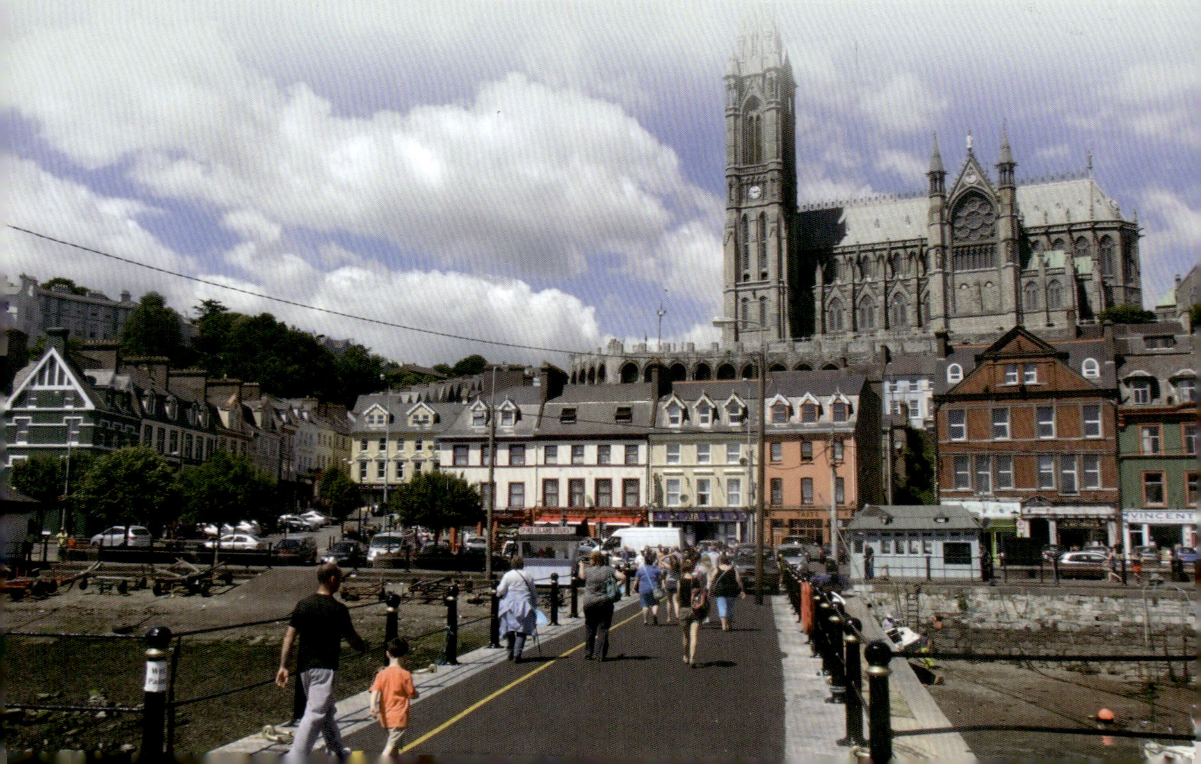

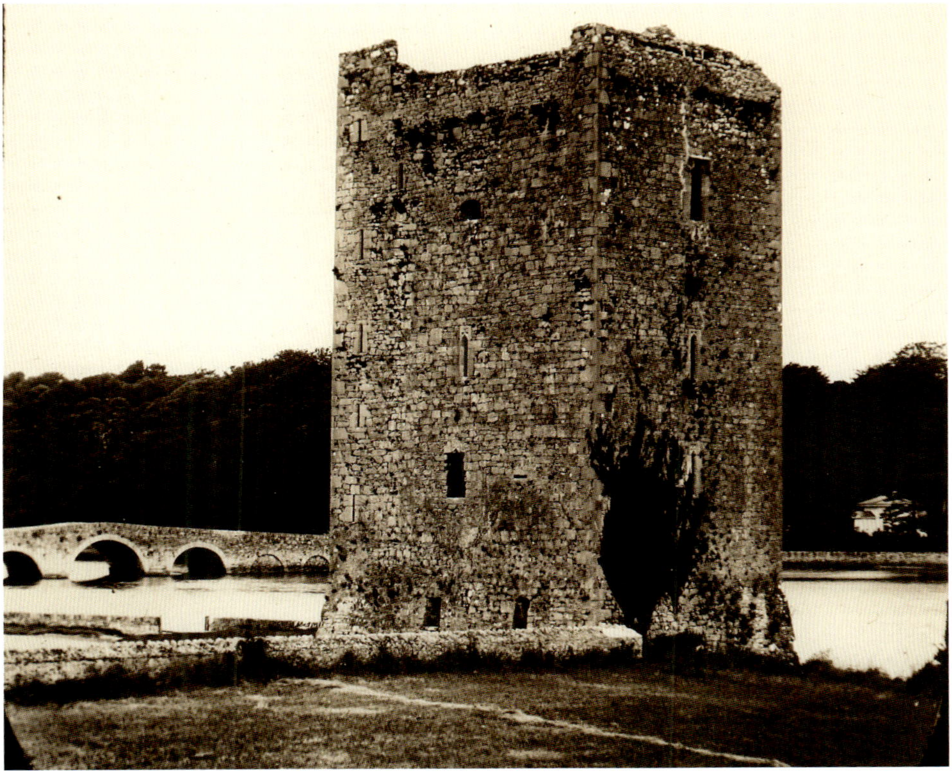

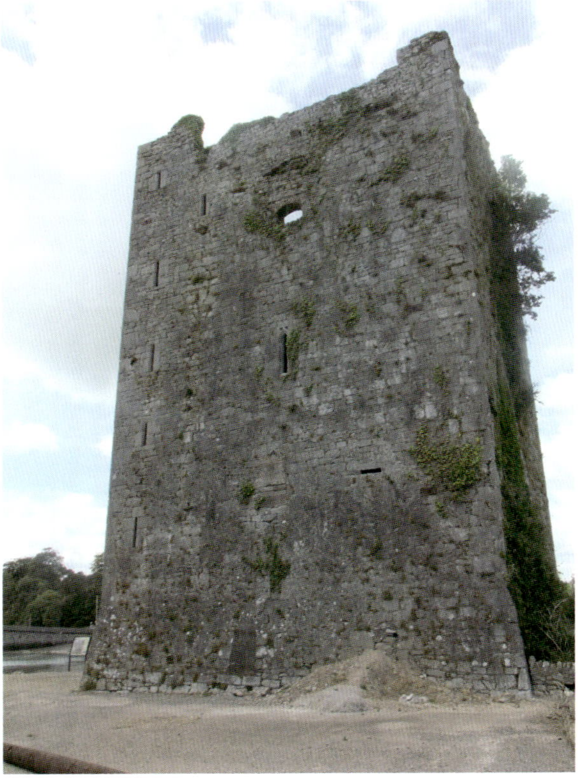

Blocks of History, Belvelly Castle, Great Island

Belvelly Castle is a typical medieval, four-storey, square tower dating from the fifteenth century. Built by the Hodnett family, it stands on a very narrow piece of land, bound by Belvelly Bridge Road (built 1807) on one side and the shore on the other. It was occupied by Sir Peter Courthorpe during 1636–51. A number of window lights have been replaced by horizontal concrete slits, built by the Irish Army during the Emergency. For such an ancient building, it is well preserved.

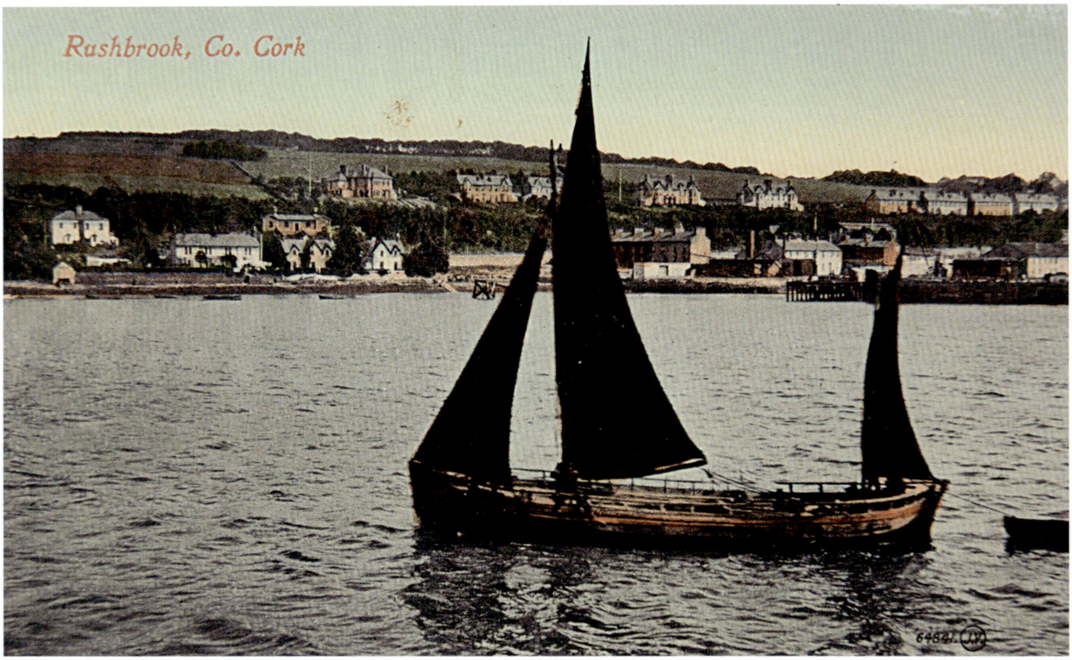

Bracing the Mainsail, Rushbrooke

Apart from busy commercial and naval dockyards, the harbour also provided a maritime space for small fishing communities, from salmon fishers working in small open boats to the large sailing trawlers. These sailed as far as Youghal to the east, and beyond Kinsale to the west. In addition, there were shrimp boats from Loughbeg and a small fishing community at Ringaskiddy. Power and speed were managed by means of brailing lines on the mainsail.

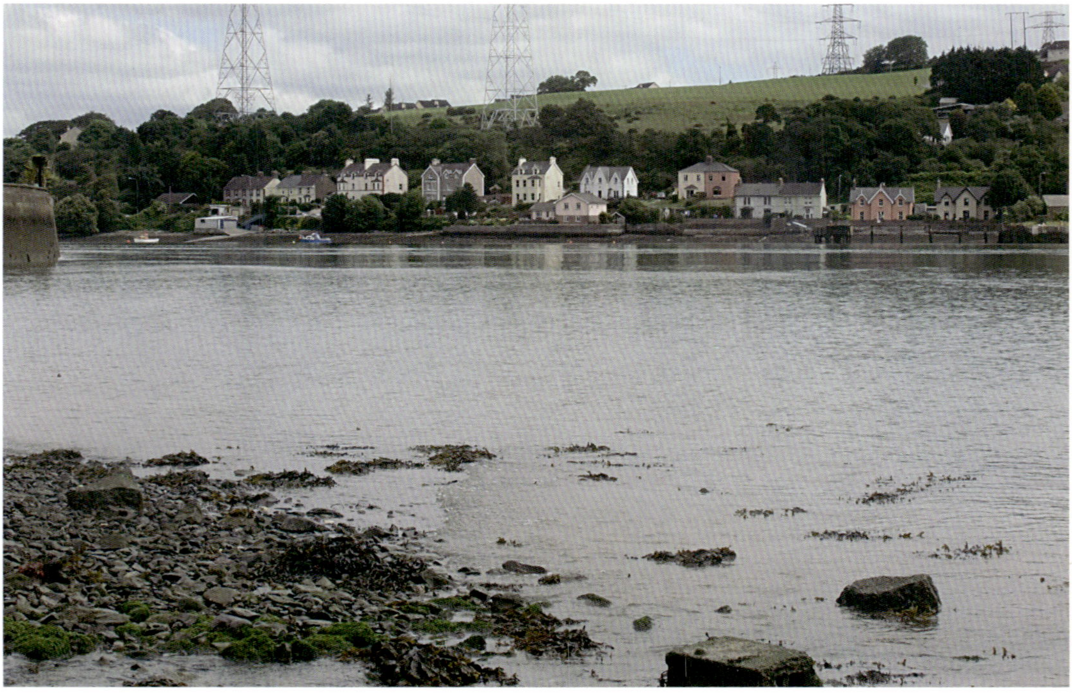

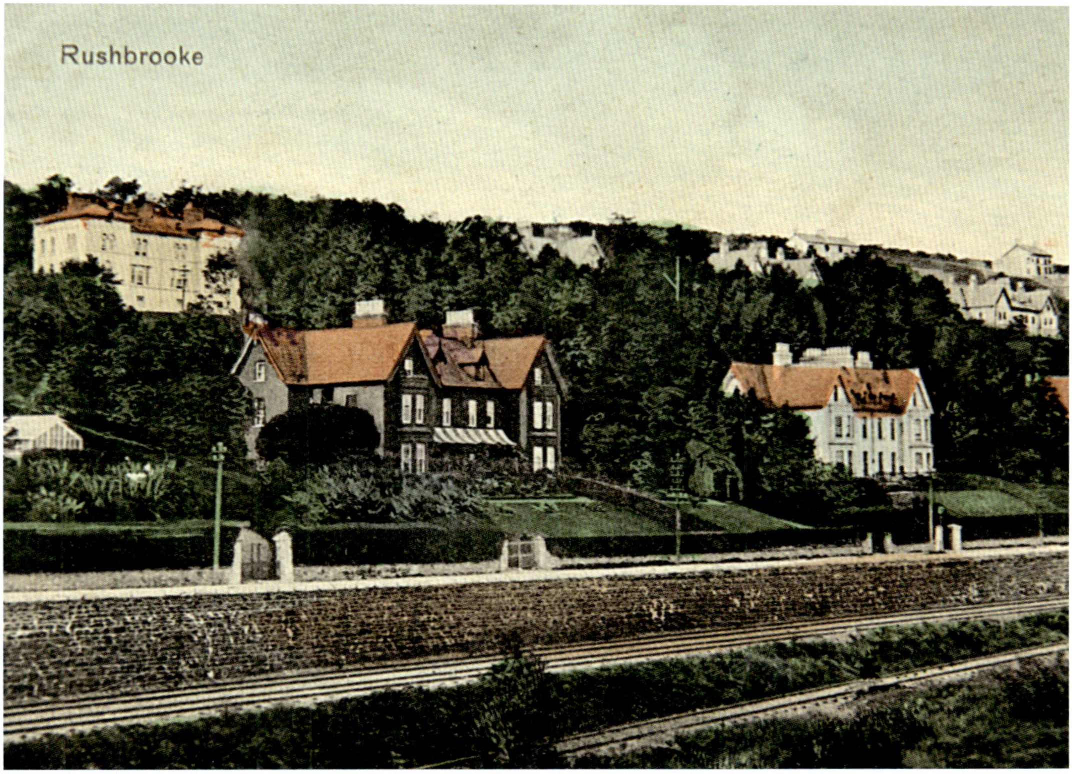

Levels and Timelines, Rushbrooke

In the 1870s, Frederica Rushbrooke of Ringmen, Queenstown, owned 1,261 acres in that county. Frederica Harriet Rushbrooke was the daughter of Col Robert Rushbrooke of Rushbrooke Hall, Suffolk, and his wife was Frances Davers. Frederica was born in 1819 and died in 1882. Her nephew, William Henry Rushbrooke of Cosford, Surrey and Whitepoint, Queenstown, was made a Count of Rome in 1892. An area on the west side of Cobh is now known as Rushbrooke. It is also the former site of the Verolme Dockyard (now partly in ruins and some operational), which opened in 1960. The site's earlier shipbuilding heritage dates back to Joseph Wheeler in 1854.

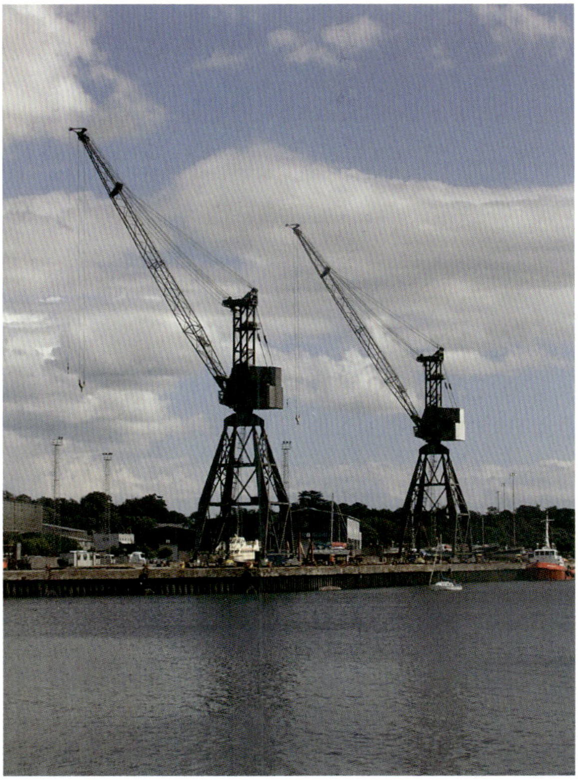

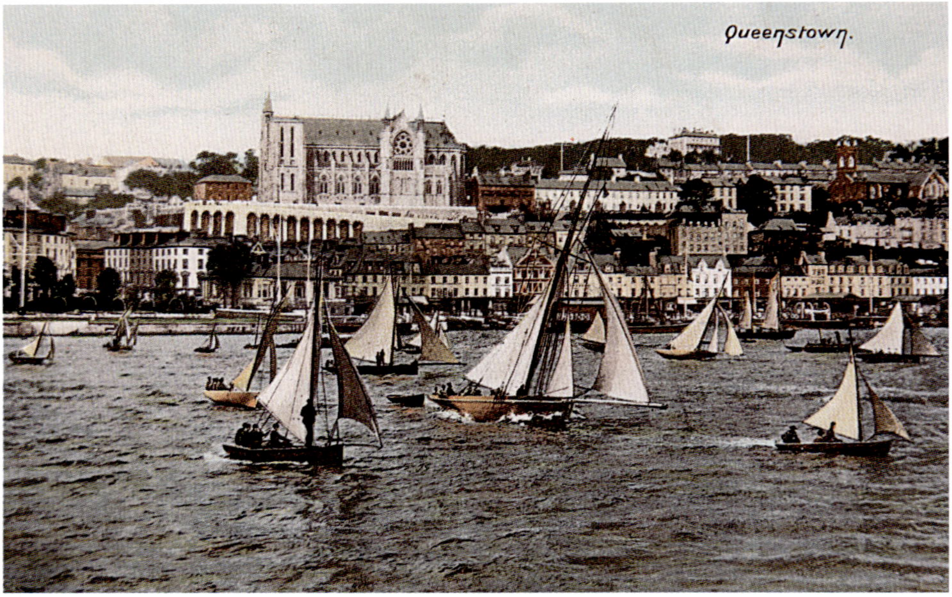

A Cove of Memories, Queenstown

In the 1780s, Cobh was a small village and was named Cove. It consisted of a few scattered houses inhabited by the tide waiters, pilots of Cork, and some miserable cabins occupied by fishermen. Its rise in population came from its convenient location for accommodating shipping in Cork Harbour. During the Napoleonic wars, 600 sailing merchant vessels were recorded at anchor there simultaneously, while 400 sailing ships left the harbour under convoy in a single day. These great fleets always lay immediately in front of the present town, and many of them were within half a cable's length of the shore. In 1849, the Queen first visited this small seaport. The port of Cove was named Queenstown after her visit. After the Irish independence of 1922, the town was renamed Cobh.

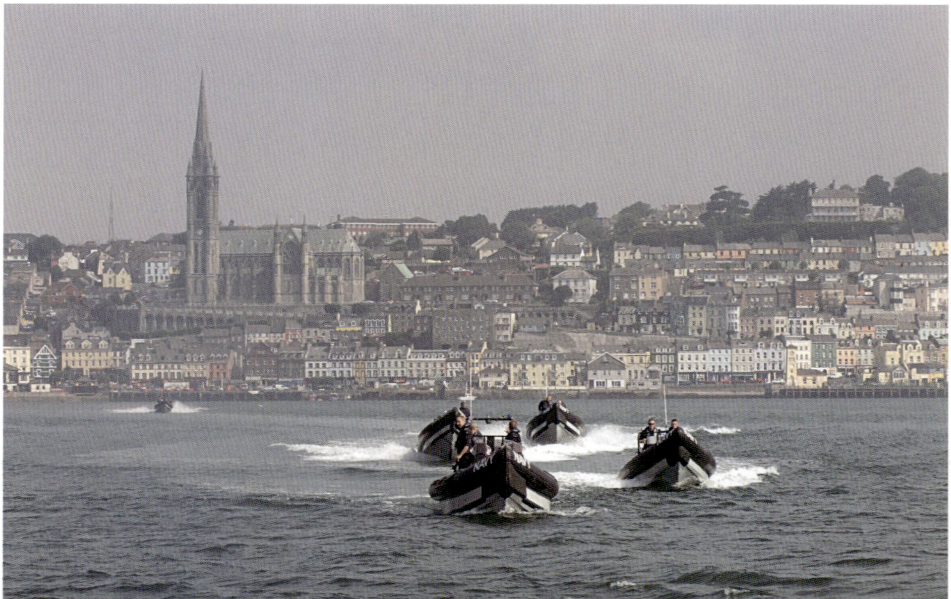

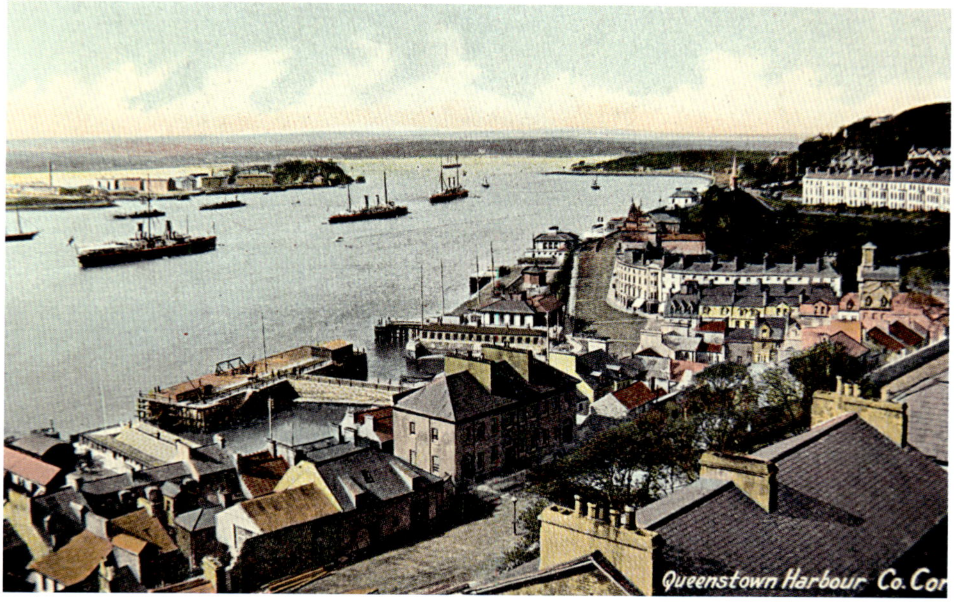

A Town Defended, Queenstown

Cobh greatly benefited by the erection of Carlisle and Camden forts; Martello towers on Great Island, Haulbowline, and Ringaskiddy; and by the bomb-proof artillery barracks on Spike Island. In addition to this, Haulbowline was fortified and made the ordnance depot, and the Lords of the Admiralty made it the only naval victualling depot in Ireland; Rocky Island was excavated and made the chief gunpowder magazine for the southern part of the country. It was also the place of embarkation for troops ordered on Foreign Service, and the station of an admiral. Vast expenditure was given by the British Navy for such works, and for the supply of provisions and other requisites for the shipping in the harbour.

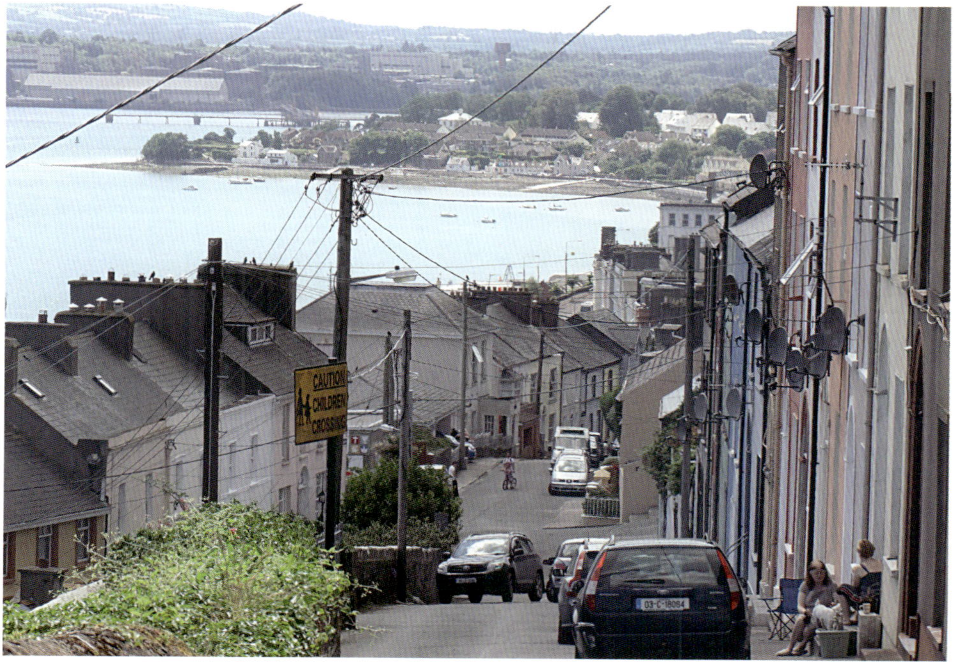

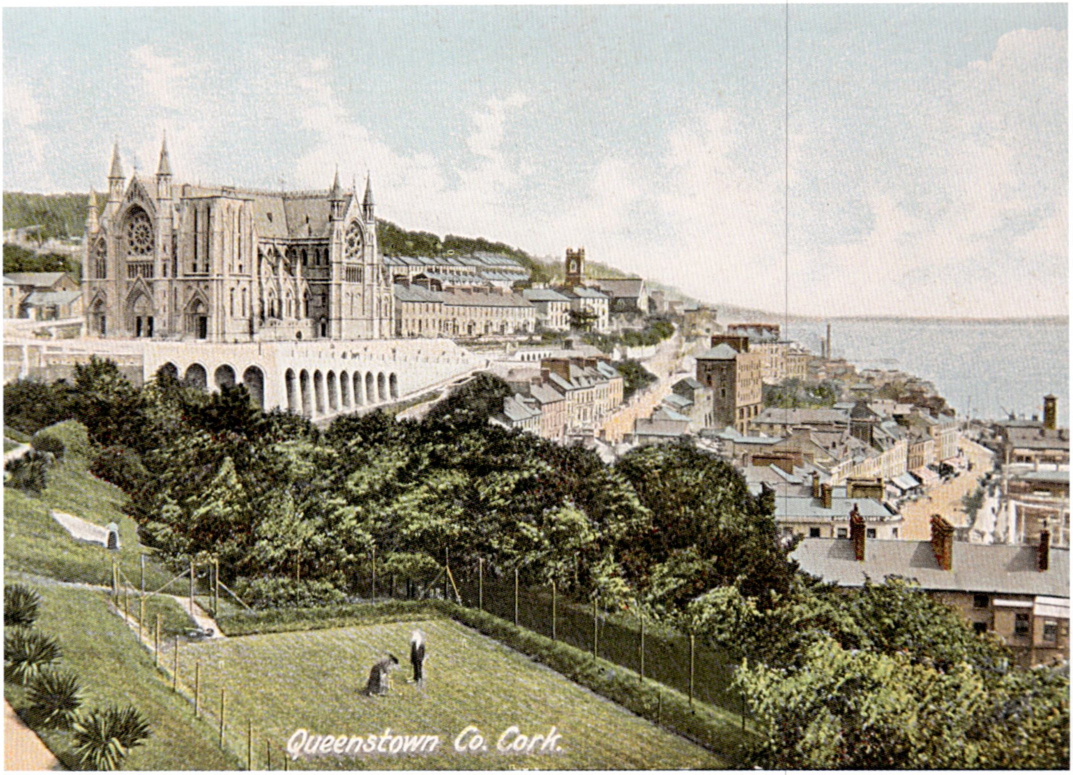

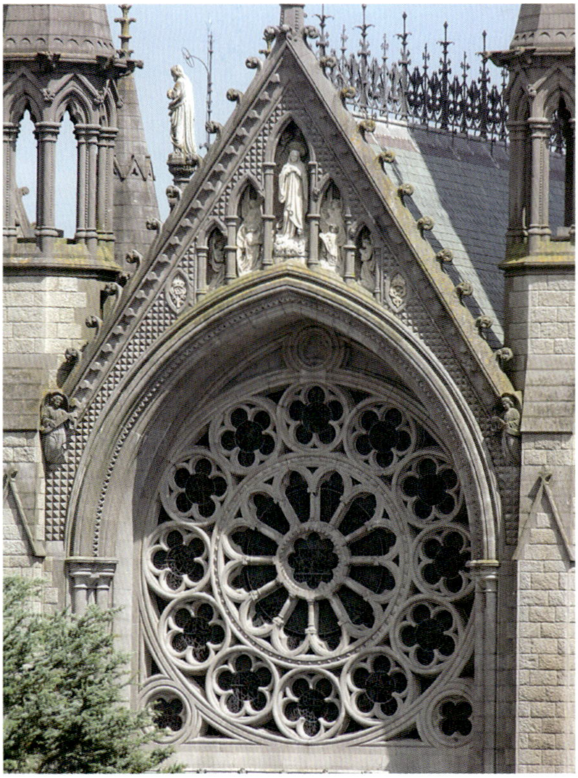

Vista Narratives, St Colman's Cathedral

St Colman's Cathedral was named after the patron saint of the diocese. The building was inspired by the great cathedrals of medieval France, such as Chartres and Amiens. Begun in 1867 and completed in 1919, the cathedral was one of Edward W. Pugin and George Ashlin's most important Irish commissions. It is one of the finest examples of ecclesiastical architecture in the Gothic revival style in Ireland. It was built at a time when leading architects had absorbed the principles of pointed architecture laid down by A. W. N. Pugin (1812–52), the father of E. W. Pugin and father-in-law of George Ashlin.

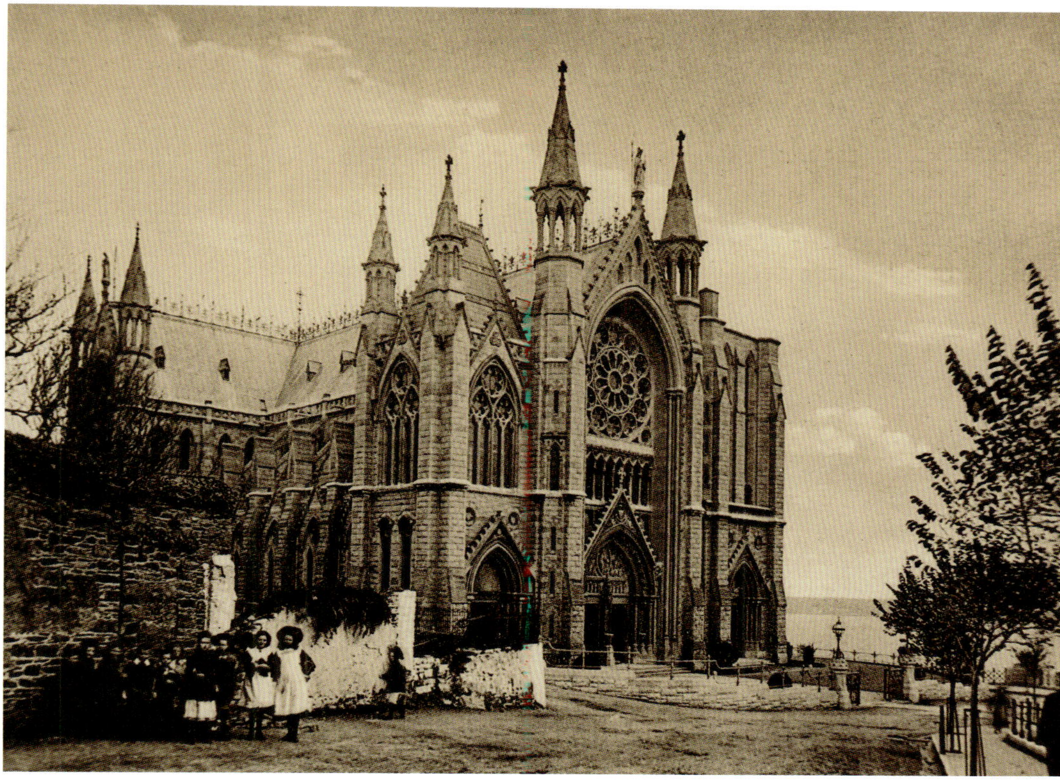

Exterior Plotlines, St Colman's Cathedral

The preparatory work for the cathedral was difficult and expensive. The widening of the roadway on the seaward side required the construction of a high, long, and thick wall of solid masonry. As the foundations were dug from steeply sloping rock, it was necessary in some parts to dig 24 feet below the level of the future floor of the church, while in other parts a firm foundation was found at a depth of only 4 feet. The first sod of the foundations were turned on 25 April 1868, and the foundation stone was laid on 15 July 1868.

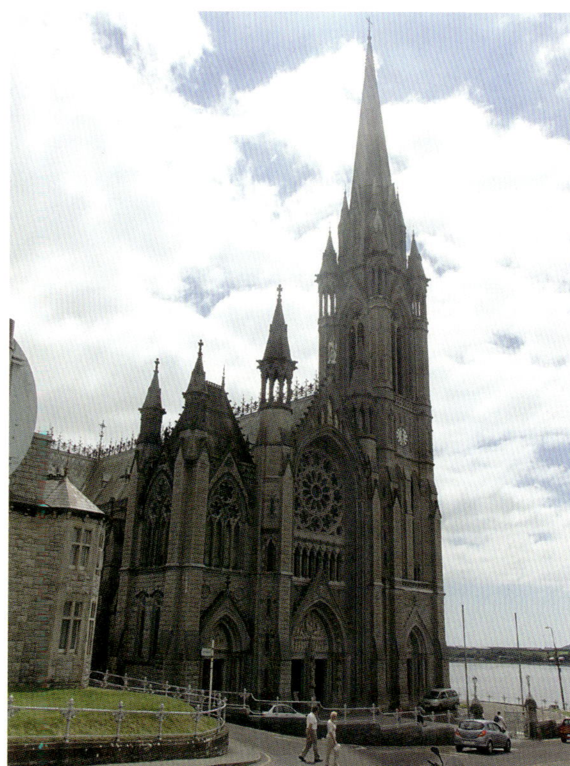

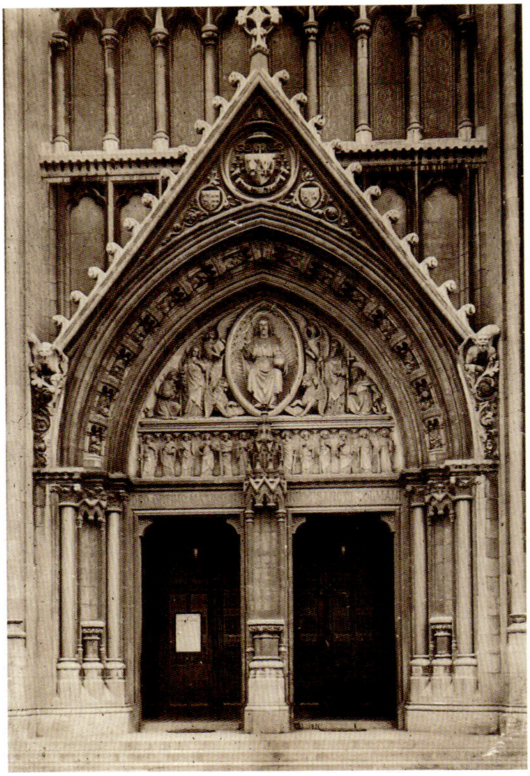

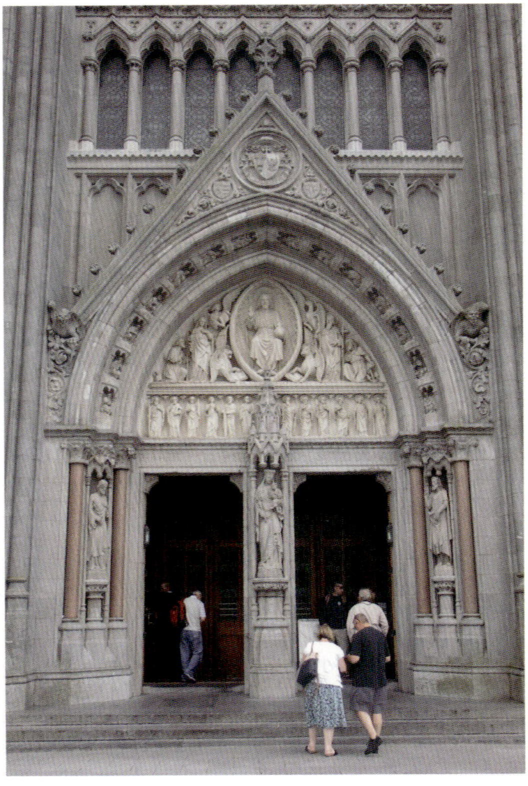

Entrance Memories, St Colman's Cathedral

Decades of careful planning went into the cathedral. The church took forty-seven years to be built, guided by three bishops. The first mass was held on 15 June 1879, with the official consecration day on 12 August 1919. A statue of St Colman stands over the west entrance. It was executed by the Dublin sculptor Joseph O'Reilly. Created in 1890, it stands 8 feet high and weighs 2.5 tons. Blue Dalkey granite and Mallow limestone were used in the external walls. The building contractors employed in the vast project comprised of local quarrymen, car men, labourers, limestone and bath stonemasons, sawyers, nailers, carpenters, smiths, plumbers, tradesmen's helpers and numerous general stonemasons.

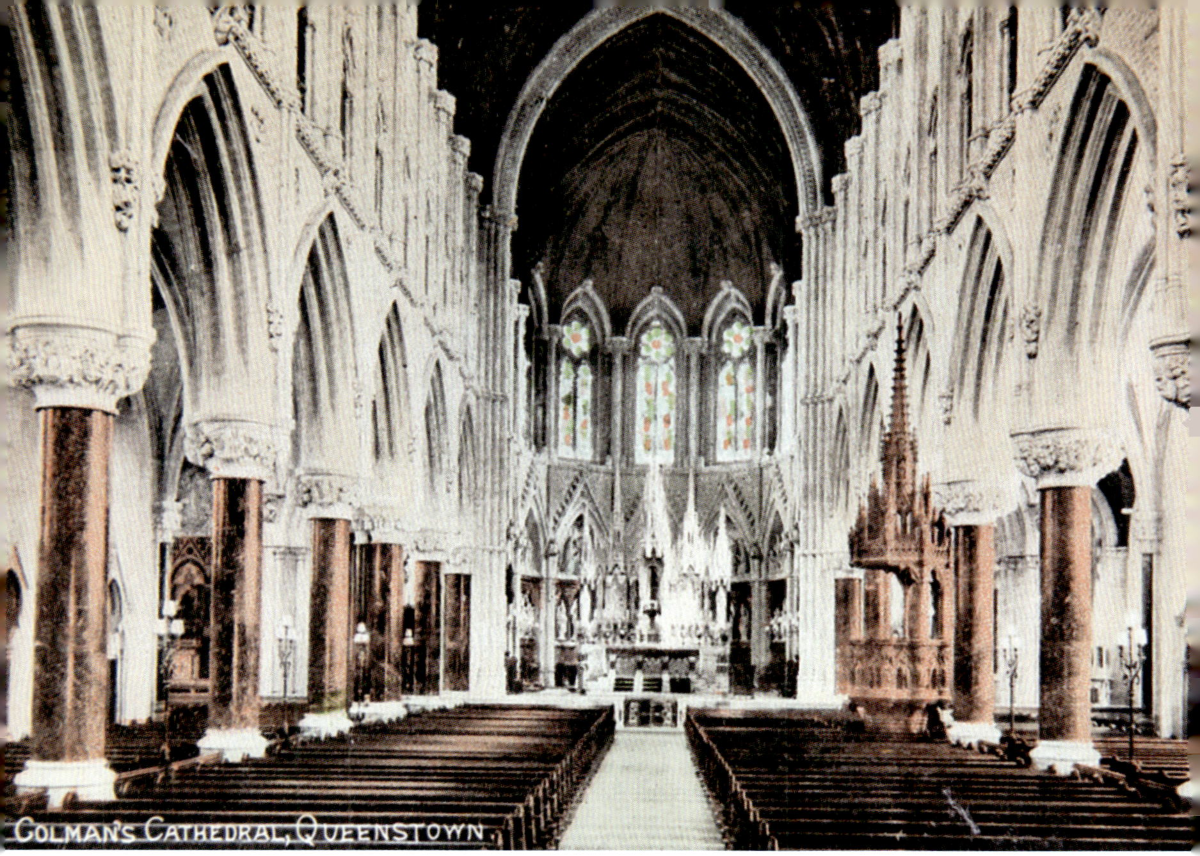

Interior Views, St Colman's Cathedral

Richly embellished and impressive in its design, the cathedral interior boasts different forms of marble. Fermoy red marble is used in the nave columns that rest on Italian white marble. Midleton red marble is used in the shrines and the first confessionals of both aisles. Connemara green marble is used in sanctuary pillars. Kilkenny black marble is used in engaged columns at the end of the north aisle. Italian white marble is used in communion raila and altar tables. Caen (Brittany) Stone is used in the Stations of the Cross. Californian Pitchpine is used in the ceiling of the nave and in seating. Austrian Oak is used in screens, the Bishop's throne, the canons' stalls and the pulpit.

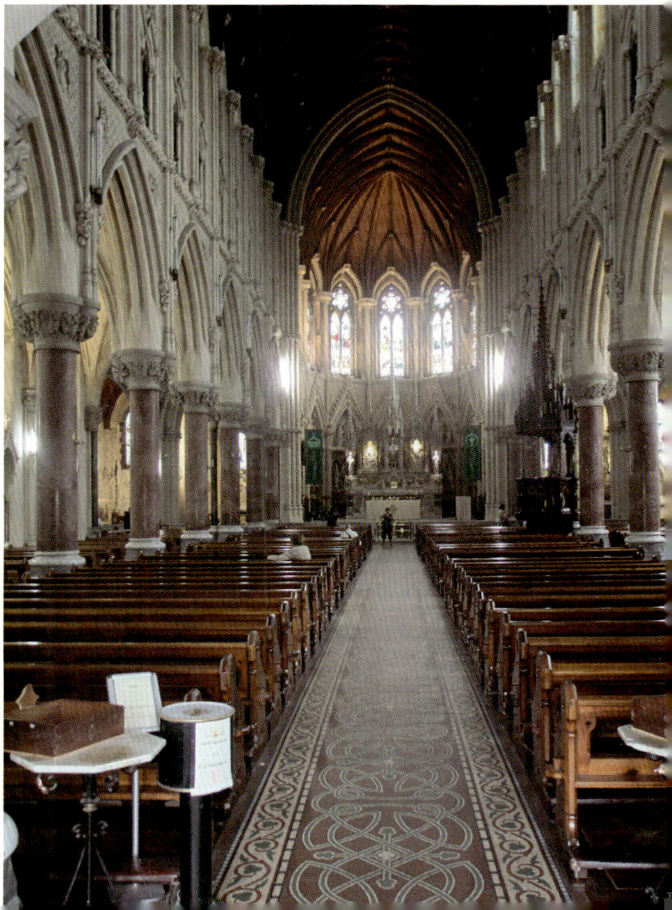

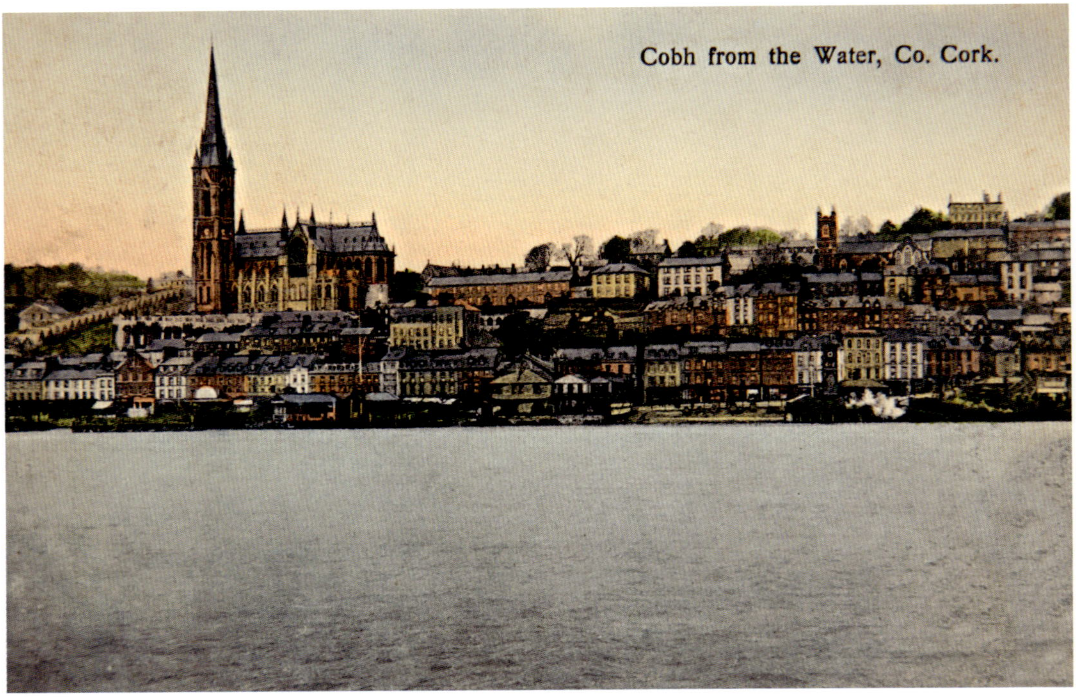

Landscapes at Queenstown

Various accounts of from 100 years ago record Cobh as built on the side of a 'clay slate hill', on the south shore of Great Island, which rises from the water's edge, and is very steep. The streets that are parallel to the shore rise tier above tier and, being on a very steep landscape, present a picturesque view from the entrance to the harbour.

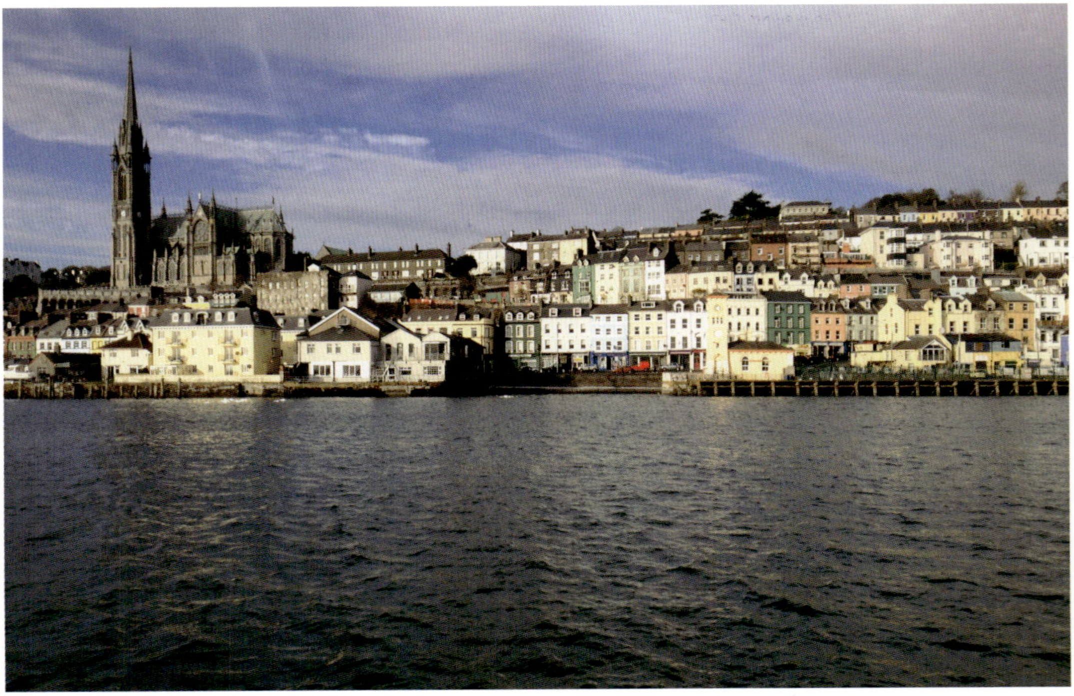

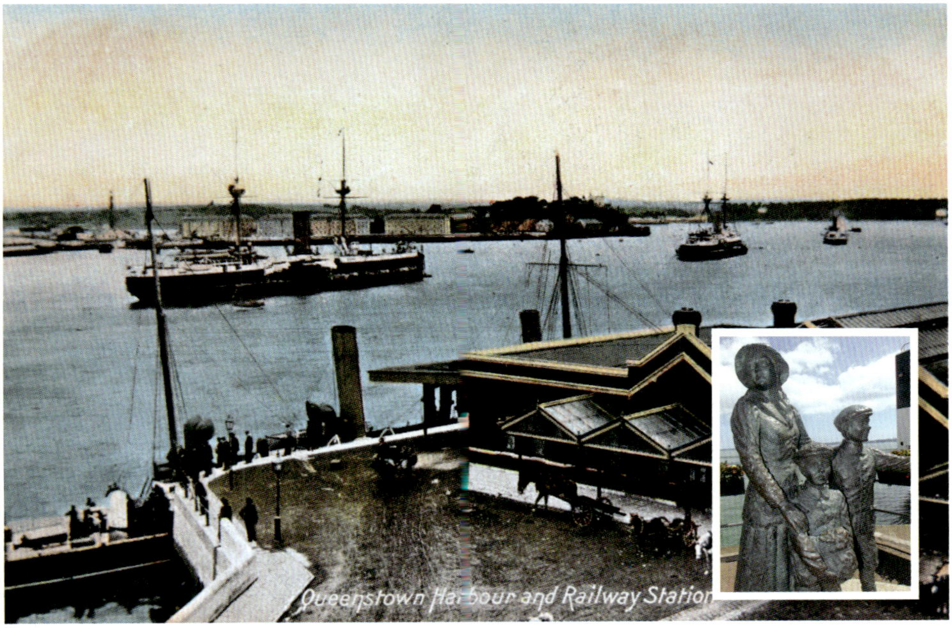

A Queenstown Story, Emigration and Annie Moore

From 1848 to 1950, over 2.5 million Irish departed from Cobh, making it the single most important port of emigration. When Ellis Island officially opened on 1 January 1892, the first passenger to register through the now world-famous immigration station was a young Cork girl named Annie Moore. Just fourteen years old and travelling with her two younger brothers, Anthony (eleven) and Phillip (seven), Annie departed from Queenstown on 20 December 1891 aboard the SS *Nevada*. There is a statue remembering her on the pier here (*inset*) and in Ellis Island.

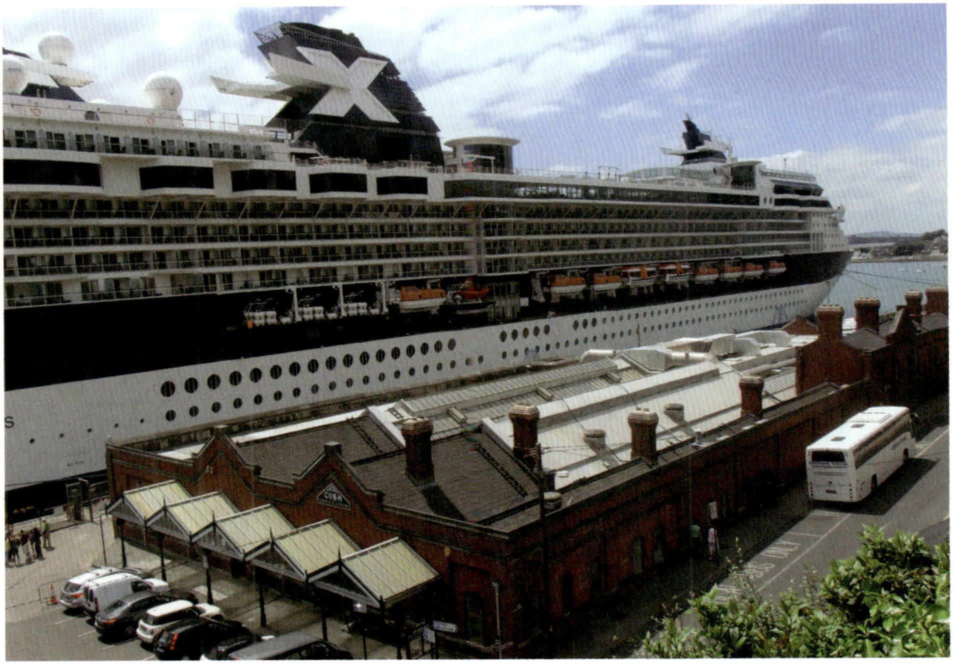

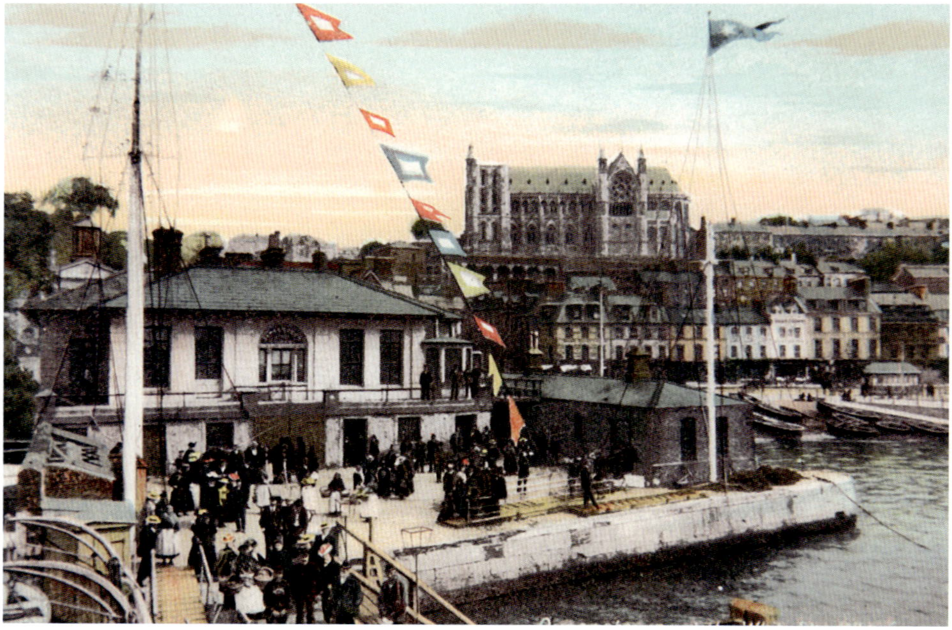

Titanic Connections, Queenstown

Cobh was the last port of call of RMS *Titanic*. The White Star Line pier is the same structure that supported the 123 *Titanic* passengers who embarked on that fateful voyage in April 1912. The *Titanic* passengers were not alone in crossing this jetty. The pier is also symbolic for the thousands of Irish emigrants who departed from the town of Cobh to build new lives abroad and in the USA. The 100th anniversary commemoration of the sinking of the *Titanic* took place in 2012, and ongoing lobbying of local and national government is still taking place to secure the future of the pier. Titanic Experience Cobh is a visitor attraction, which is located in the original offices of The White Star Line (as shown above and below).

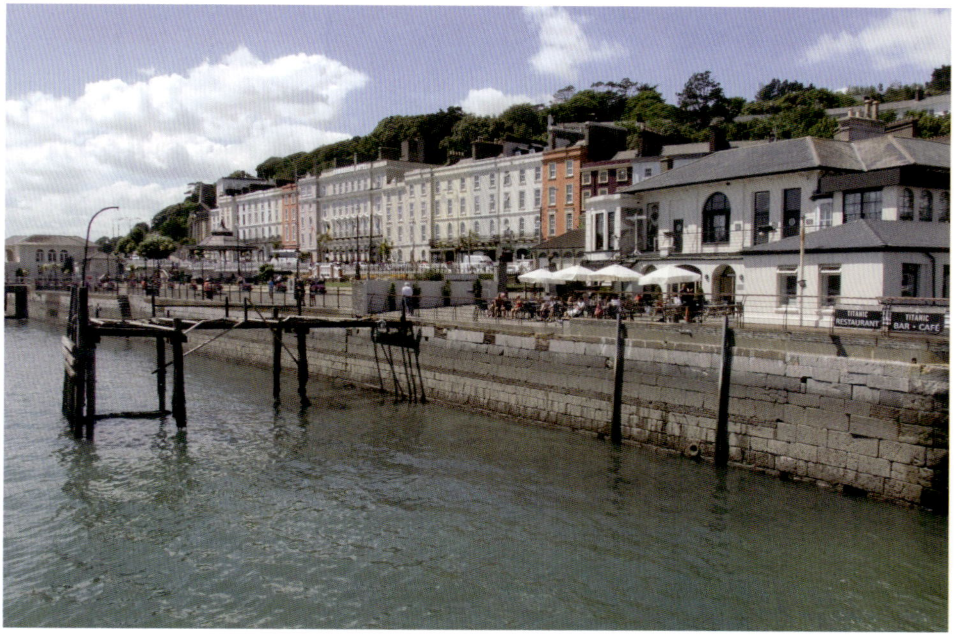

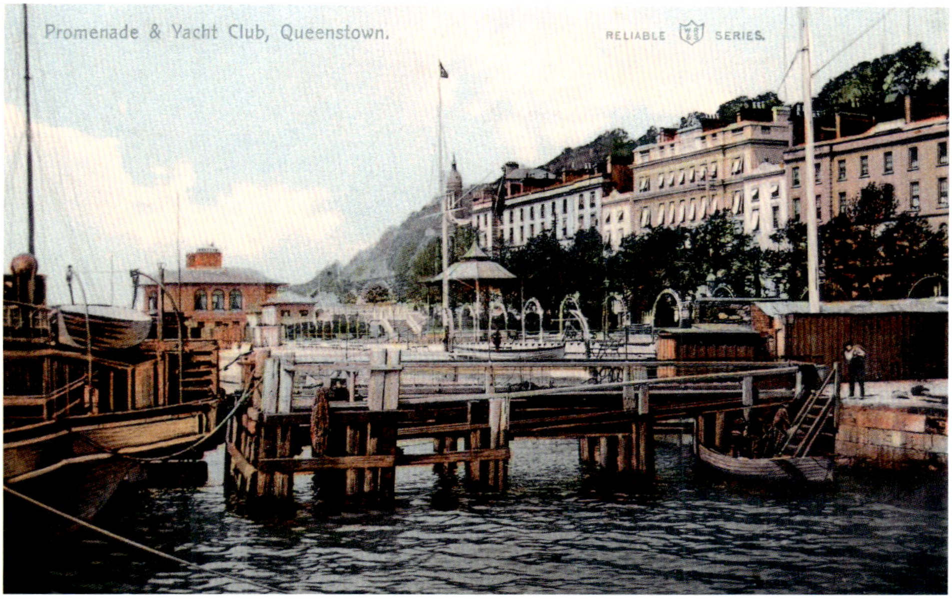

Royal Cork Yacht Club, Queenstown

The Royal Cork Yacht Club (RCYC), whose station was at Queenstown, is the oldest of its kind in Britain and Ireland. It owes its origin to the Water Club of Cork Harbour, established in 1720. The RCYC received an Admiralty warrant in 1831 to fly the old flag (burgee) of 1720, with a harp and crown on a green field in the centre. Near the custom house quay was the club's splendid edifice in the Italian style, now the Sirius Arts Centre. The celebrated regattas of Cove took place in July or August, and the prizes numerous and valuable. Many of the best yachts in Ireland, with some from England and Scotland, attended the event.

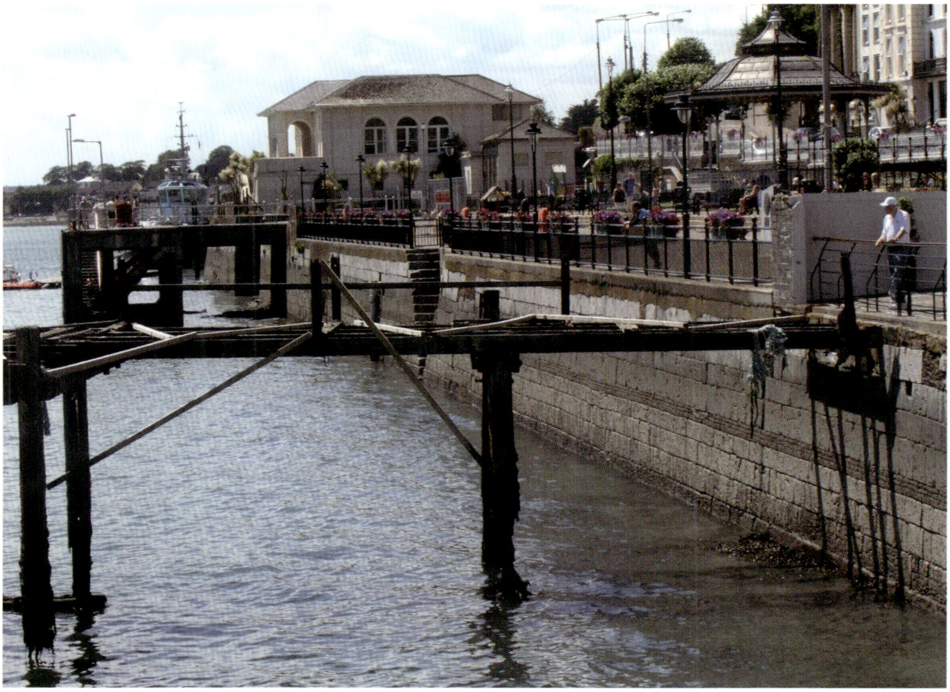

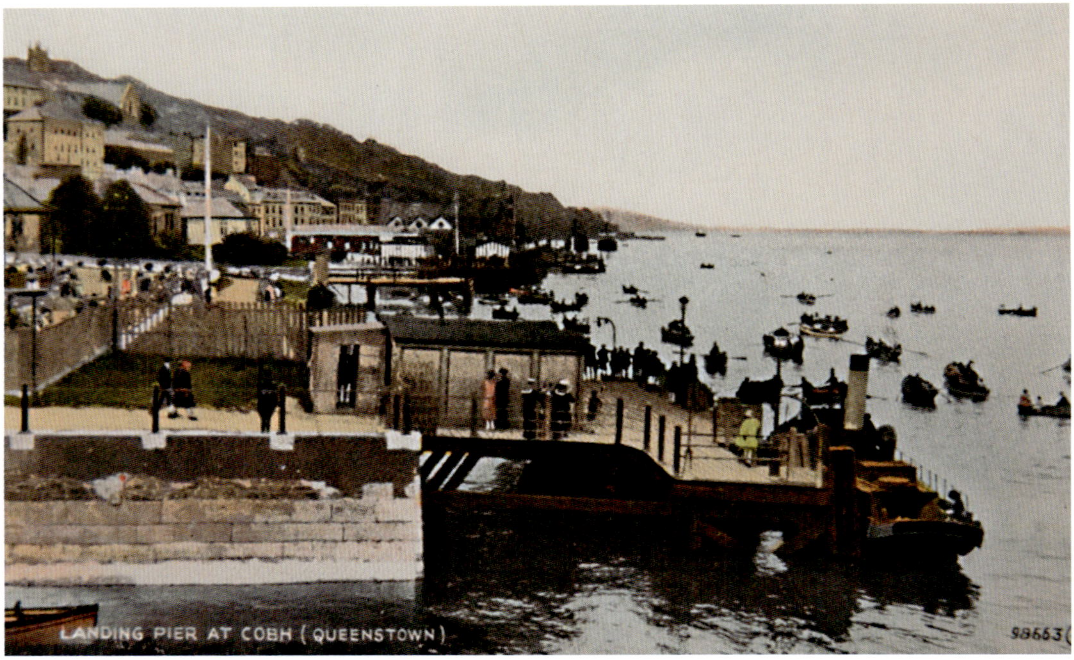

Pier memories, Royal Cork Yacht Club

The Royal Cork Yacht Club had been using various premises in Cobh as clubhouses, but eventually, in 1854, it moved into a magnificent new building built on land given by the then Admiral, J. H. Smith Barry. The building, which stands directly on the waterfront, was to become not only a major yachting centre, but also an essential meeting place for Cork society. In 1966, the Royal Cork and the Royal Munster Yacht Clubs agreed to merge, and the Royal Cork moved to its present premises in Crosshaven. Since 1988, the Cobh building is now the Sirius Arts Centre.

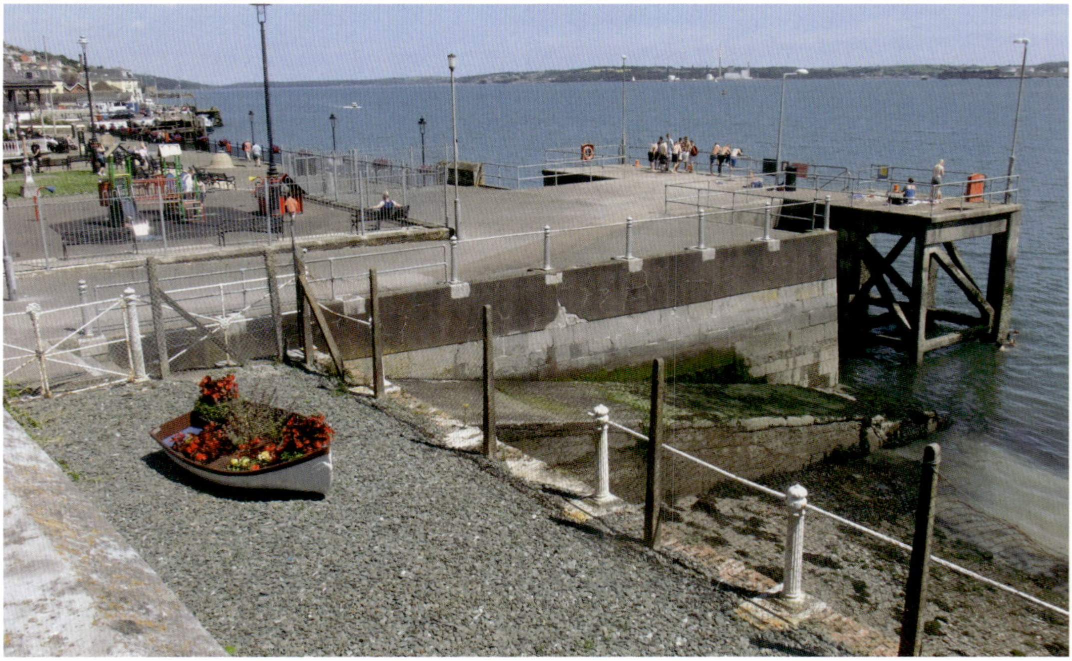

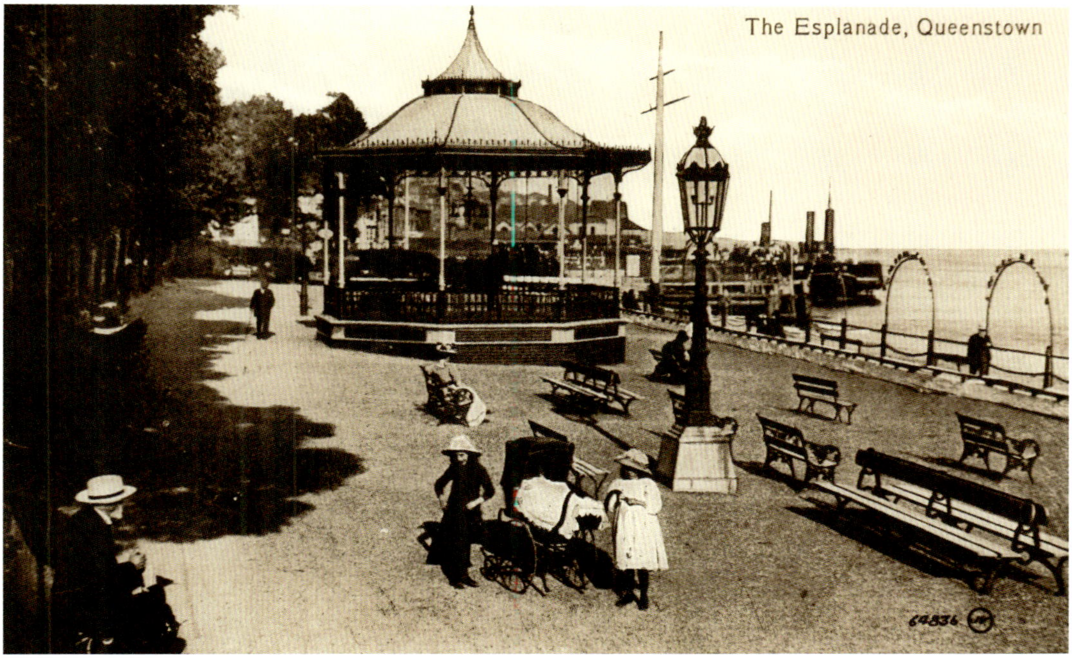

At the Water's Edge, John F. Kennedy Promenade, Cobh

This promenade on the water's edge is a favourite place for locals and visitors to relax. The bandstand was originally built for the visit of Queen Victoria in August 1849. During the summer months, regular band recitals take place here. The two cannons in the promenade were returned from the Boer and Crimean Wars in 1899 and 1854 respectively. Later on, the promenade was named after US President, John F. Kennedy.

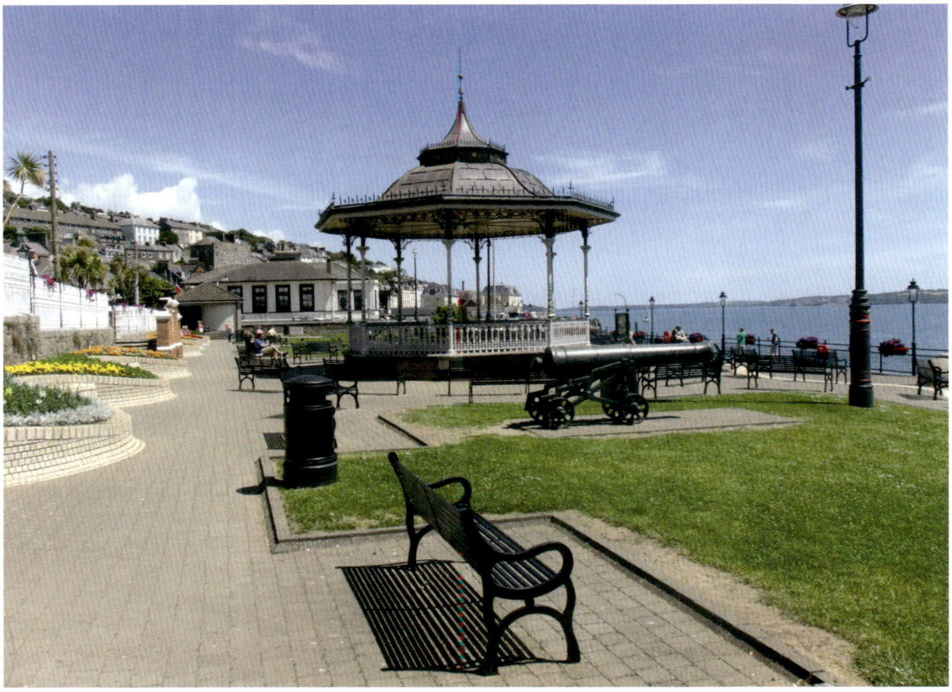

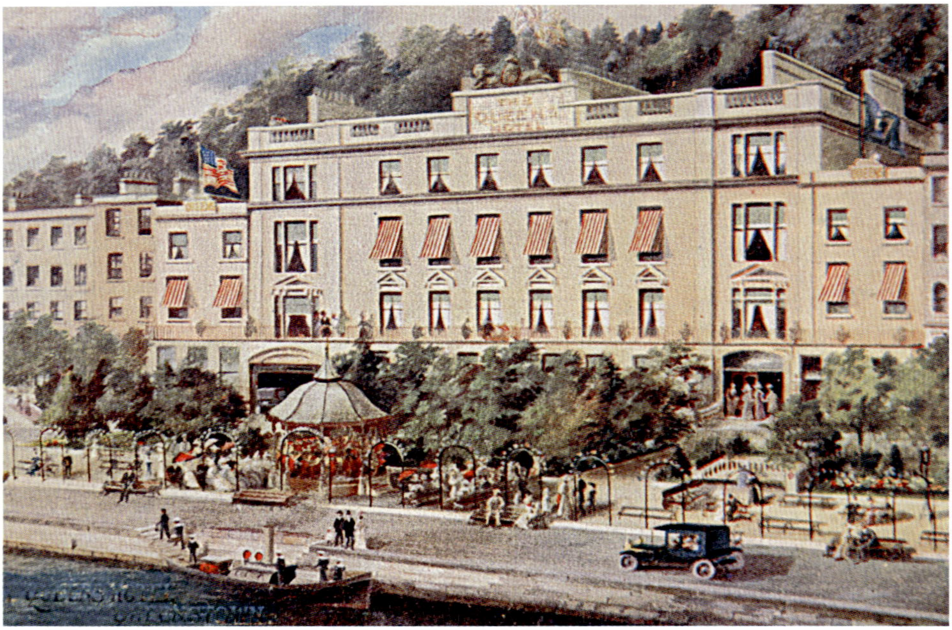

States Hotel, Queenstown

The States Hotel, now the Commodore Hotel, was built in 1854 and consisted of fifty sitting and sleeping arrangements, two coffee rooms, a billiards room and fresh and saltwater baths. The hotel is recorded to be one of the first purpose-built hotels in Ireland. The hotel ownership changed hands in 1874 and was taken over by Mr Raymond. However, the most noted owner of the hotel was Otto Humbert, who owned the hotel during the time of the *Lusitania* sinking in 1915. The family had just taken over the hotel and began focussing on attracting passengers from the liner traffic that passed through the harbour.

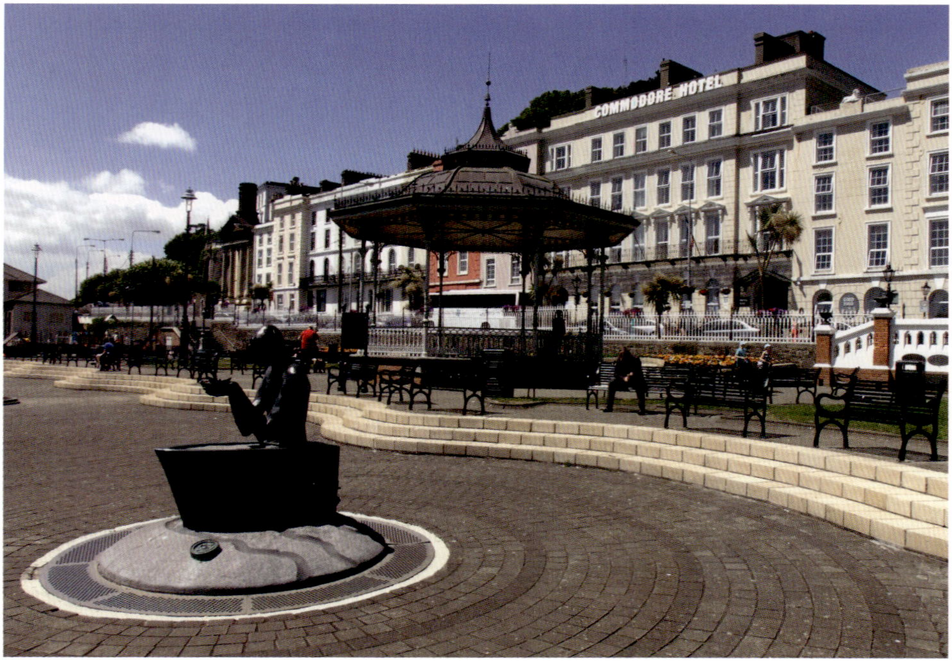

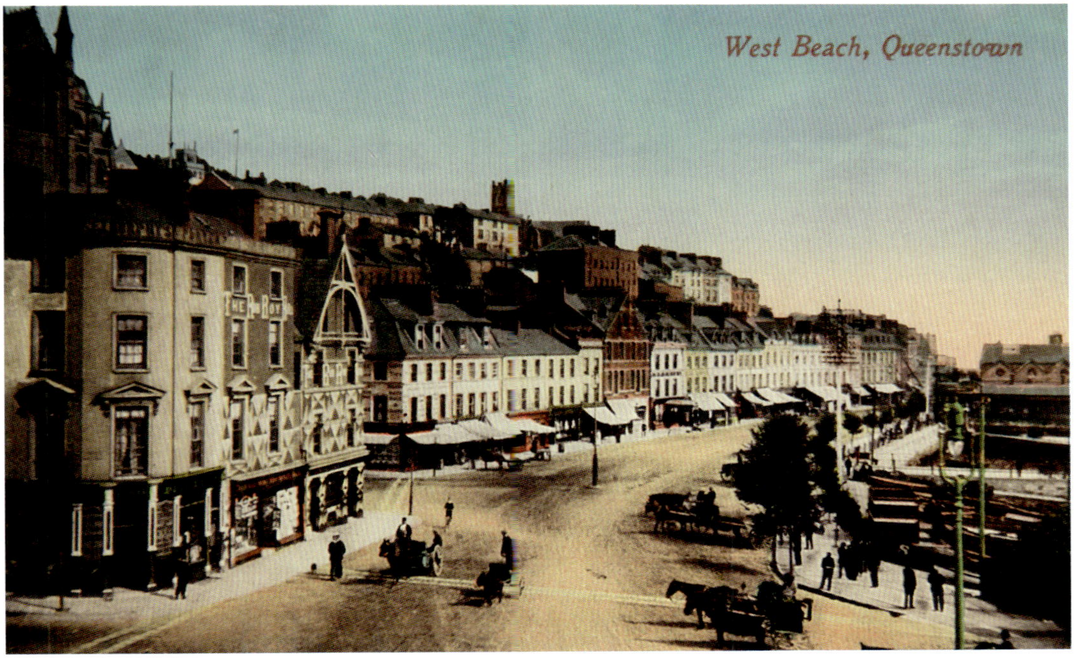

Visually Striking West Beach, Queenstown

In the early part of the nineteenth century, there were still very few streets or buildings in the developing town of Cobh. The successive Lords of Midleton were mostly responsible for the development of the thriving town and commercial port. Lord Midleton had quays and houses built along what is currently known as the East and West beach. What is now the courthouse and library was built in 1806 as a market house. St Mary's Protestant church and parts of the Midleton Road were also built around this time.

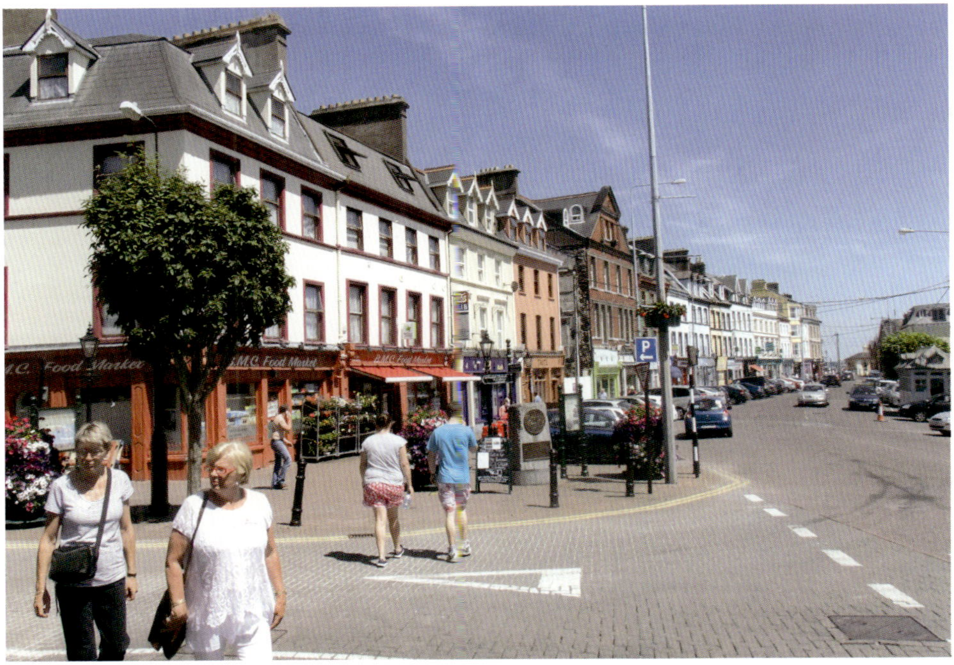

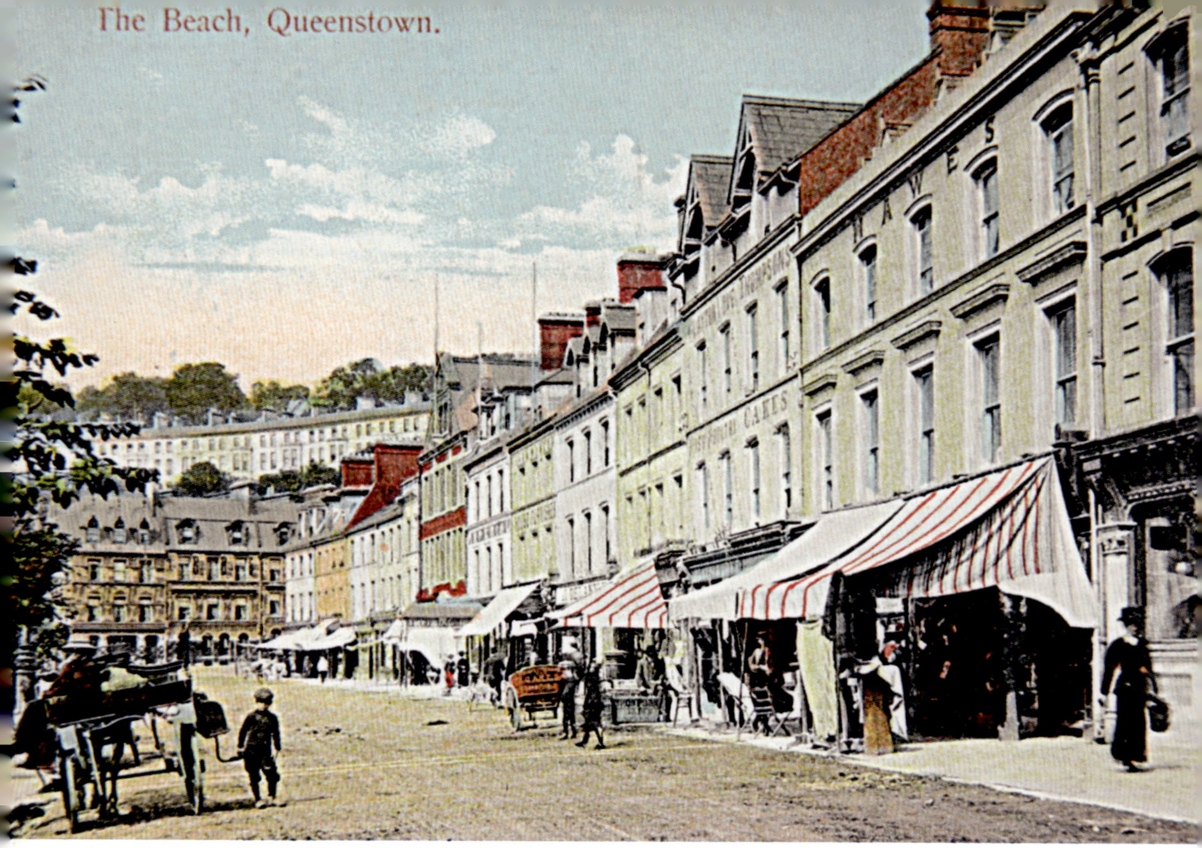

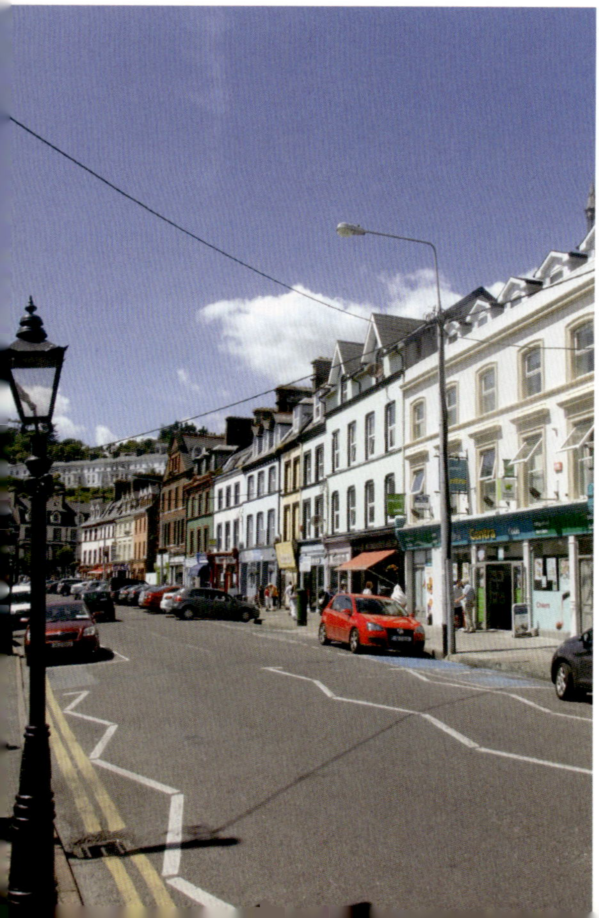

West Beach, Queenstown

A read through the businesses on the street in a County Cork Directory for 1914 reveal an eclectic mix of businesses on this visually striking street, but also a focus of the sale of provisions. In 1914, West Beach could boost 2 bakers, 1 boot and shoemakers, 1 coal merchants, 1 confectioners, 1 dairy, 6 drapers, 1 fish store, 3 fruiterers, 5 grocers and provision dealers, 1 general naval and military contractors, 1 Irish lace manufacturers , 2 ironmongers, 1 jewellers and watchmakers, 1 lodgings boarding houses, 1 emigrant lodging house, 1 printer, 1 ship chandler, 2 stationers, 3 tobacconists, 2 victuallers, and 2 vintners.

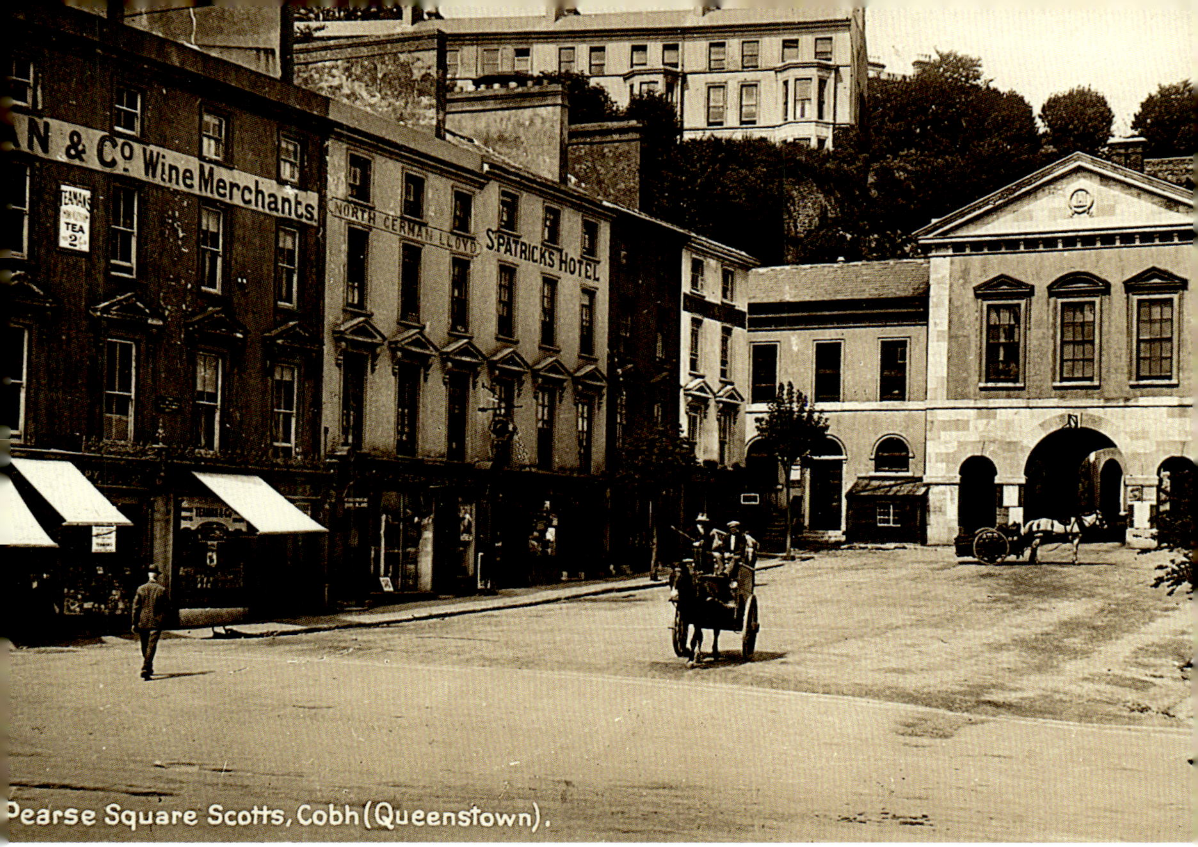

Remembering the *Lusitania*, Pearse Square
The sinking of the *Lusitania* on May 7 1915, after it was torpedoed by a German U-boat, had a prominent impact on Cobh. Survivors were brought to local Cunard Line offices and the rescue operations were launched out of the town by fishermen and naval personnel based there. The old church graveyard also contains the remains of 193 people who died in the tragedy. Of those, forty-five were unidentified and their coffins merely marked with a number. The monument pictured below is by Irish American sculptor of note Jerome Connor and was unveiled in 1968. Seamus Murphy was responsible for the stone carvings. To underline the importance of the local fishermen in rescuing the survivors, two of them are depicted in the memorial below the so-called Angel of Peace. The Lusitania Peace Memorial Committee included Franklin Roosevelt, Gertrude Vanderbilt and other leading public figures.

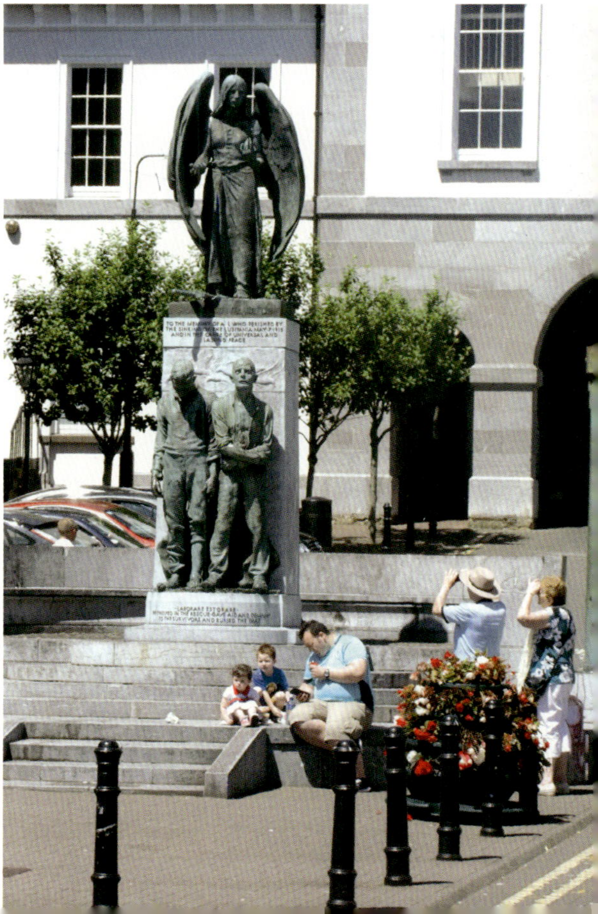

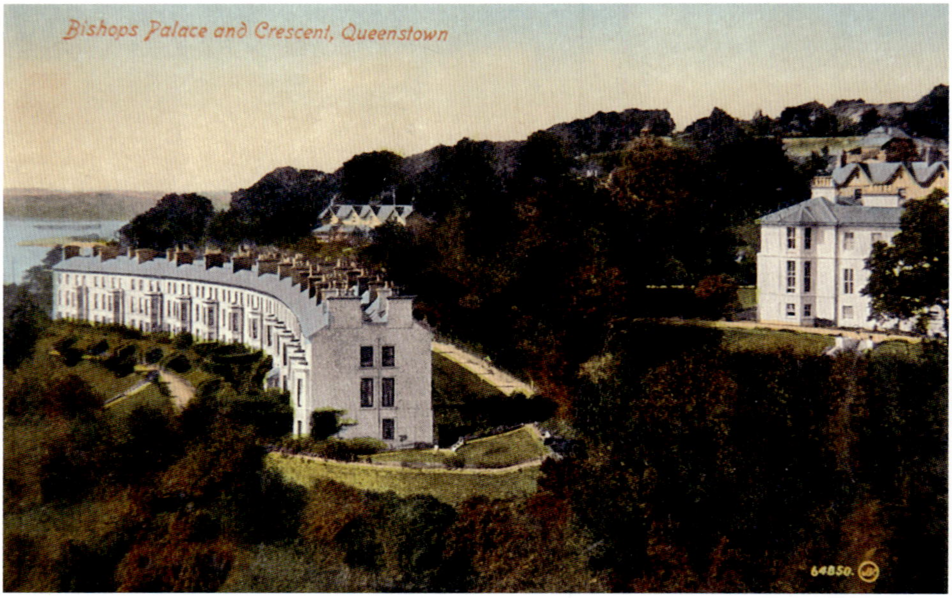

A Gem of a Crescent, Queenstown

Following the repeal of the Corn Laws in 1846, Cobh enjoyed a half century of prosperous port trading. In the same year, Cobh again became a naval station and the admiral returned. Lord Midleton improved the road into the town, now known as high Road, the Esplanade and vill-type houses in Midleton Park. The fine crescent of thirteen houses above Market House was also built during this period. In the 1800s, Cobh was promoted as a health resort on account of its climate and location, and was on par with Bournemouth in the south of England and Ventnor on the Isle of Wight.

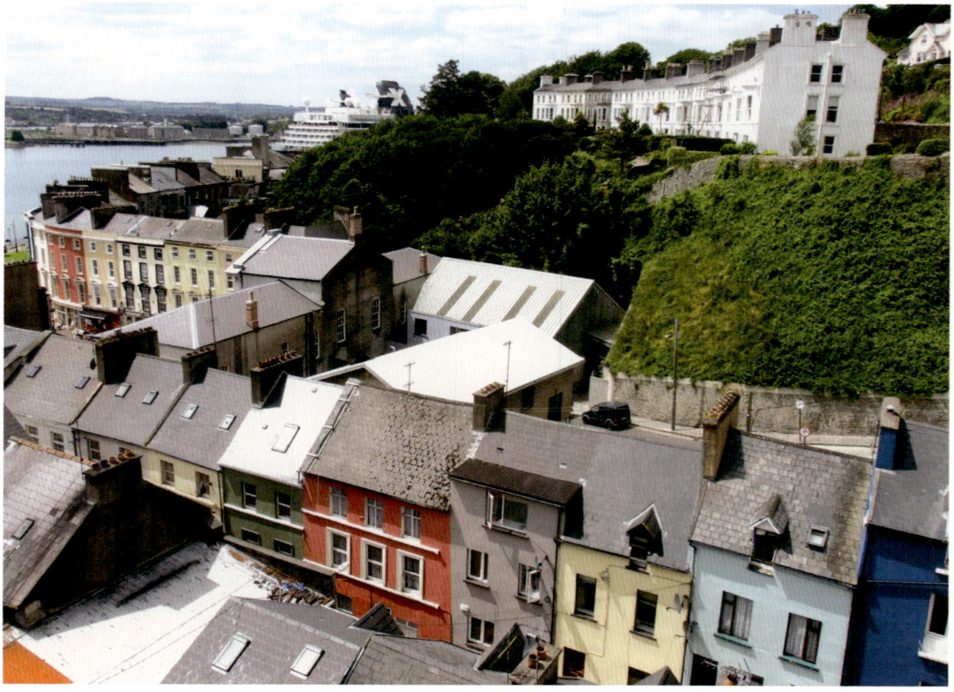

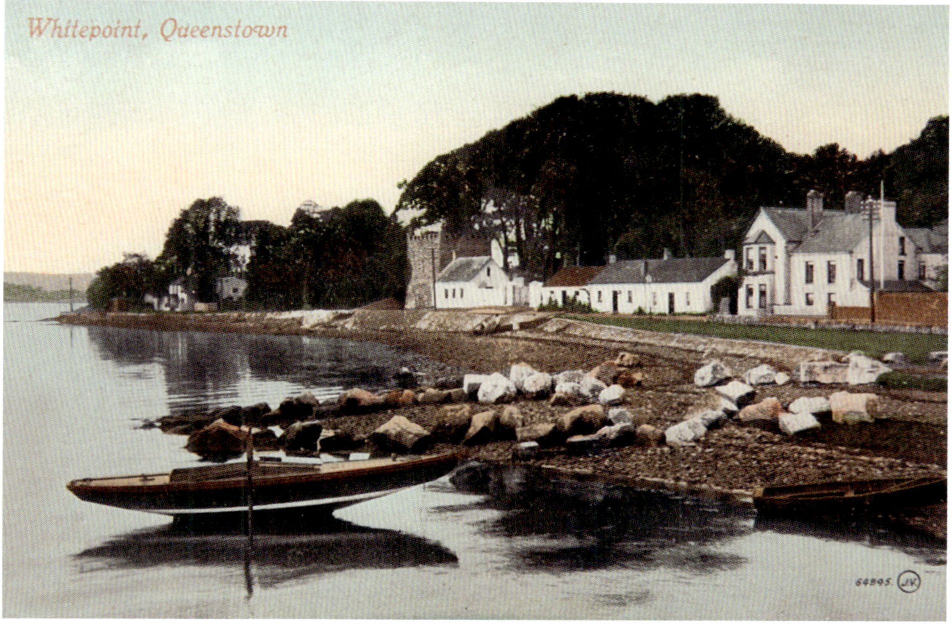

A Fishing and a Naval Hamlet, Whitepoint

A little village of a handful houses and near to Queenstown, Whitepoint was once a fishing hamlet. Its adjacent Victorian residence, built *c.* 1820, was utilised as an American naval hospital during the First World War. After the US Navy entered the war in 1917, America sent a USA destroyer division to Cobh. The first destroyers arrived in Cork Harbour on 4 May 1917 under the command of Commander J. K. Taussig, who was met in Queenstown by Admiral Sims and British Admiral Baylay. At first, they were not quite sure of the role of the destroyers, but quickly it became clear that the best role was for the destroyers to help convoy merchant ships.

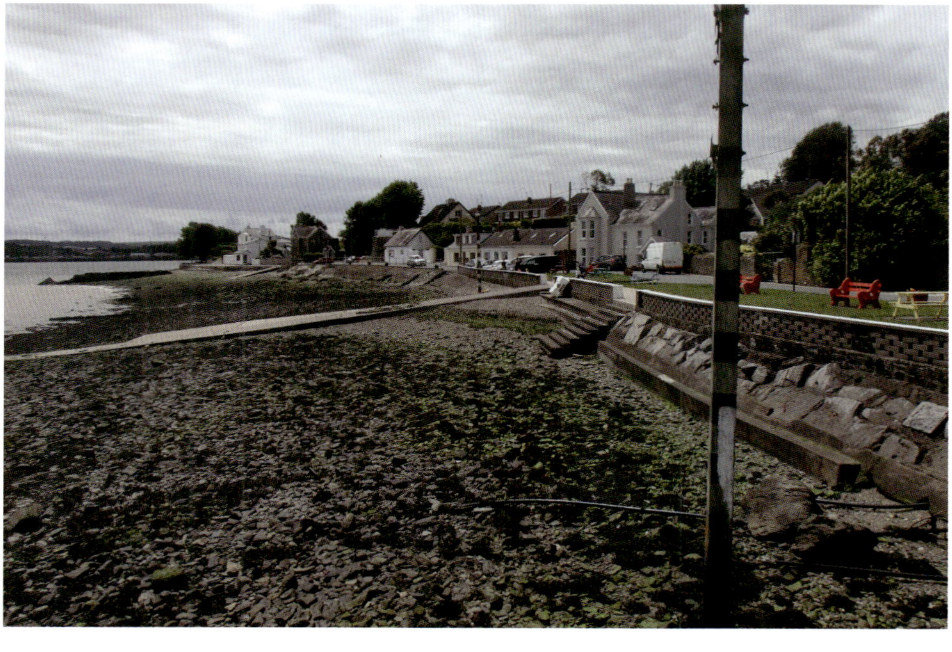

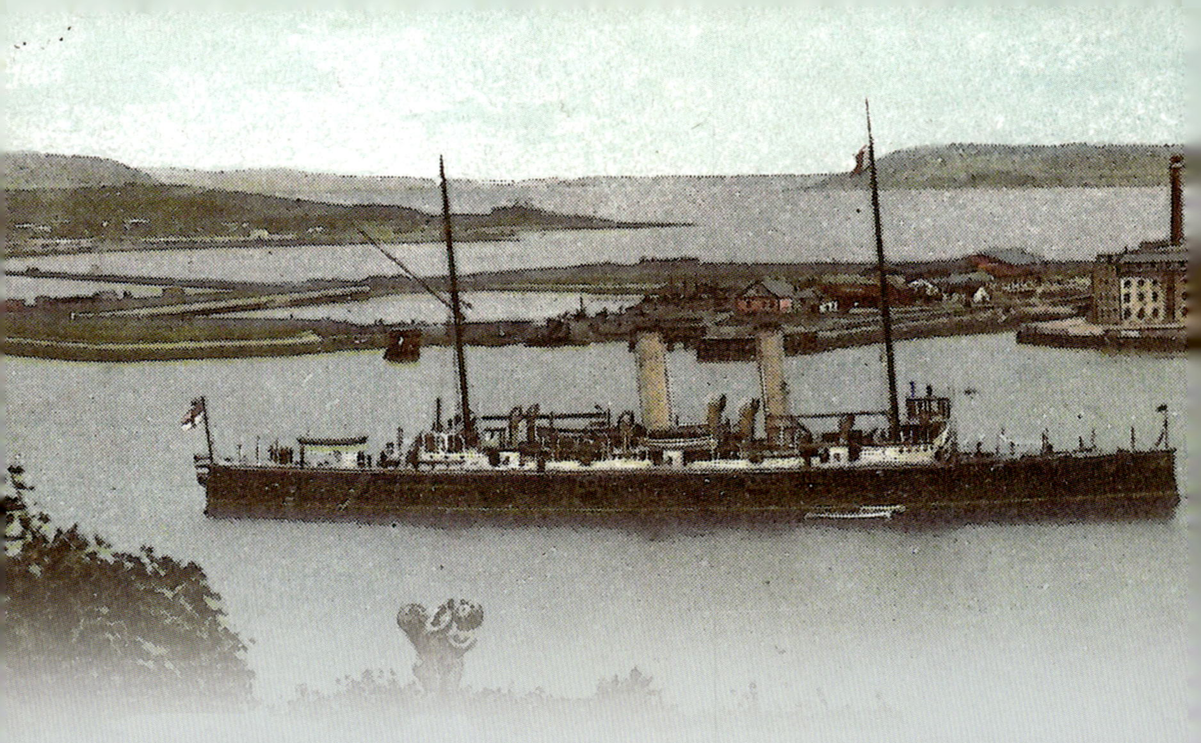

CHAPTER 3

Hidden Corners, Island and Bays

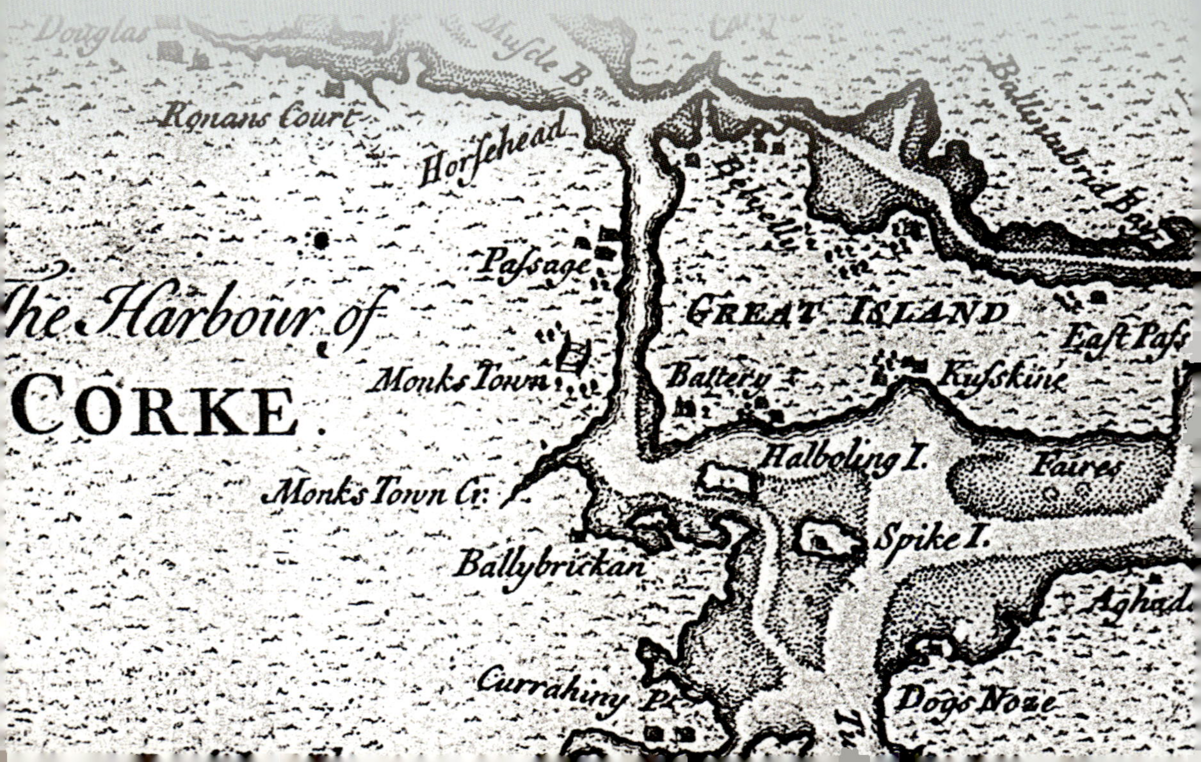

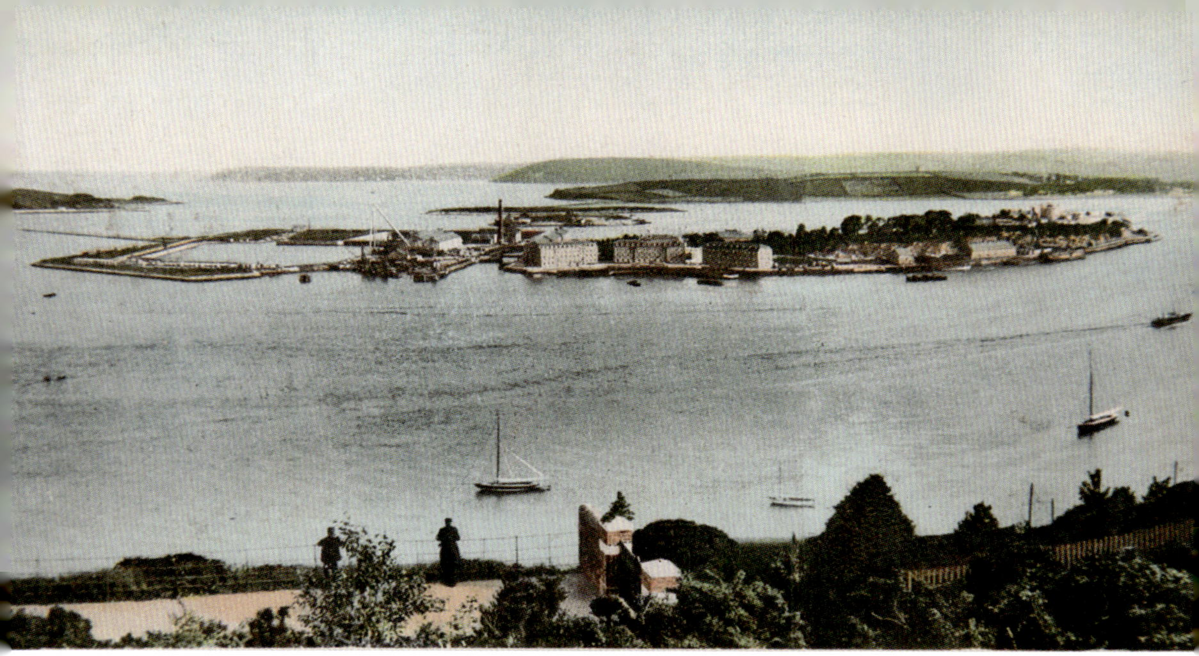

Defending an Empire, Haulbowline Island

In 1602, Haulbowline was considered for fortification as part of a coastal defence scheme for the south coast, after the Battle of Kinsale (1601) exposed a potential weakness in the defence of the harbour to raiders and marauders. For the defence of Cork Harbour and the city, the construction of the bastioned fort commenced on the northern side of Haulbowline at its highest point. By 1624 the fort was abandoned, and by 1665 it was probably in complete ruin. It is not mentioned on subsequent military reports and did not play any part in the 1690 attack of Cork Harbour and City.

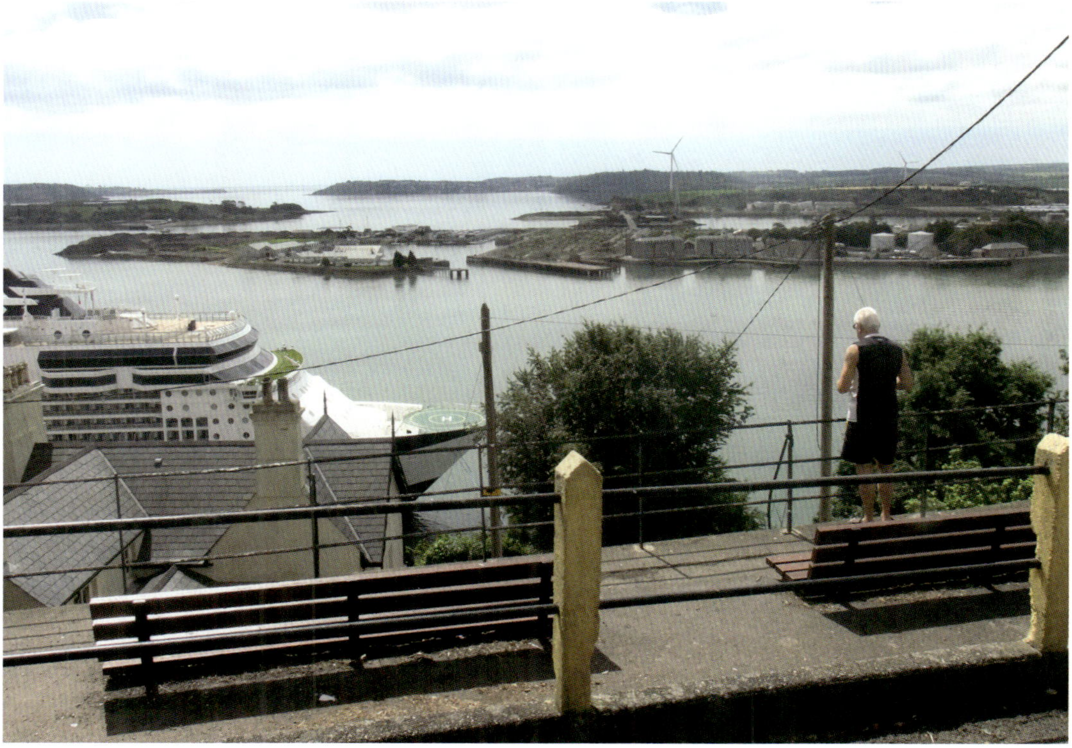

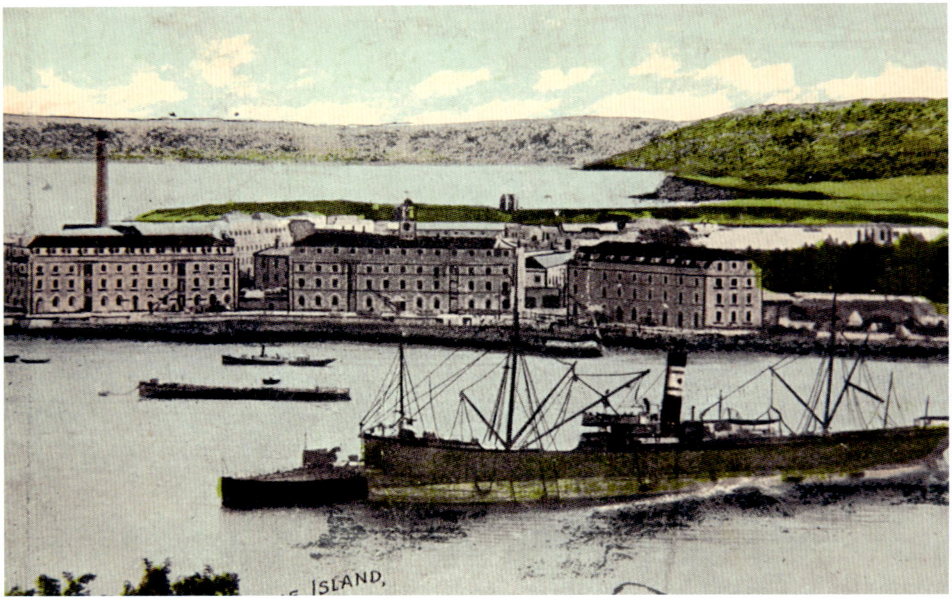

Haulbowline Dockyard

In 1806, when the British Army moved to Spike Island, directions were given by the Order in Council to erect a naval establishment at Haulbowline. The Martello tower was constructed in 1813–15 on the high ground at northern edge of Haulbowline island. A barracks to accommodate three officers and sixty men, two storehouses, a gun carriage yard, smithy and carpenters' workshop, and other installations were constructed *c.* 1813. On the naval side of the island (the eastern side), a large victualling yard containing six large storehouses, living quarters for the supply staff and medical officers, houses for the chief surgeon, the coopers and other workshops were erected. The island was extended by 4.5 acres of reclaimed land in order to construct the flat wharfage area. The building contractor was Mrs Deane of Cork.

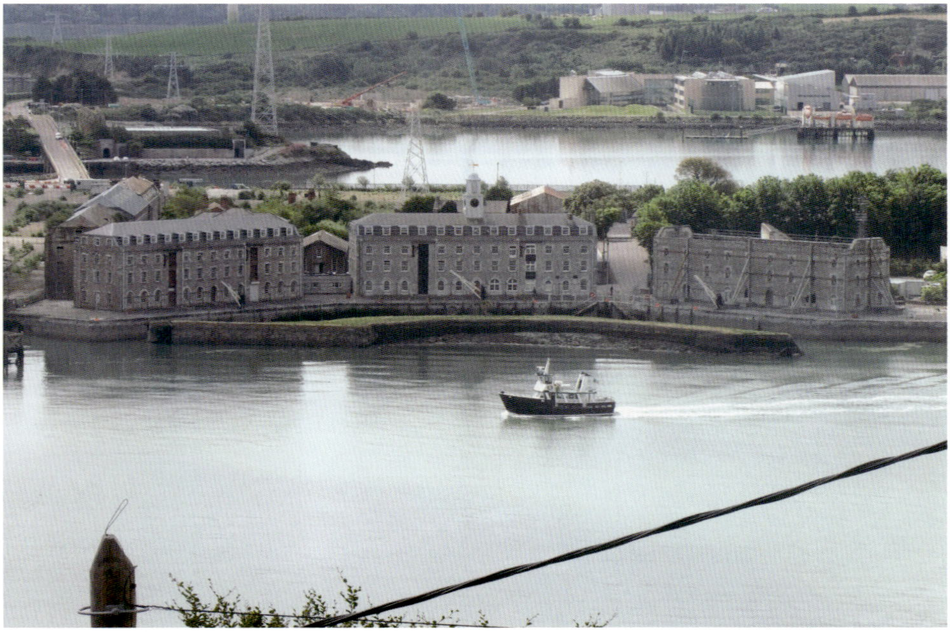

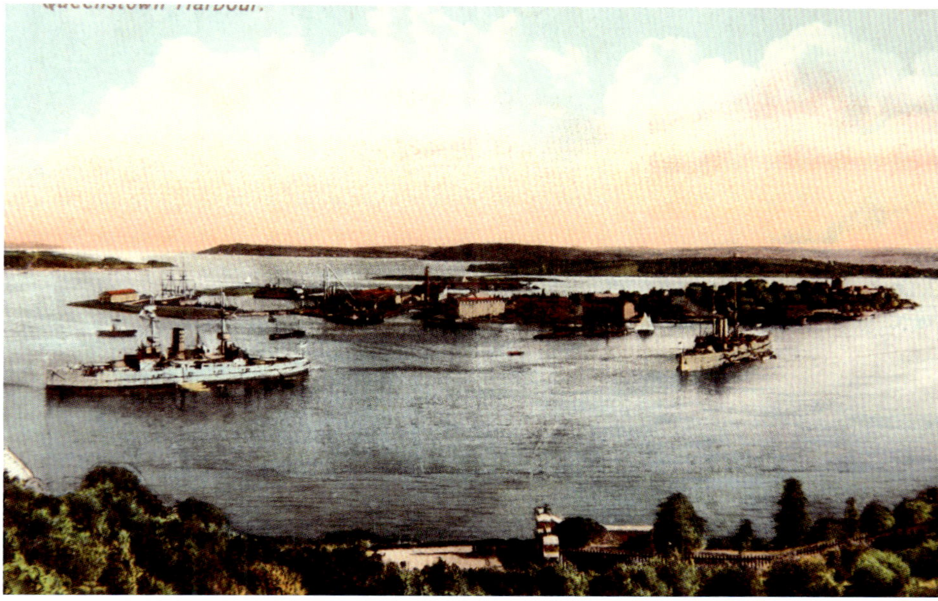

Irish Naval Service, Haulbowline

On 11 July 1938, the port of Cobh was handed back to the then Irish Free State. The Haulbowline Island was developed into a steel plant in 1938 to assist Cobh in recovering from the loss of income from the departing British forces. Since, 1946, Haulbowline has been home to the Irish Naval Service. In 2014, the Irish Government bought the €48 million ship LÉ *Samuel Beckett*, which is not only the fastest ship in the Irish fleet, but also boasts 'Star Wars' capabilities for Remotely Operated Aerial Vehicles (ROV drones), as well as robotic submersibles. Since 2008, the Navy has intercepted €1.7 billion worth of drug shipments in Irish waters. This year alone, the Navy has carried out 407 vessel boardings and arrested four fishing trawlers.

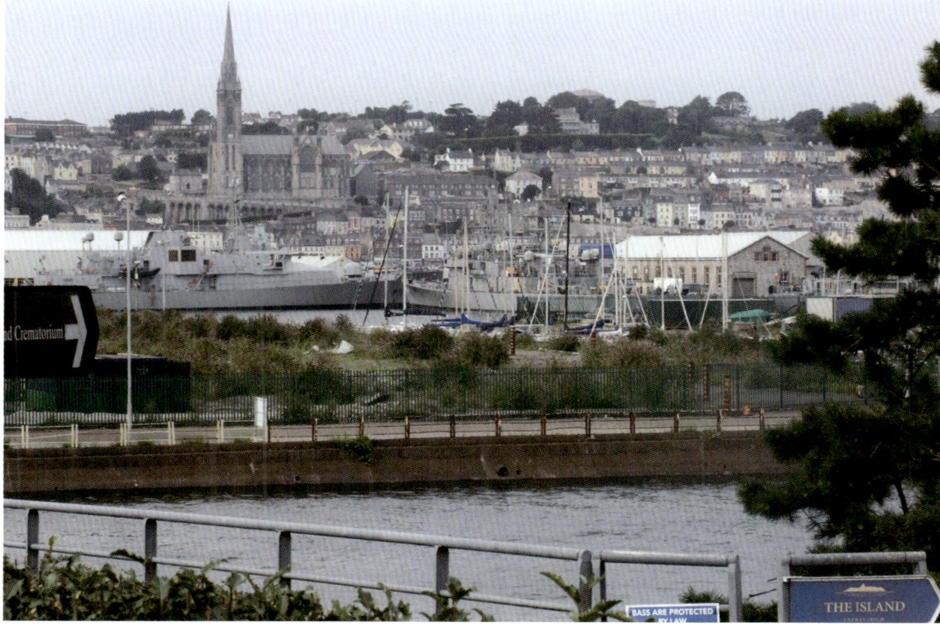

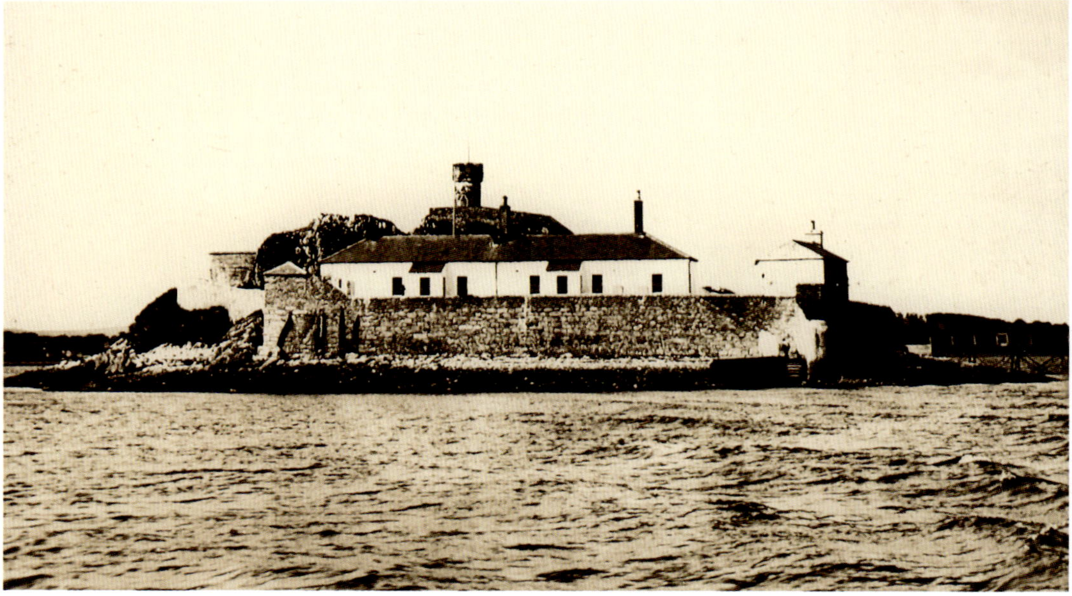

The Magazine, Rocky Island

In 1810, a magazine was constructed on Rocky Island, a small rocky outcrop located to the south of Haulbowline. It was designed to contain 25,000 barrels of powder. The island was originally conical, and the east and west shoulders of the rock were dug out and large vaults excavated beneath the levelled surface. Into these vaults, two magazine buildings were built, of which only one survives. One month before the Second World War, in August 1939, the Haulbowline Steel Syndicate began production of steel. The company built the bridge that bisects the island in 1966, allowing for easier access to Haulbowline from the mainland. The steel plant was closed in 2001 after sixty-two years of production. Rocky Island and its magazine building were purchased by The Island Crematorium Co. Ltd in February 2005.

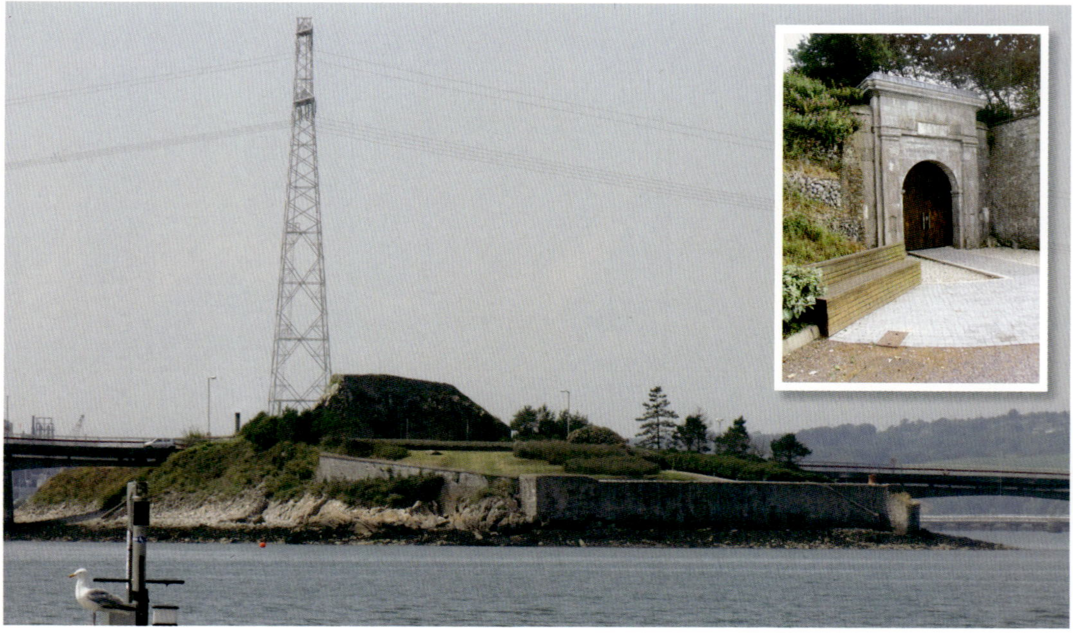

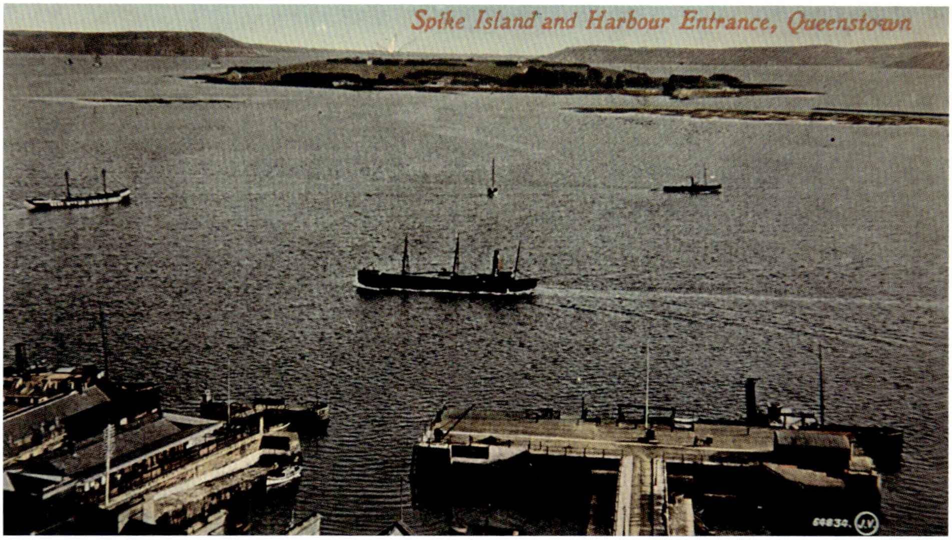

Fort Westmoreland, Spike Island

There is some evidence that a monastery was founded on Spike Island in the seventh century. The well-known St Mochuda, or St Carthage, is said to have founded a monastery here in AD 635. Fast forward to the 1770s, during the turmoil of the American War of Independence, and Cork harbour replaces Kinsale as the principal royal navy base on the south coast. To strengthen the defences of the harbour, a decision was taken to build a fort on Spike Island. It was named Fort Westmoreland and was completed by 26 July 1779. In time, the British military quickly realised the strategic importance of Spike, and decided to replace the old fort with a much larger structure. Gen. Charles Vallancey and architect Michael Shanahan were responsible for the new fort, the foundation stone was laid on 6 June 1804.

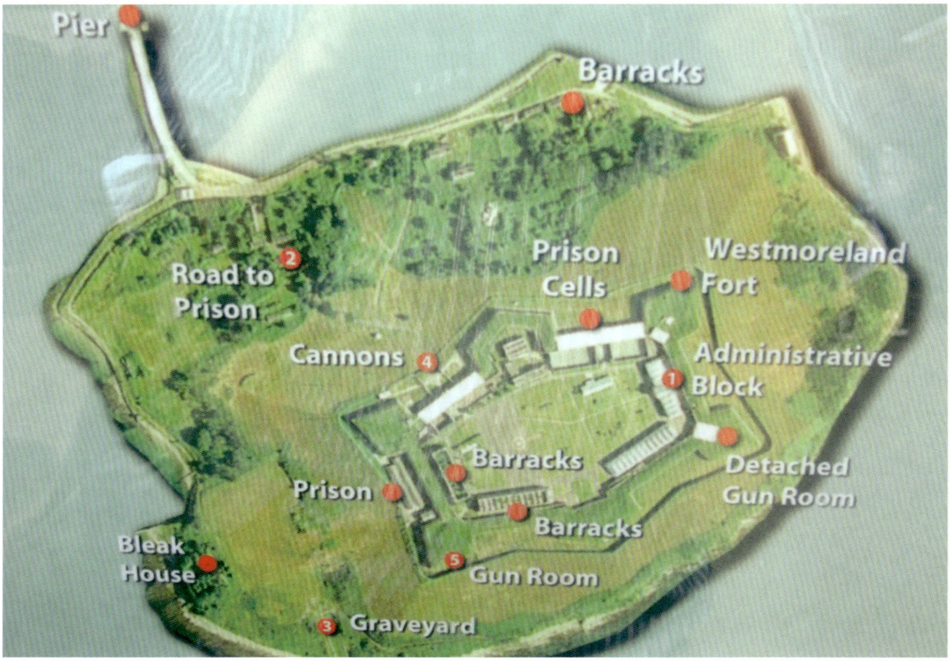

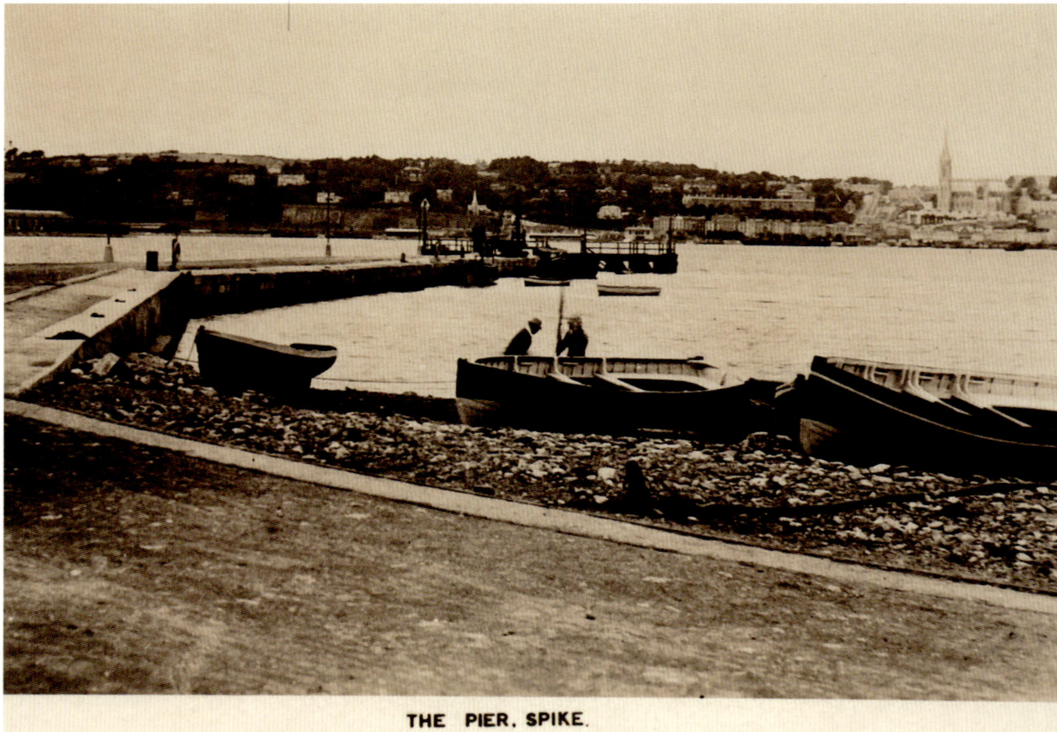

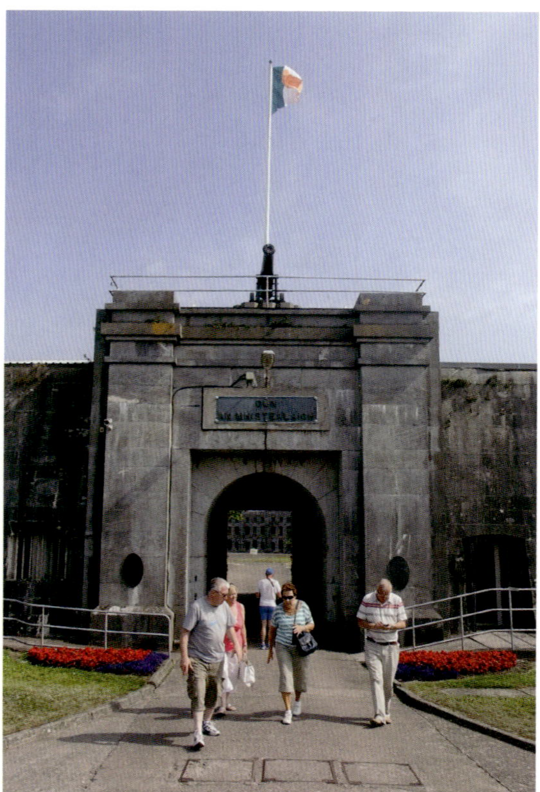

Spike Island

The fort also holds the cell of John Mitchel (1815–75), who was an Irish nationalist activist, solicitor and political journalist. Born near Dungiven, County Derry, he became a leading member of both Young Ireland and the Irish Confederation. He was an outspoken critic of British rule and, in 1843, he was convicted of sedition and sentenced to transportation to Bermuda for fourteen years. On 27 May 1848, Mitchel was sent from Dublin on board HMS *Scourge* to Spike Island, where he was incarcerated for three days. Mitchel was sent to the penal colony of Van Diemen's Land – now Tasmania. It was during this journey he wrote his famous *Jail Journal*. Mitchel escaped from the colony in 1853 and settled in America. He returned to Ireland and was elected to the British House of Commons, only to be disqualified because he was a convicted felon. In 1961, the Fort on Spike Island was renamed Fort Mitchel in his honour.

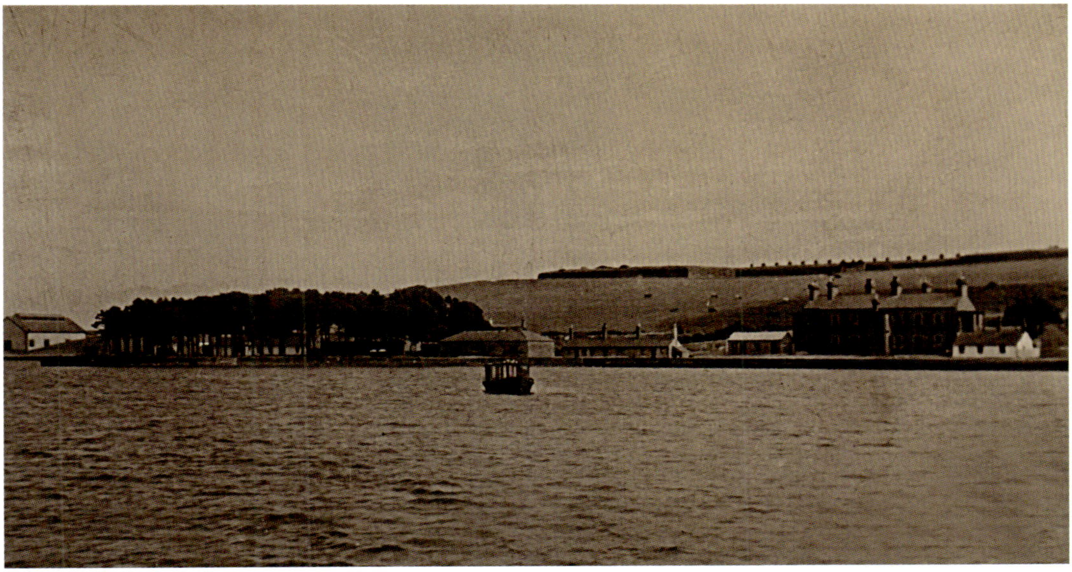

Twentieth Century, Spike Island

The transfer of Spike to the Irish Government took place on 11 July 1938. In 1980, the first Naval Service recruits came to the island and, during the next five years, up to four classes per annum were enlisted. In 1985, the government decided to convert the fort into a prison and the order was given for the naval garrison to stand down. In July 2010, a new phase in Spike Island's history began, as the state, specifically the Department of Justice and Law Reform, officially handed control over to Cork County Council, thus ending over two centuries of institutional use. Cork County Council entered into a contract with experienced tour operators to conduct walking tours of the island. The picture below shows the southern battery of Spike Island, 10 July 2013, an event to mark the 75th anniversary of the handing over of Spike Island by the British to the Irish Free State.

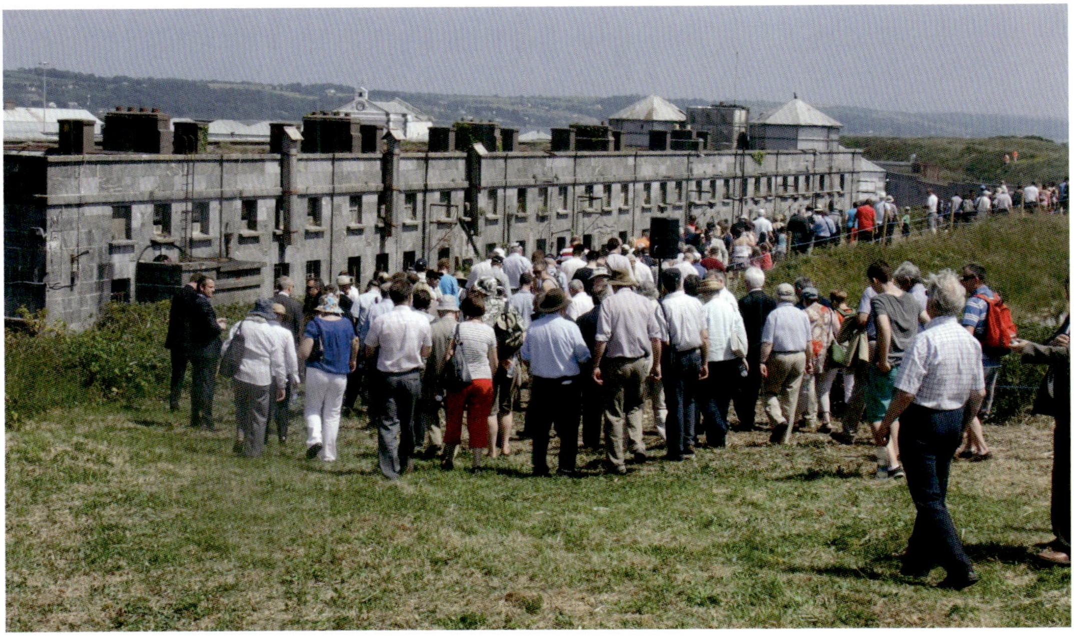

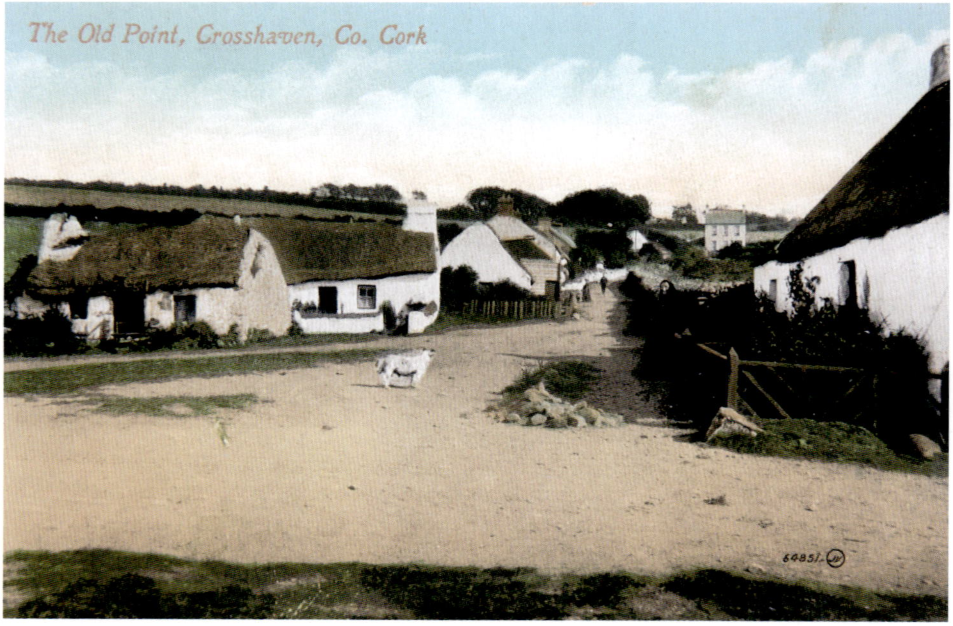

The Old Point, Crosshaven

Old Point represents the probable site of the first Anglo-Norman settlement at Crosshaven in the thirteenth century. There was a small village protected by a castle and linked with a larger manor in Carrigaline. Crosshaven took its name from a cross erected in honour of St John near the settlement. Fast forward in time and Castle Point was an embarkation point called the 'old Quay' in the nineteenth century. In addition, the Castle Point village comprised of twenty-one houses. Today, the Old Point settlement is built upon by modern housing and the Crosshaven boatyard, which provides much employment.

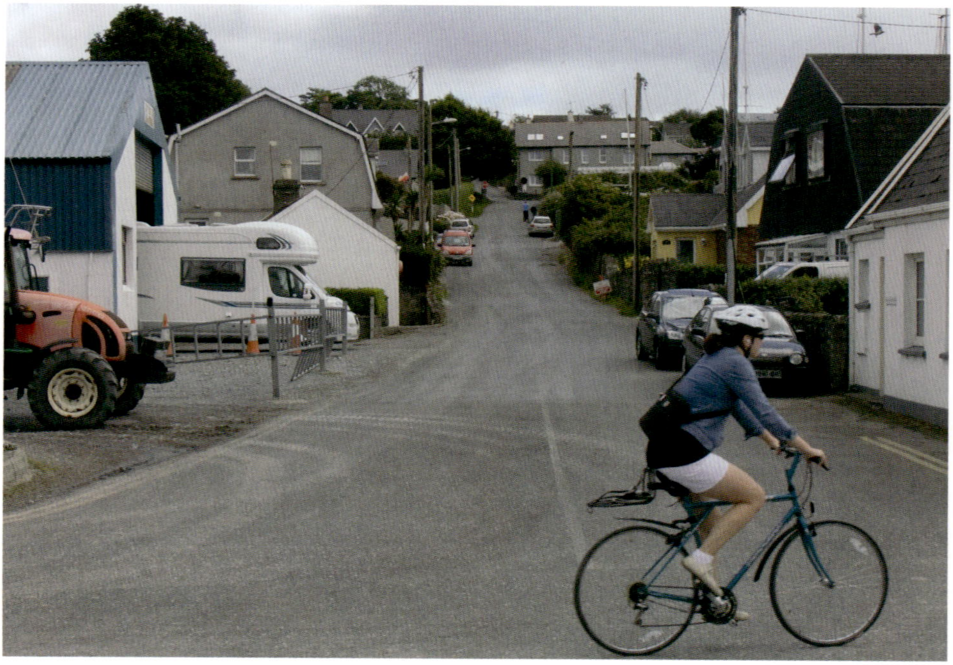

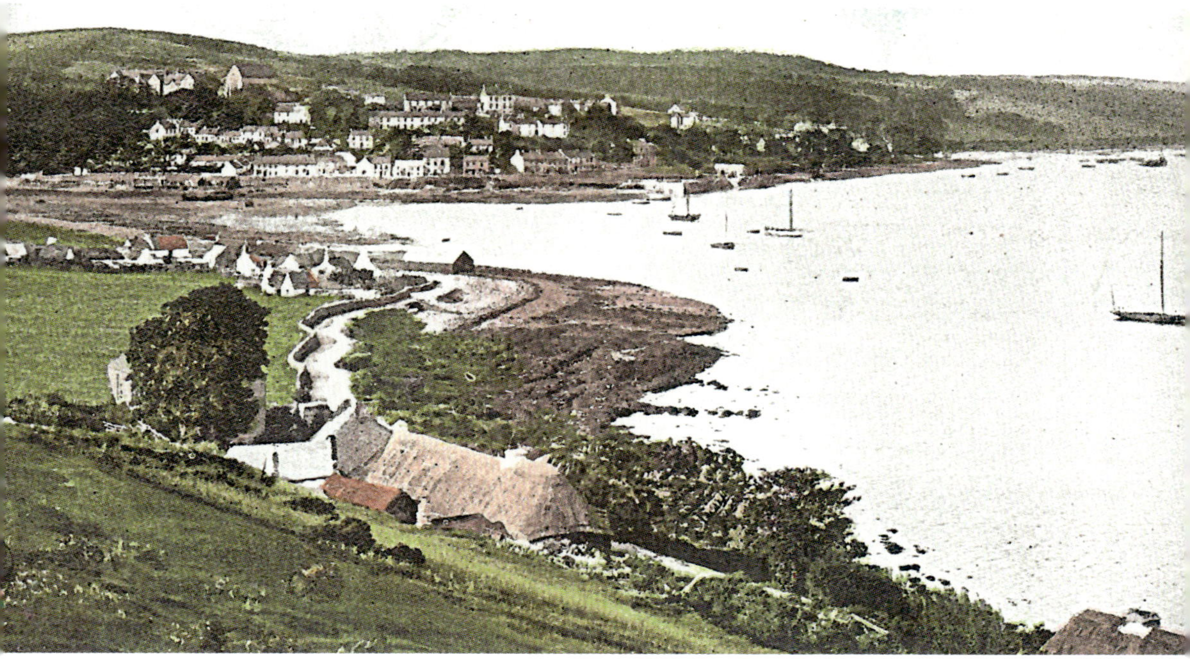

Crosshaven

Crosshaven village, as people know it today, is situated on an estuary to which it gives its name, but is more generally known as the river Carrigaline. A century ago, it comprised of around 100 houses, which were small but well built. It also had one of the eight coastguard stations in the district of Queenstown. Several handsome villas and lodges closely adjoined the village, and these were the summer residences of those who visited the coast for seabathing,

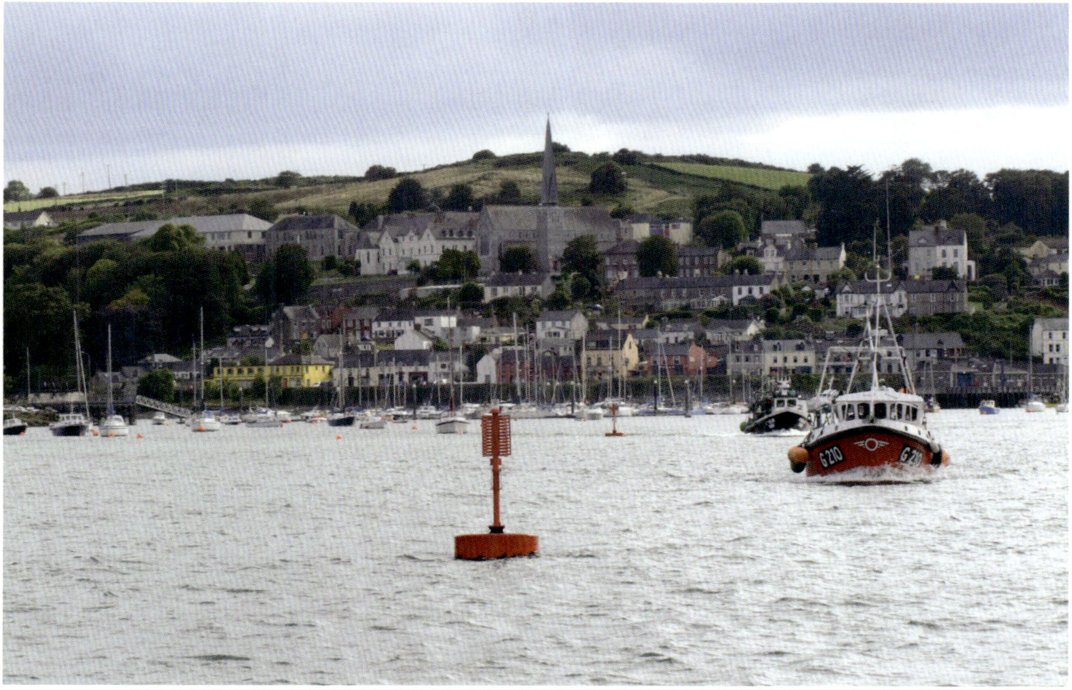

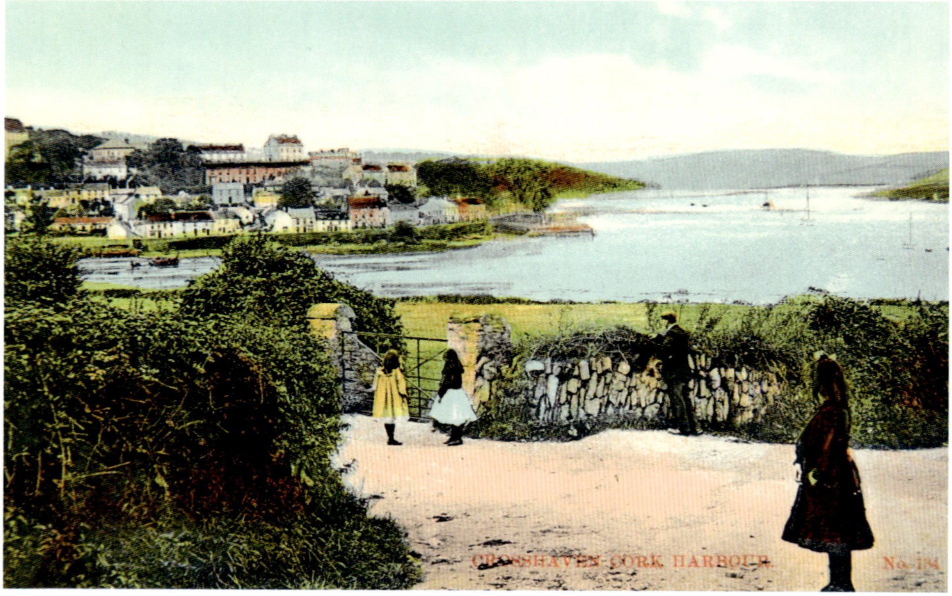

Vistas and Estates, Crosshaven

Thomas Hayes of Crosshaven was the owner of almost 1,600 acres in County Cork in the 1870s. Over 1,000 acres of his estate in the baronies of Kinalea and Kerrycurrihy were offered for sale in the Landed Estates court in October 1872. At the heart of Crosshaven is an eighteenth-century country house. Built in the Palladian style of 1750, this fine, cut limestone, ashlar building has a three-storey central block with two detached pavilions to the east and west. Although the house was built in 1750, it remained unoccupied until the early nineteenth century, so all joinery and decorative features date from after 1800. It remained in the ownership of the Hayes family until the early 1970s. The house is still extant and occupied and is open to the public for heritage tours.

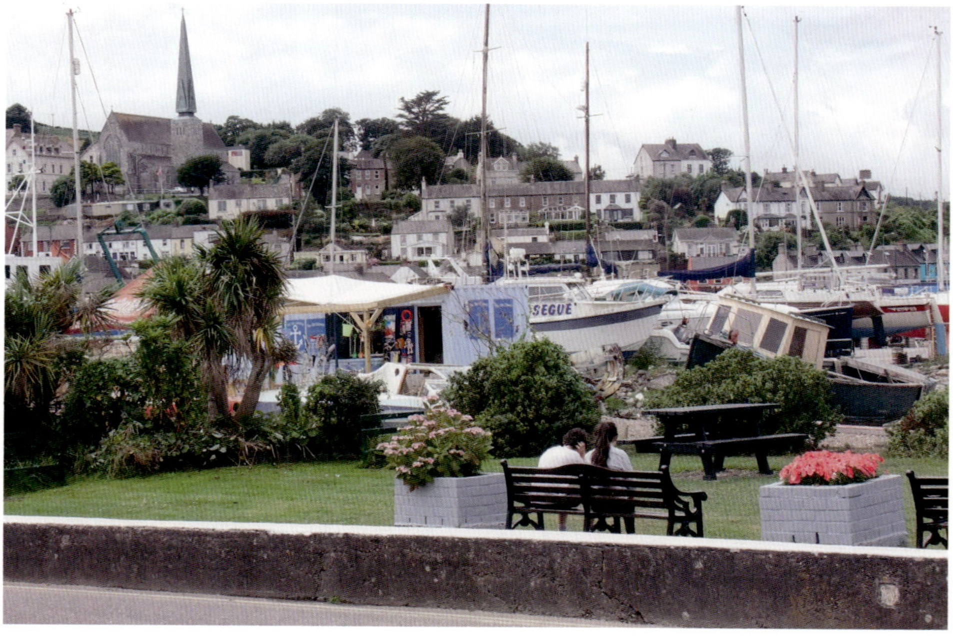

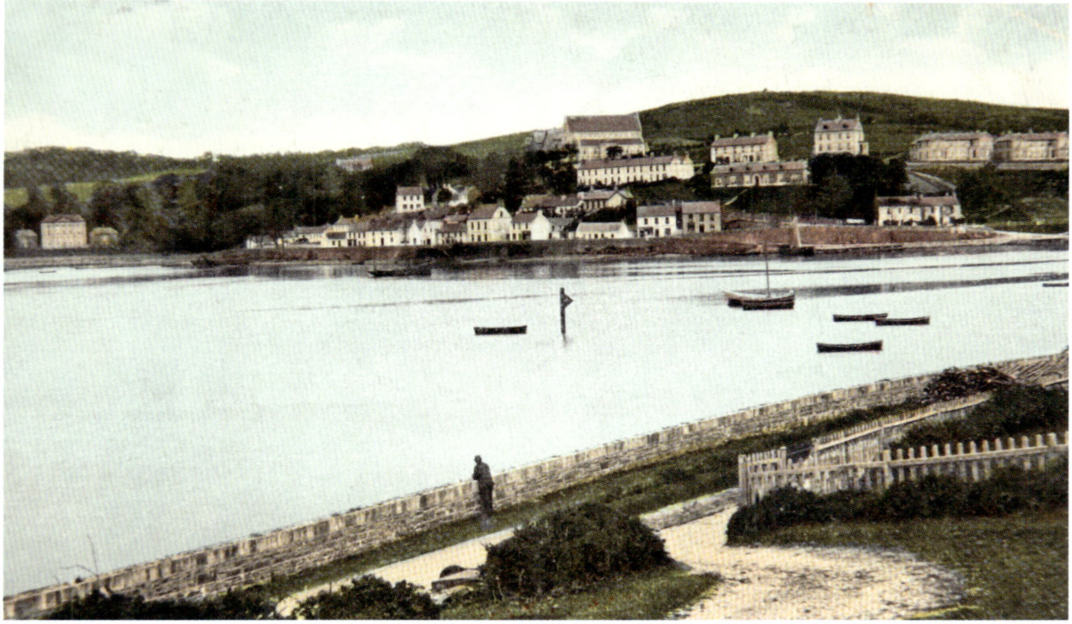

Church Stories, Crosshaven

Two churches stand out on the landscape of Crosshaven. Holy Trinity, Church of Ireland, was designed by the famous architect William Burges after he had won the commission for St Finnbarre's Cathedral in Cork. Between 1866 and 1868, through the energy and zeal of the Revd Mervyn Archdall, Rector of Crosshaven, the church was erected by Robert Walker of Cork at a cost of around £2,000. After the main body of the church was complete, it was decided not to build the proposed round tower that would adjoin the building. The Catholic St Brigid's church is also an impressive structure. It was designed by well-known architect Edward Welby Pugin. Its foundation stone was laid in 1869, constructed of Little Island limestone and named after the patron saint of Crosshaven.

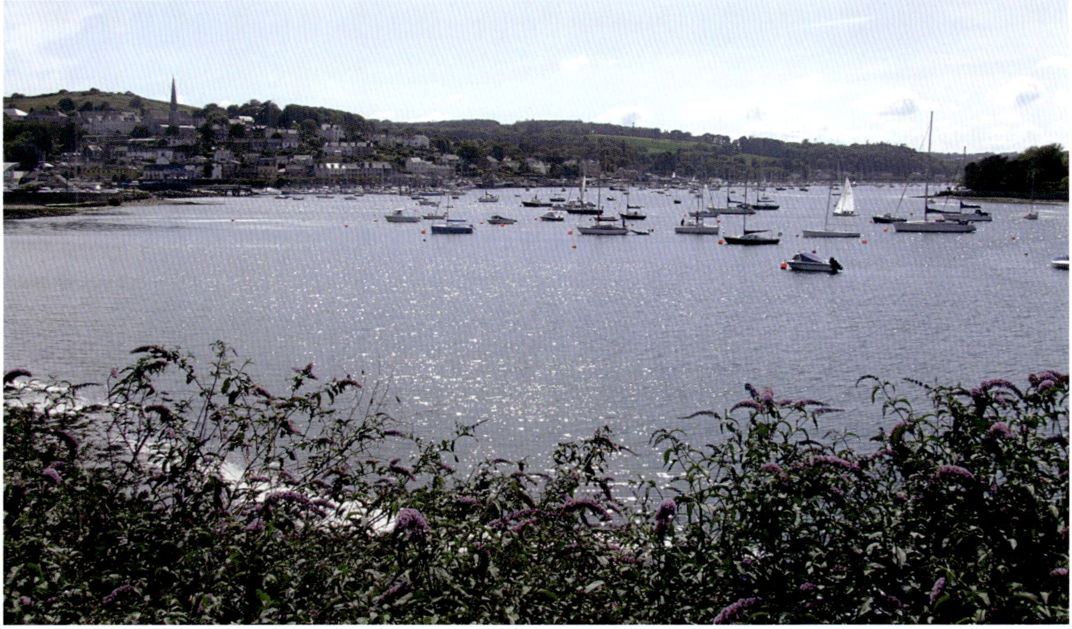

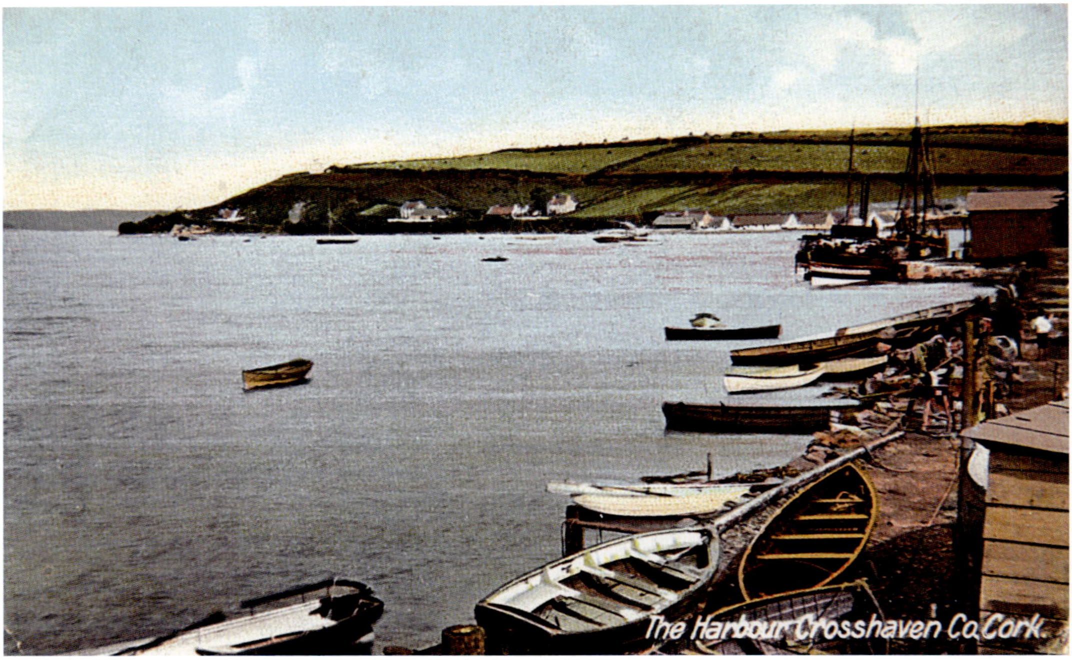

Fishing for Memories, Crosshaven

An extensive fishing trade existed in the early nineteenth century, but declined due to the high price of food during the Napoleonic wars. By 1910, small boats with oars, as seen in the postcard, were used by the men of Fountainstown, Myrtleville and Fennel's Bay. The fishing grounds were located around the harbour mouth. Those without boats waited for the mackerel to come inshore and caught them by the hundred with large pocket nets. A barrel of salted mackerel could be seen in every fisherman's cottage in preparation for winter each year.

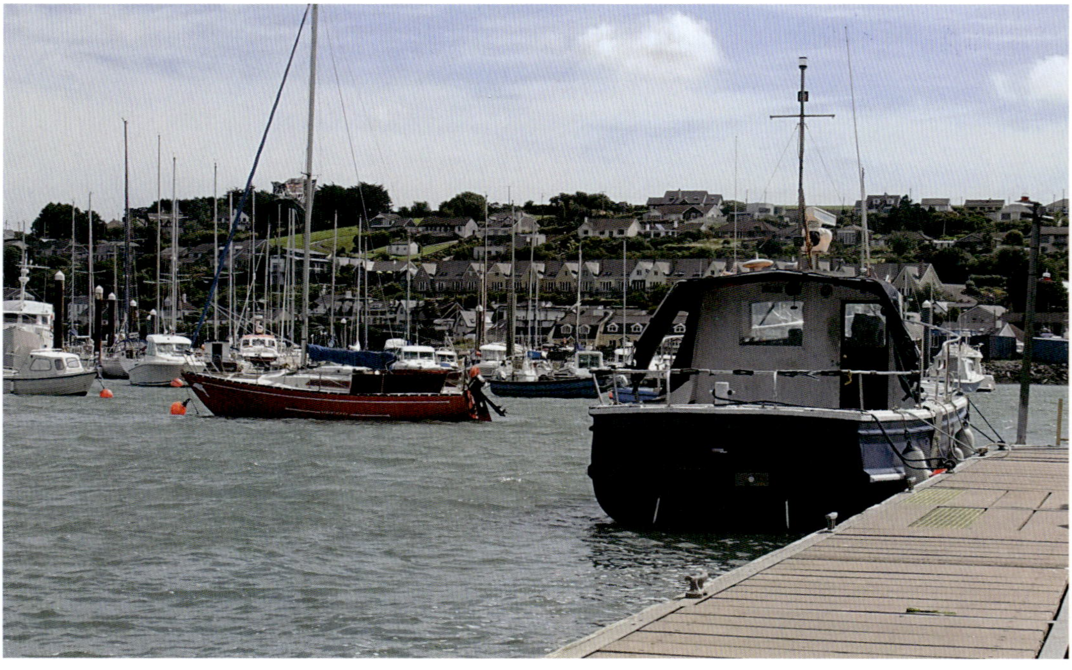

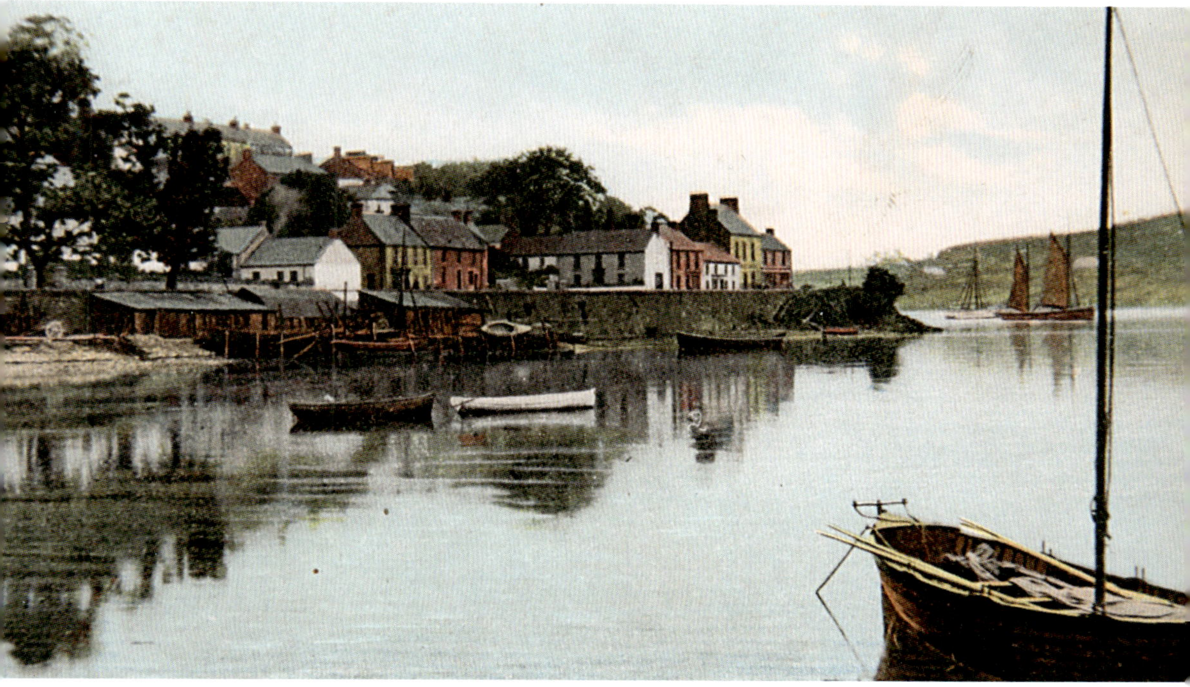

Reflections, Crosshaven Village

Crosshaven village grew rapidly in the late eighteenth and early nineteenth centuries. One cause of growth was the construction, in the mid-eighteenth century, of houses for revenue officers or coastguards, whose responsibility was to prevent smuggling. It became popular for many family members in the area to serve a term in the navy before coming home to marry and settle down.

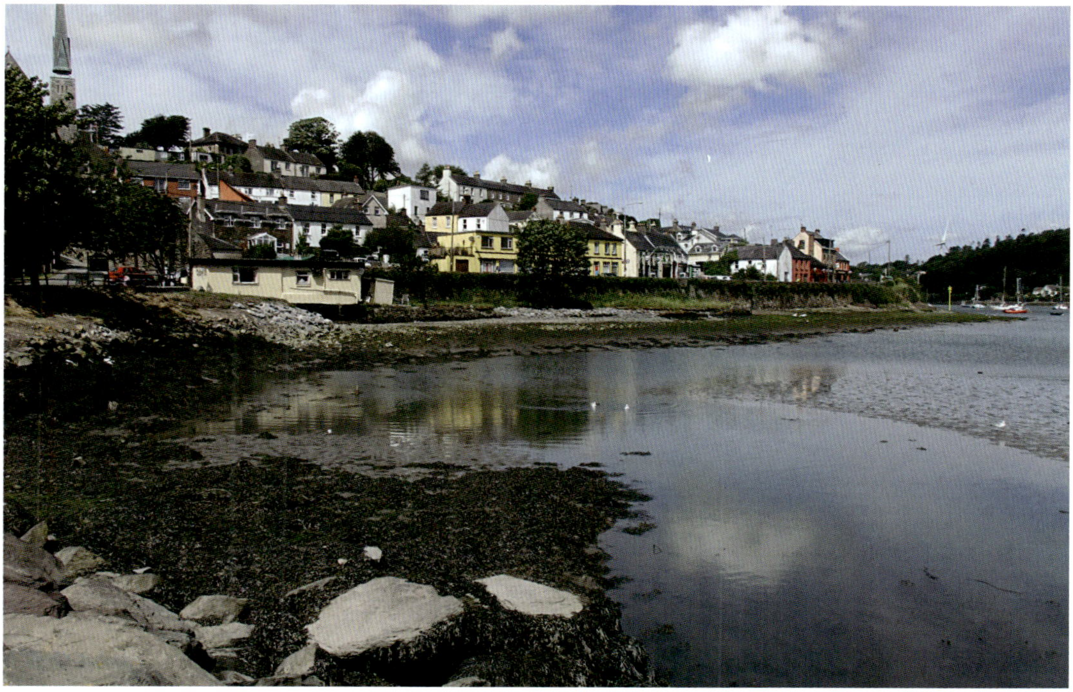

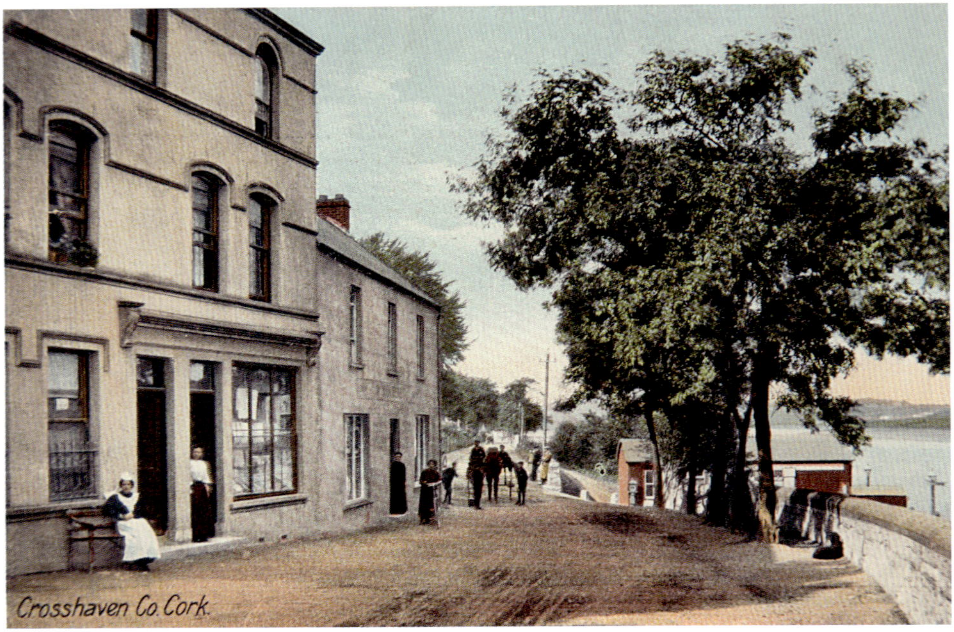

Connecting Crosshaven

Crosshaven Village in 1914 could boast a post, money order and telegraph office. Transport was by train to Cork with trains every hour. There was also transport by steam to Queenstown and Monkstown. A growing tourism town, it had five hotels, twelve shopkeepers, and four vintners. Today, it is regularly visited by Corkonians and visitors who indulge in its great pubs and renowned food. The village is known in the region for its season of amusements more affectionately known as 'The Merries', operated by the Piper family for generations.

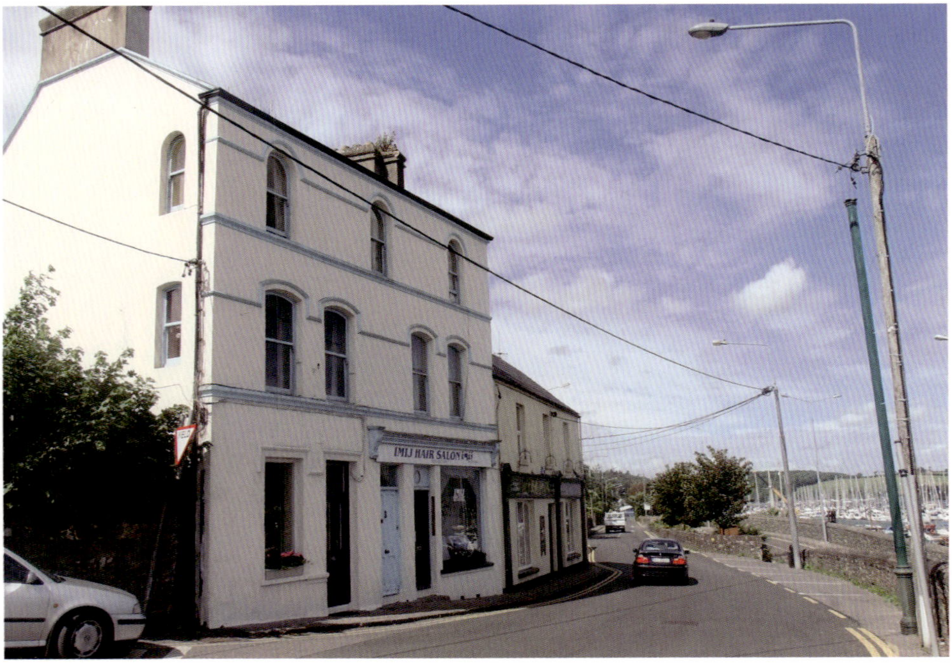

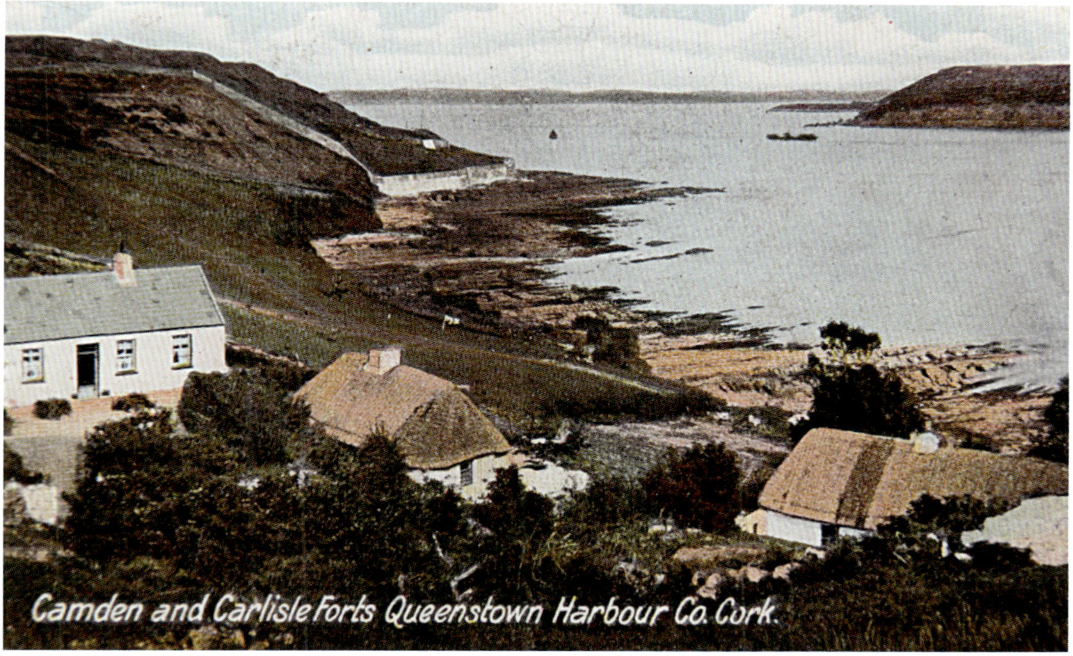

Camden Fort Meagher, Crosshaven

Fortifications on the left of this postcard date back to 1550; for almost 400 years the fort played an important role as a strong strategic position for the defence of Ireland and the west coast of England and Wales. However, most of what the visitor now sees was built during the 1860s by British Forces and finished around 1871. It is documented that it took 500 men forty years to carve out the moat, which goes around three sides of Camden Fort Meagher.

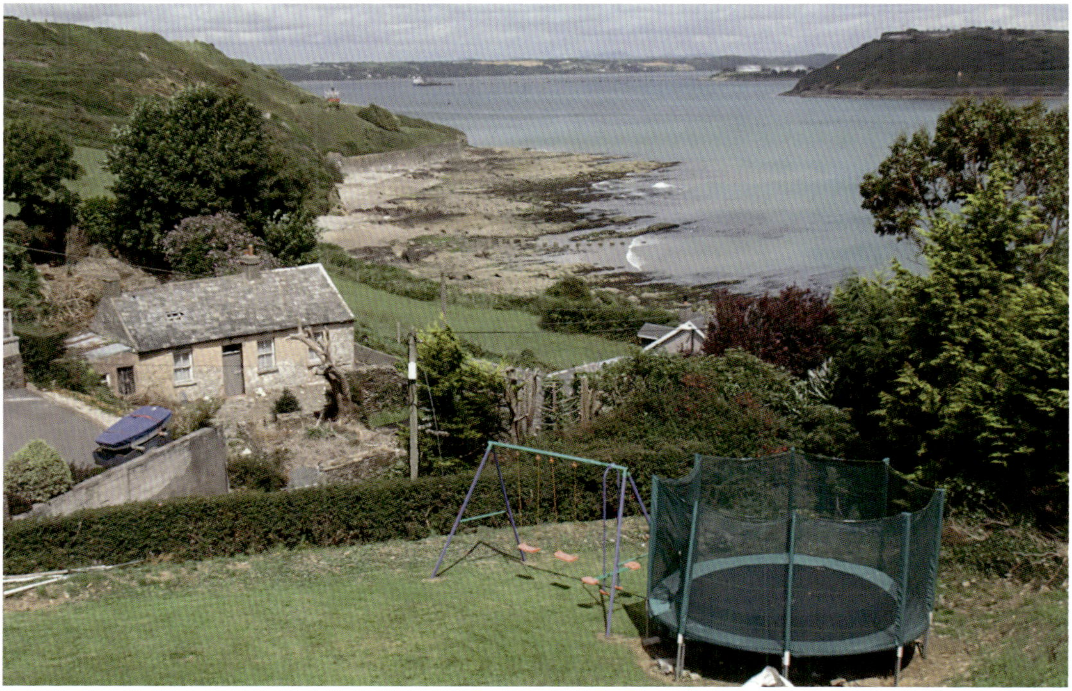

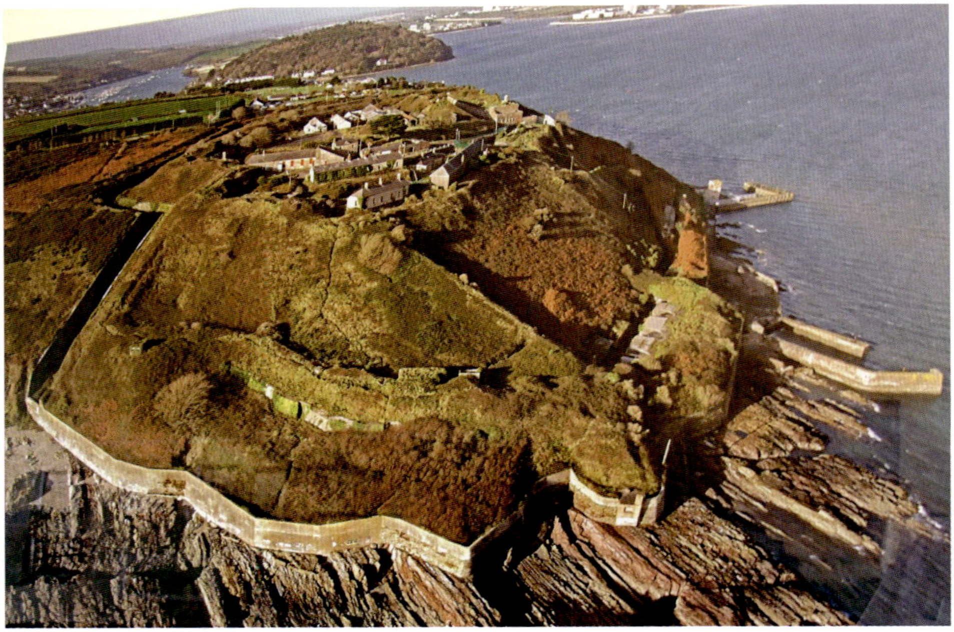

Camden Fort Meagher

At the gate to the fort, you can see the original pillars of the fort and they are inscribed with *Dun Ni Mhecair*, which is the Irish for Fort Meagher. The fort was named Fort Meagher (from Fort Camden) in 1938 after Thomas Francis Meagher, who was the leader of the Young Irelanders. Ninety years previously, in 1848, Meagher and fellow patriot William Smith O'Brien went to France to study revolutionary events there, and returned to Ireland with the new flag of Ireland, a tricolour of green, white and orange made by and given to them by French women sympathetic to the Irish cause.

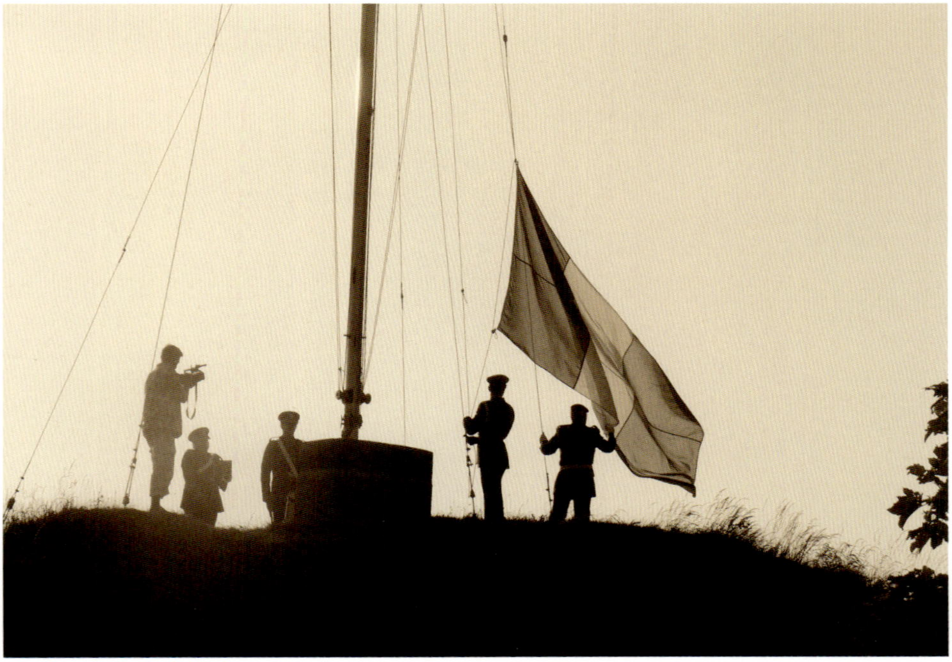

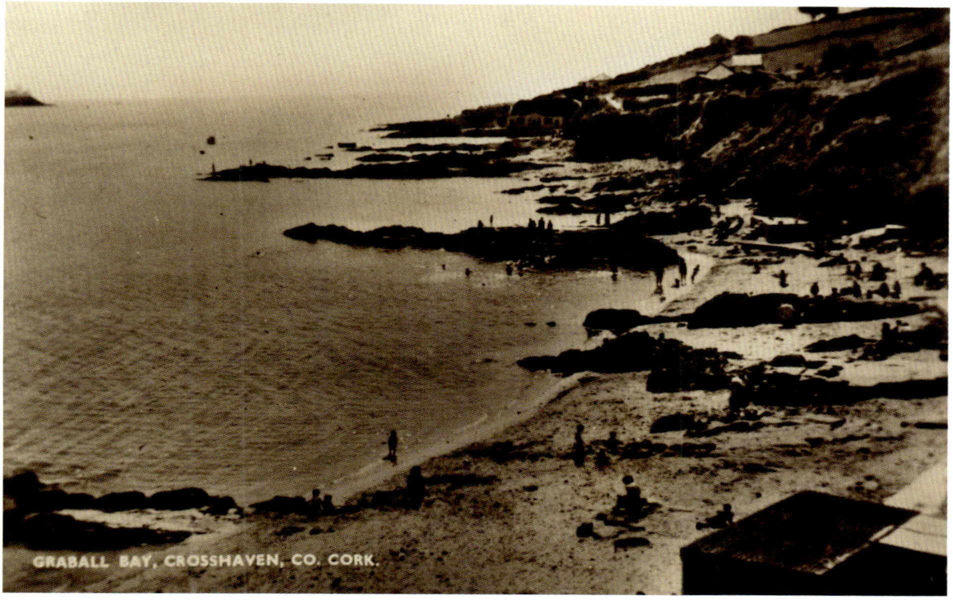

Tourist Urges, Graball Bay

In the late 1800s, Crosshaven flourished from a quiet backwater into a tourism resort. The numerous bays like Graball Bay were unrivalled for bathing – even bathing dresses and towels could be attained. One media story records a local lady who erected two comfortable tents that could dine at least fifty people, and which were in constant demand. In time, the area by the 1930s witnessed many light, wooden holiday bungalows constructed by Cork's citizens. Many were constructed from disused Ford delivery crates in the mid-twentieth century.

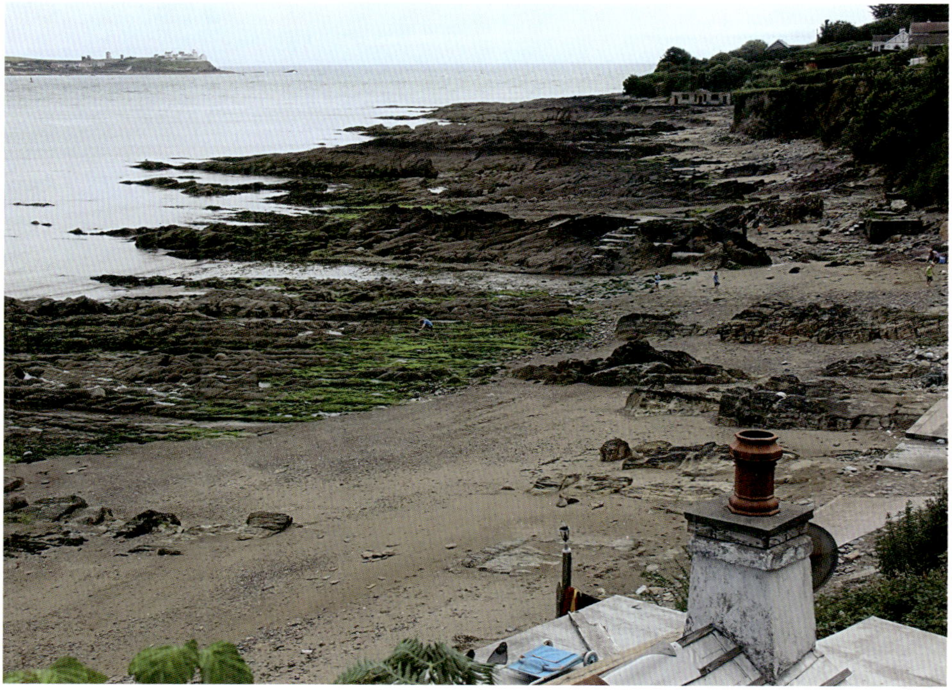

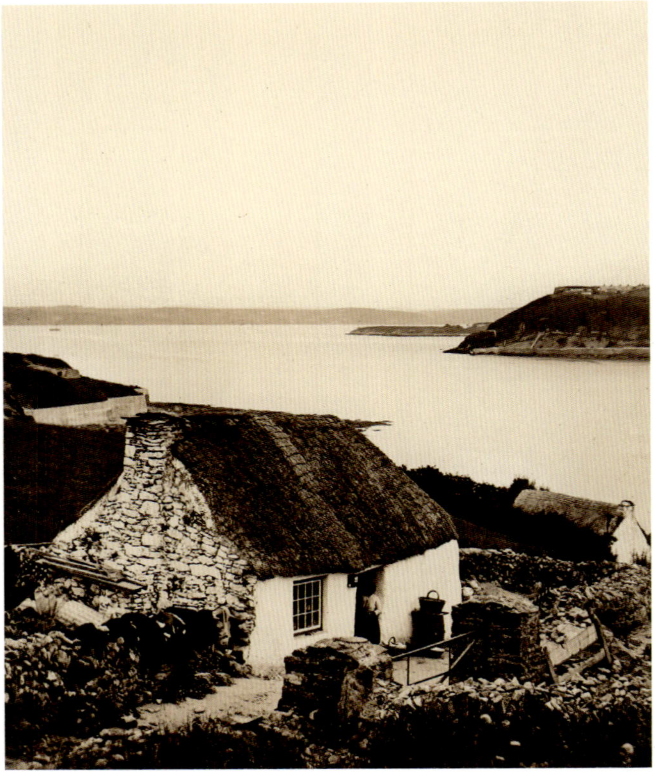

Negotiating the Harbour, Graball Bay, Crosshaven

Many pictures of the harbour show a wide mass of water to negotiate. Apart from fishing, another community of pivotal importance were the harbour pilots. In 1875, when 2,280 overseas vessels entered the Port of Cork, sixty-four harbour pilots and two Ballinacurra pilots were employed. Prior to 1892, there were sixty-seven sea pilots within Cork whose average weekly earnings were from 12 to 15*s*. Subsequently, the number of sea and river pilots was reduced to fifty, but pilot boats were still stationed at Mizen Head, Galley Head, Old Head of Kinsale and Cork Harbour's mouth. Pilots still escort large ships into the heart of the harbour today.

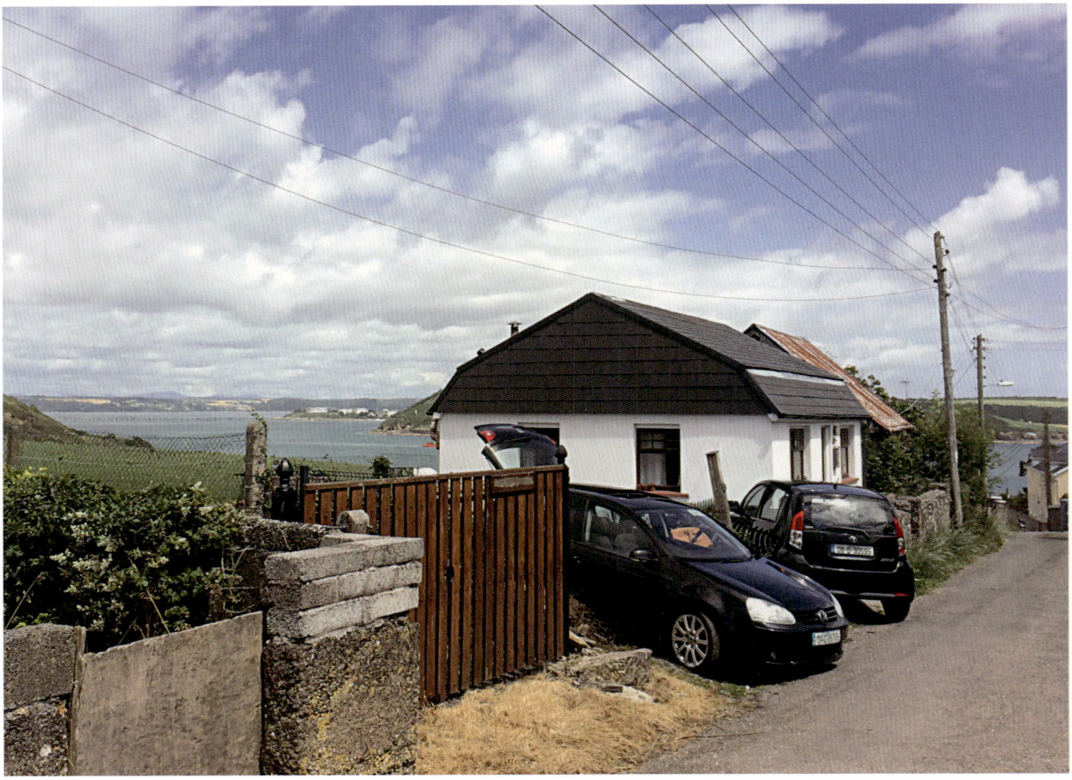

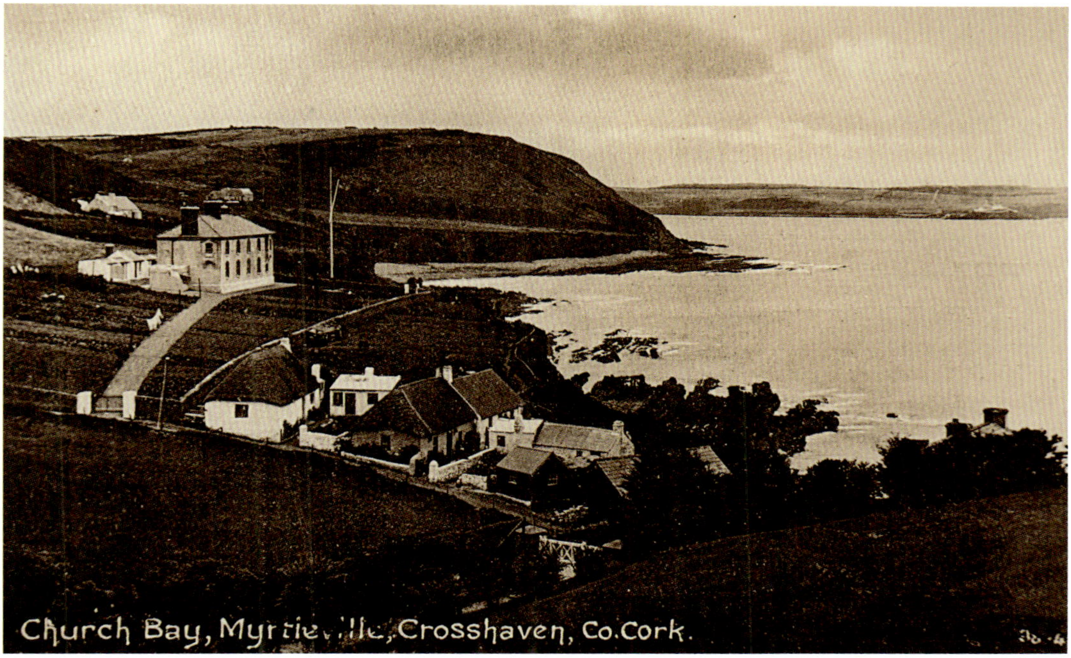

By the Seaside, Myrtleville

Myrtleville is a small seaside village near Crosshaven. Frequented by Cork people and families through the ages, the old coastguard station is shown on the left of the old picture. Today, many holiday homes dot the local landscape. Nearby are the famous Fennel's bay and the popular beach of Fountainstown. A shipping and merchant family, the Trants owned Myrtleville House (still there today) and farm. They built a cottage for family members – Myrtleville Cottage – which is now the well-known Bunnyconnellan Bar and Restaurant.

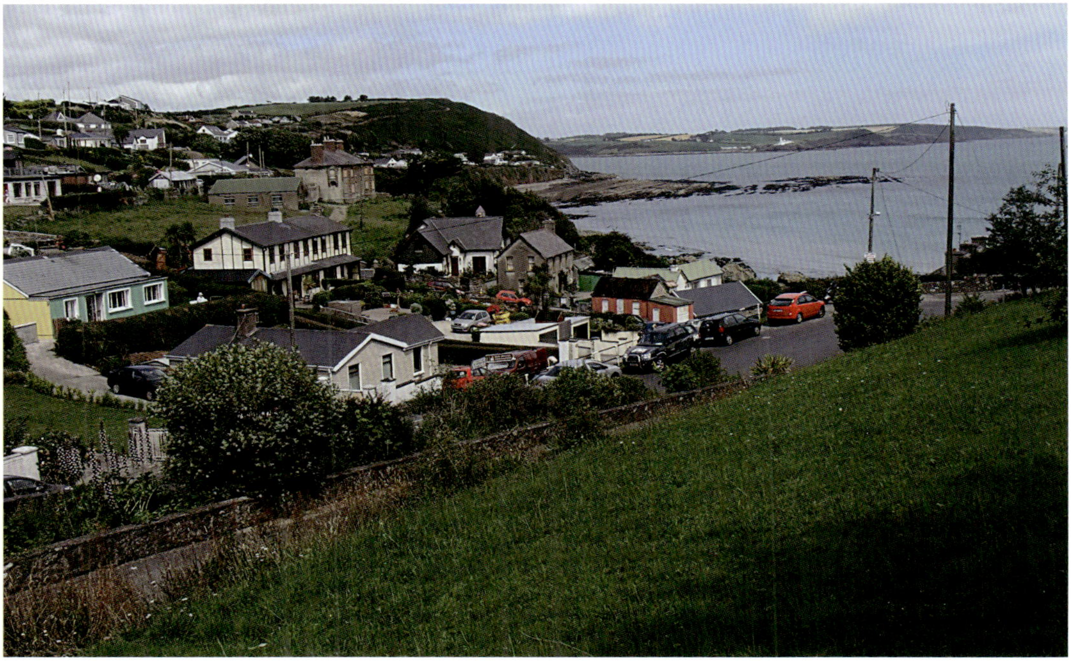

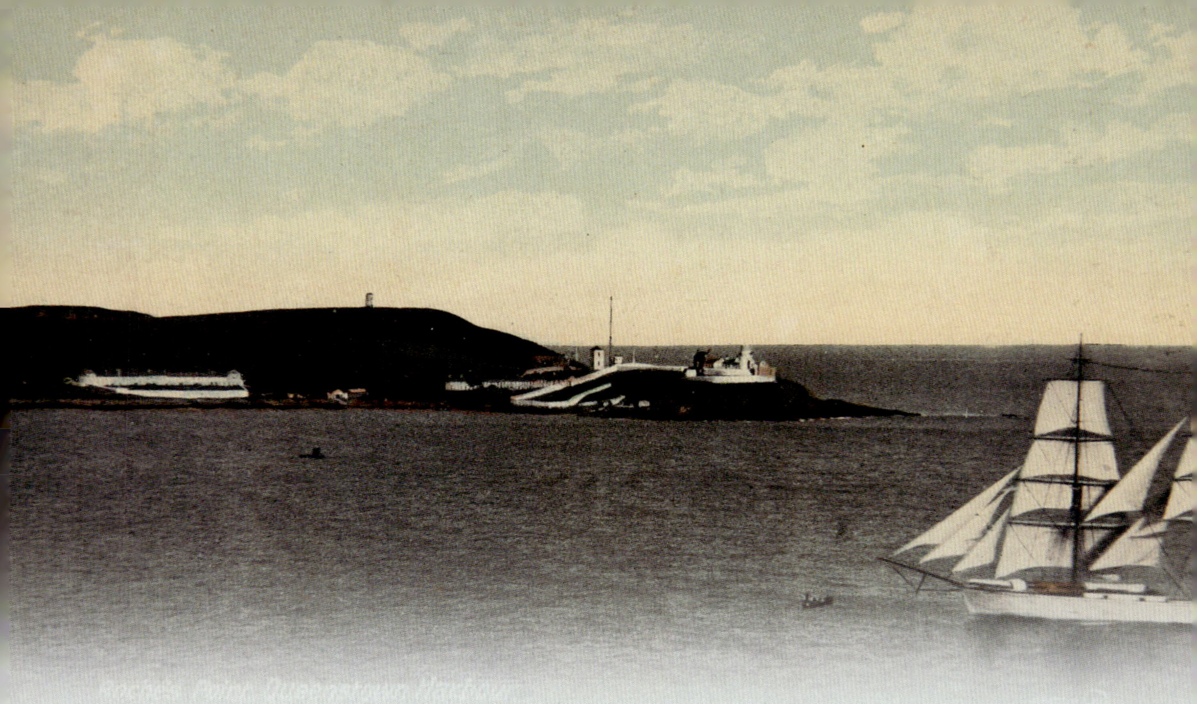

CHAPTER 4

Eastern Shores

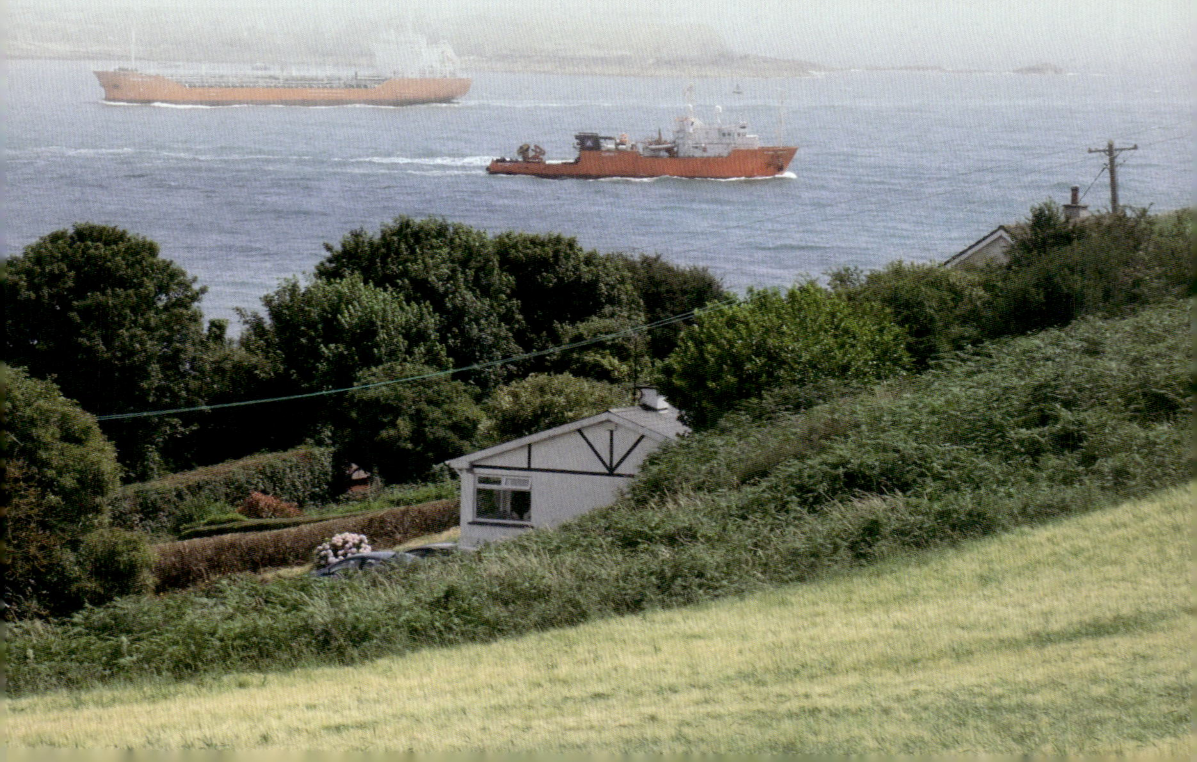

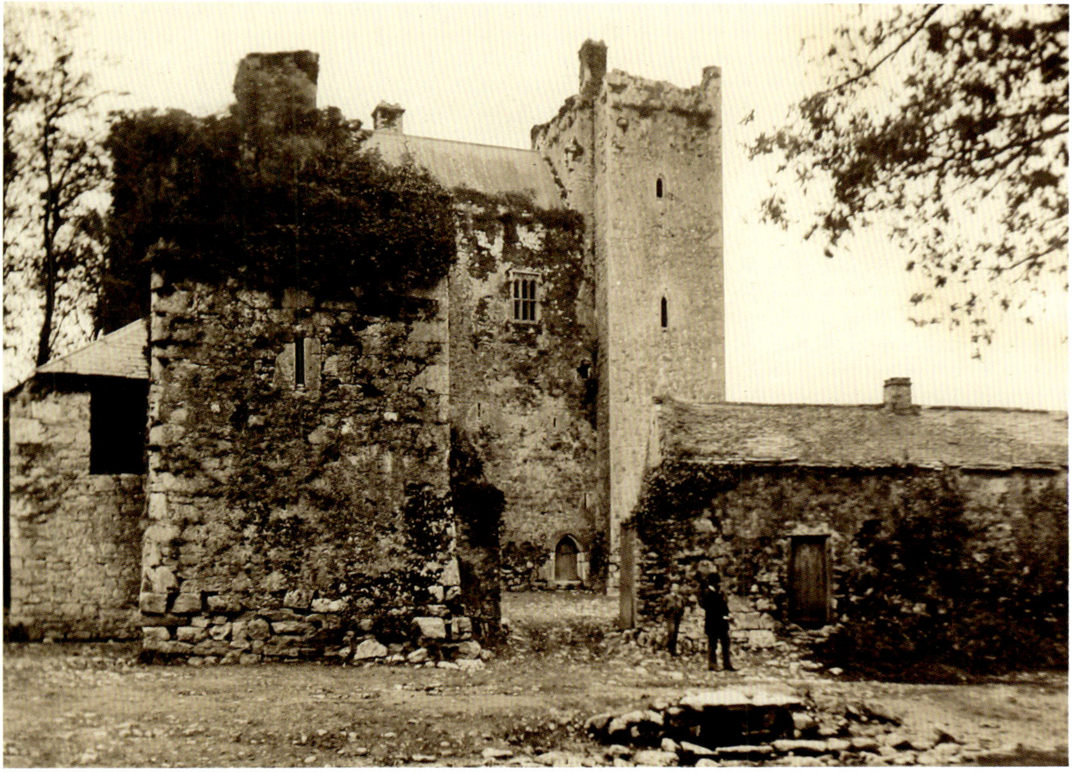

Open for Exploration, Barryscourt Castle

Barryscourt Castle was built on a strategic site in 1206 by Philip de Barry. It was the seat of the Earls of Barrymore until about 1700 when the hunting house at Fota was built. In May 1990, Barryscourt Castle was reopened to the public after extensive and continuing restoration, and is now managed by the Barryscourt Trust. The present castle, with its largely intact bawn wall and corner towers, is a fine example of an Irish tower house. Both the first-floor main hall and the second-floor Great Hall have been extensively restored, with fittings and furnishings reinstated. The Orchard has been restored to an original sixteenth-century design, and a herb garden has been reinstated in the bawn.

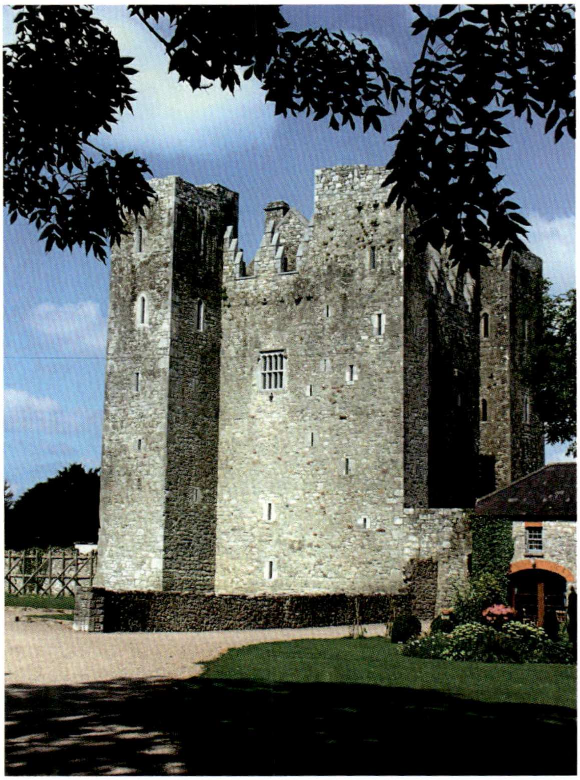

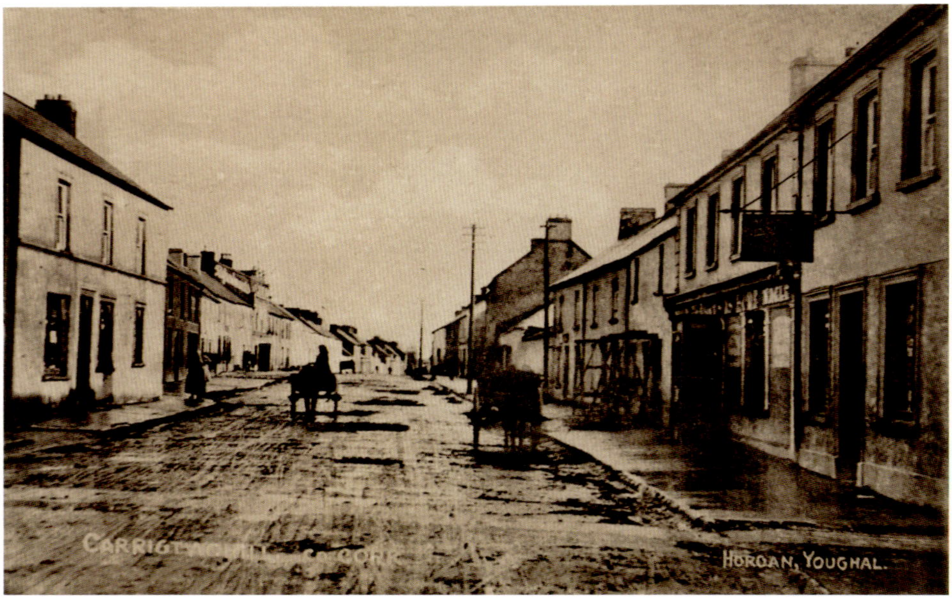

A Rock of Culture, Carrigtwohill

Carrigtwohill, in Irish *Carraig Tuatail*, means 'a rock worked leftwards' or 'to the north or wrong direction'. This huge rock is about half a mile north-eastwards from the village itself, and in the townland of Carrigane. The rock is honeycombed with caves; some are very extensive, extending for miles underground, where beautiful stalactites are to be found. The village was part of the common of Barryscourt Castle. This village is now one of Cork's satellite towns, with modern housing estates and a population of 6,665 individuals (2011). In recent years, it has seen a 64 per cent increase in population, which has earned it the title of the fastest growing town in Munster, and the fourth fastest growing town nationally.

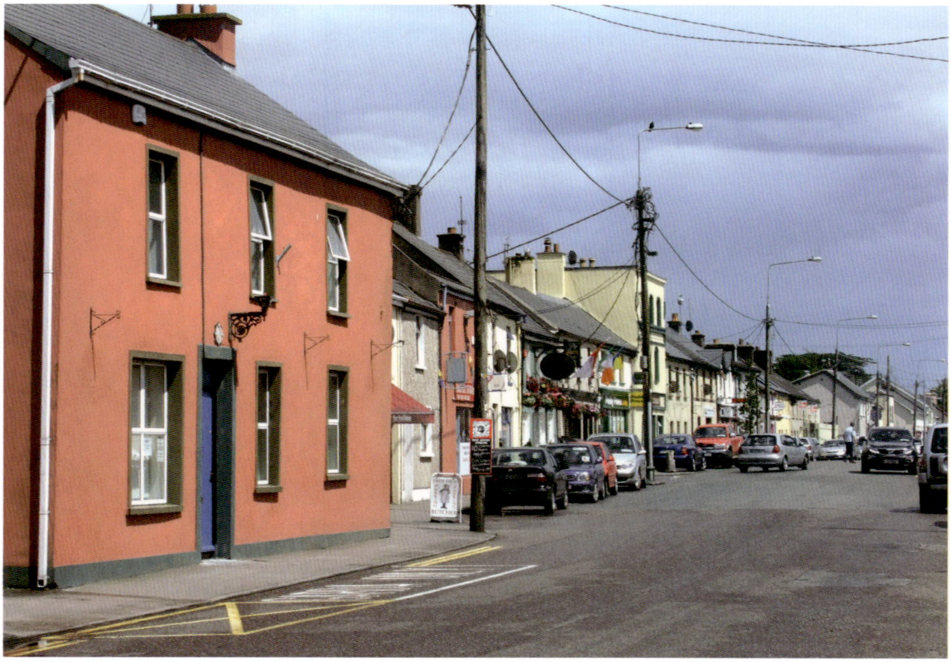

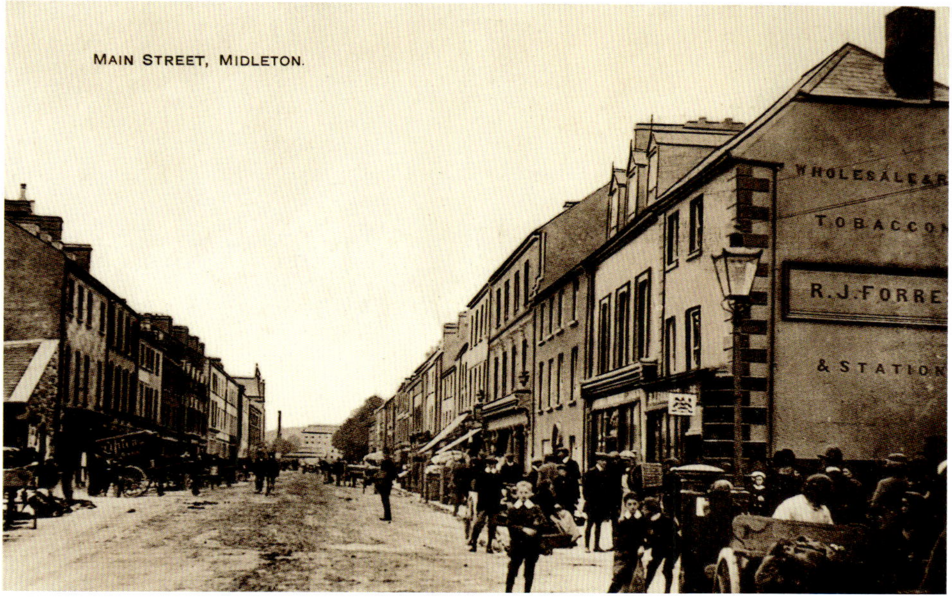

Along the Main Street, Midleton

Midleton was previously called Chore Abbey, and derived both its origin and ancient name from the 1182 foundation of a Cistercian monastery by the Barrys or Fitzgerald Anglo-Norman families. The abbey is commemorated in the Irish name of the town, *Manistir na Corann*. The present town's English name is derived from its equal distance on the road from Cork to Youghal. The town received its charter of incorporation from Charles II in 1670, which was granted to Sir John Broderick. His estate constituted the manor of Midleton, both his castle and lands were made a free borough and he was granted a corporation to run it.

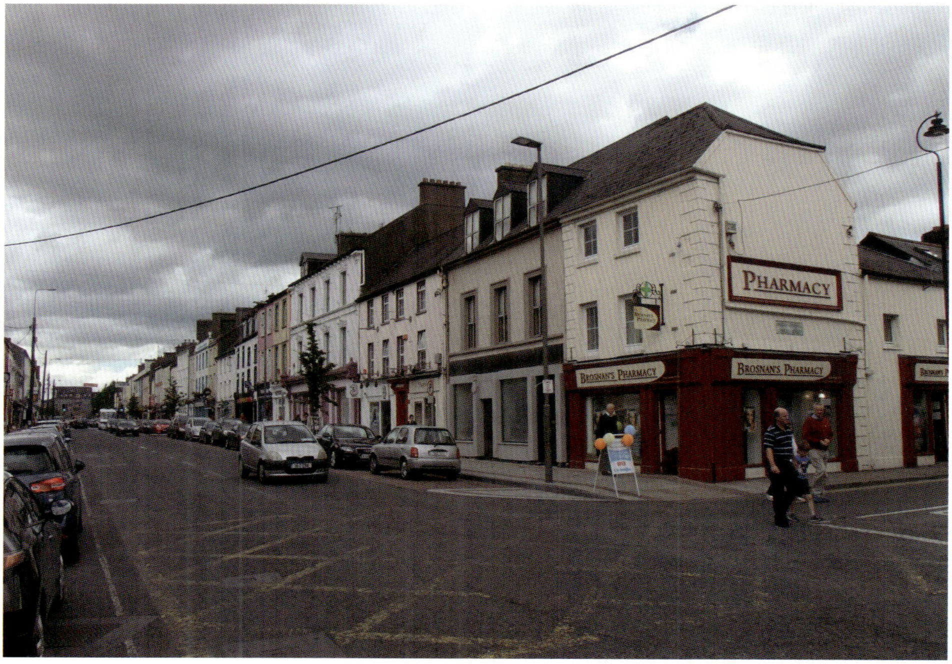

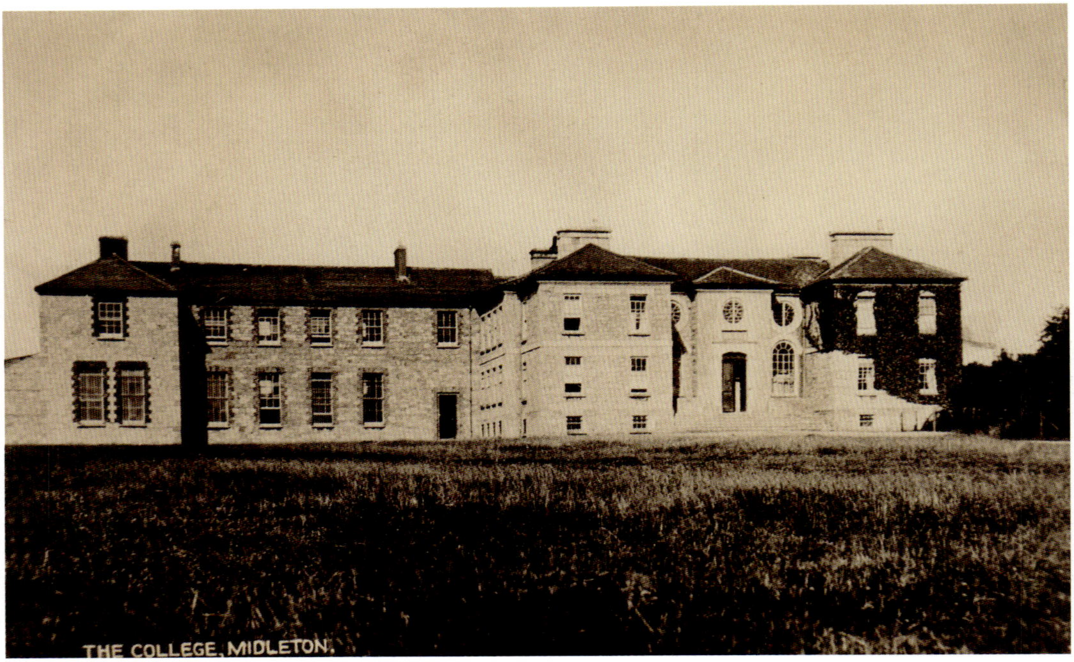

Education and the Past, Midleton Past

Midleton College was founded in 1696 by Elizabeth Villiers, a favourite of King William. It was housed in a newly constructed, handsome limestone building, which is still in use today. It took in its first pupils in 1717. Some famous pupils include Isaac Butt (founder of the Irish Home Rule Party), John Philpott Curran, (lawyer and father of the famous Sarah Curran), Edward Hincks (orientalist), Standish O'Grady (literary pioneer), Revd W. Spottiswood Green (mountain explorer), and Rachael Kohler (international hockey player).

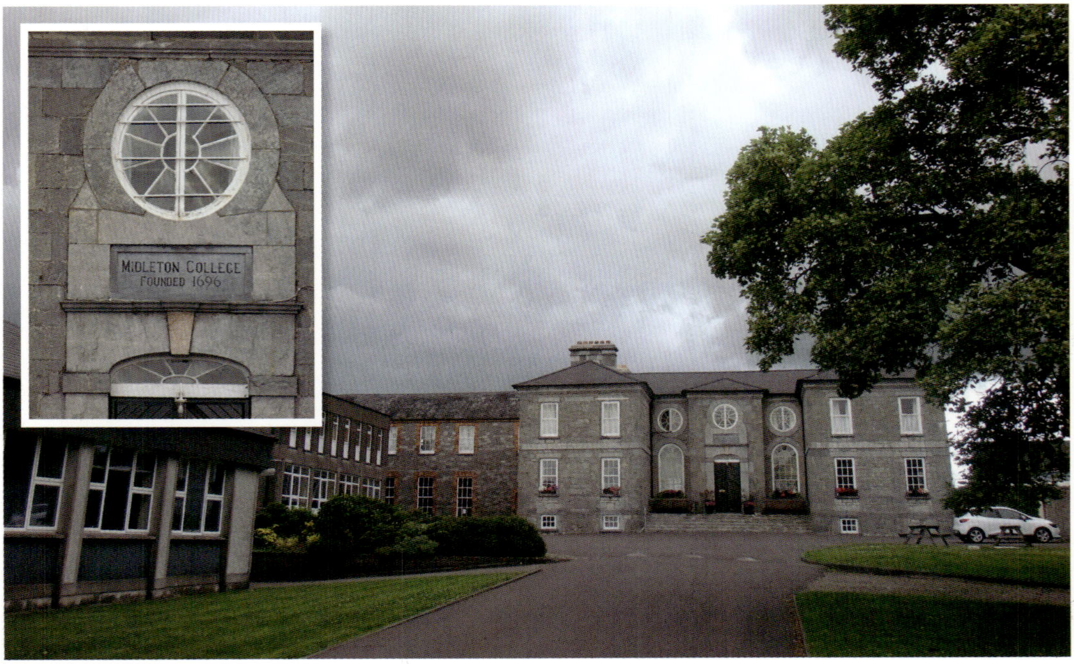

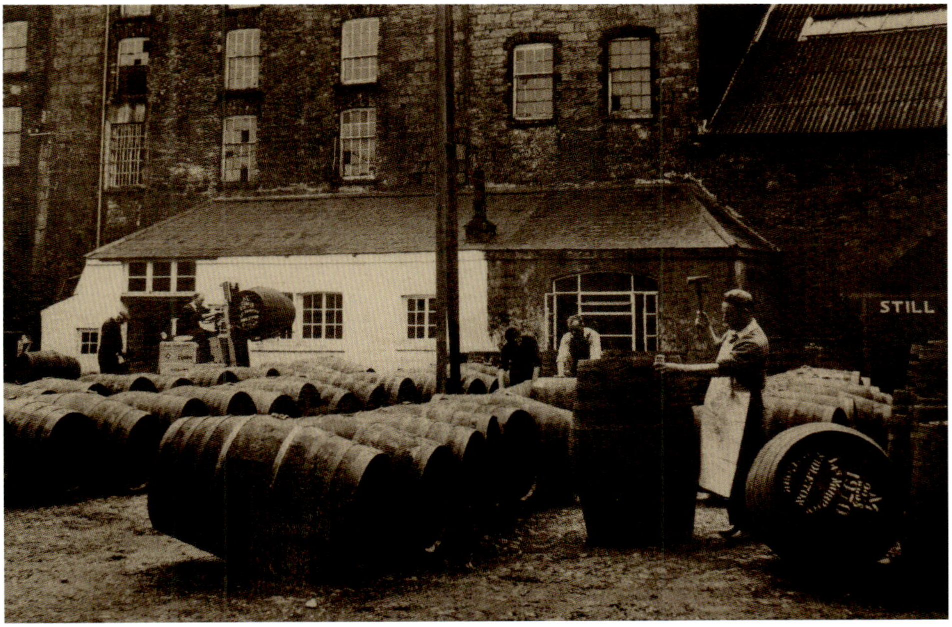

Distilling the Present, Midleton Distillery

The old Cork Distilleries Co. operated for 150 years from 1825 until 1975, when the workers then clocked off on a Friday evening in July to start work in the new Midleton Distillery the following Monday morning. The old distillery was kept intact and beautifully preserved. It is now one of the most striking and interesting tourist attractions in Ireland. Some of the original buildings date back to 1795, built as a mill before being converted for use as a distillery. The water wheel, which once operated all the machinery at the distillery, still turns, operating the cogs and wheels in the mill building today.

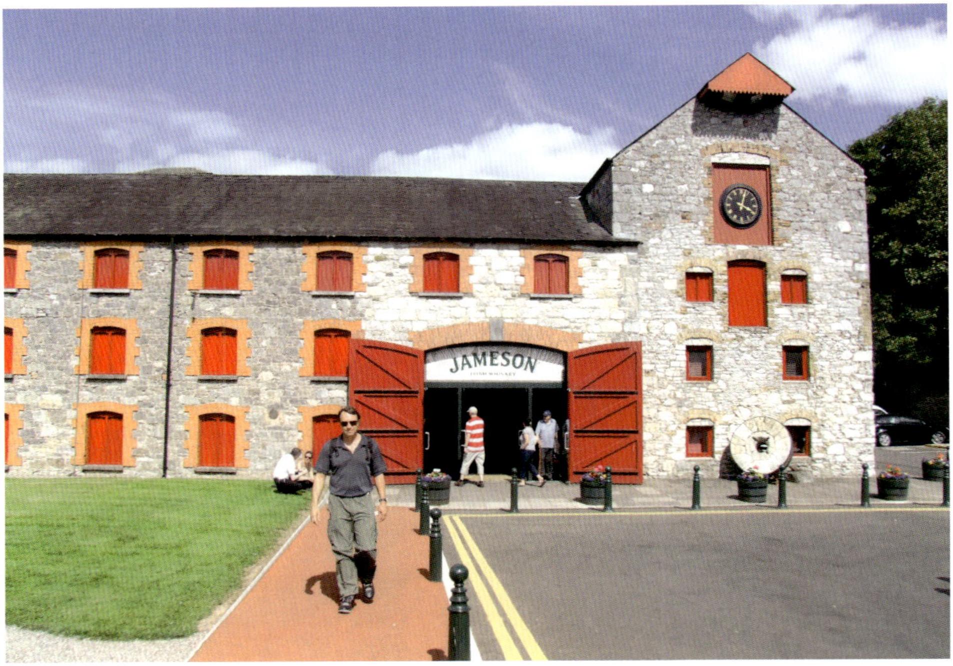

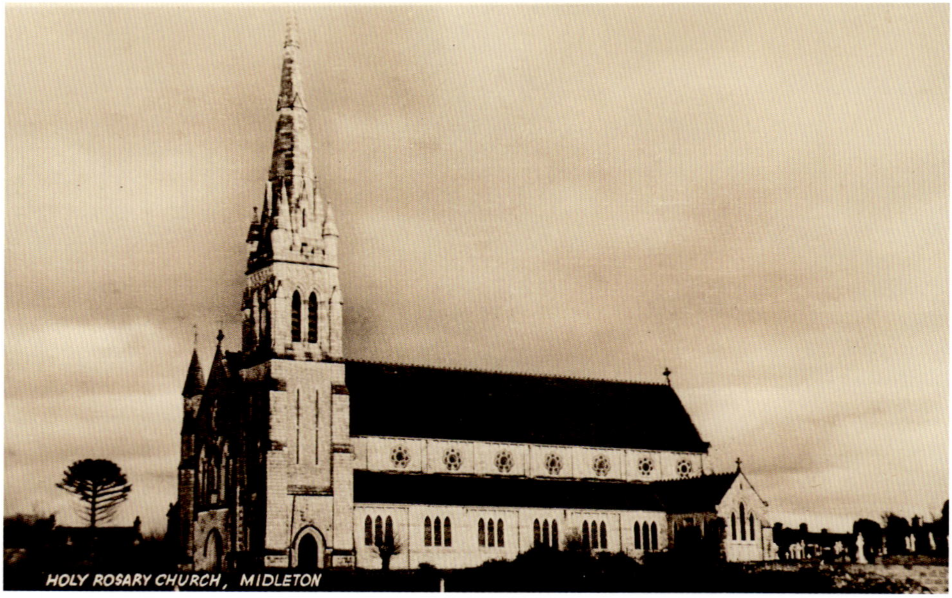

Towards the Skies, Holy Rosary Church, Midleton

This impressive church was designed by George Coppinger Ashlin, a leading church architect of the Gothic style, and was dedicated in 1896. On 28 June 1908, the spire, tower and belfry was completed and blessed. It took eighteen months to be constructed by local builder and contractor, Mr J. J. Coffey. The spire rises to 189 feet, and the beautiful copper cross, which surmounts it, is 12 feet in height. The masonry in 1908 was noted by the *Cork Examiner* as 'bold, pitch-faced ashlar, butressses being finished by neatly wrought iron weatherings'. The bell is one of the largest in County Cork, and is cast by Mathew O'Byrne of Dublin.

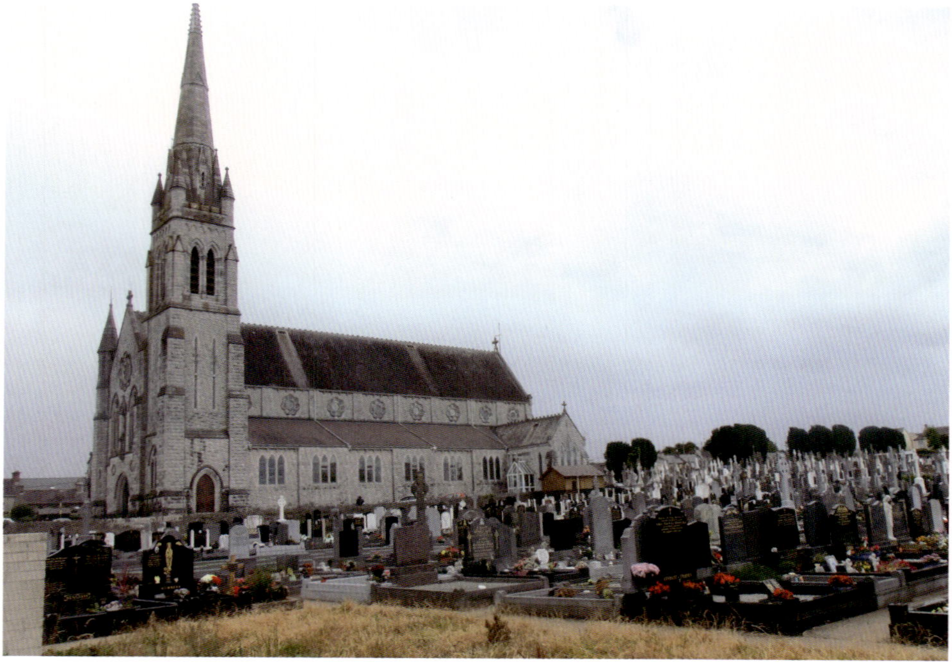

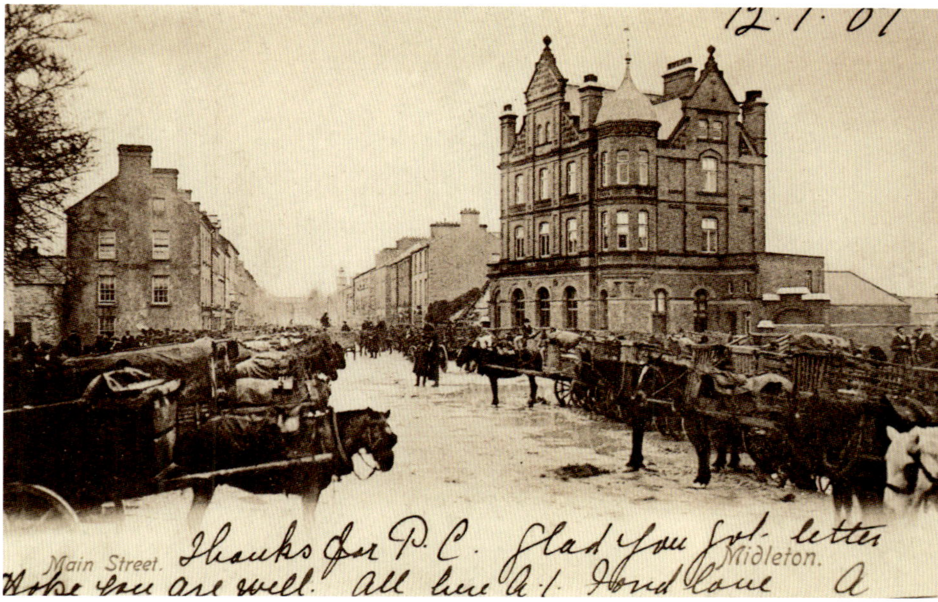

Traditions and Trades, Midleton

In 1914, Midleton was noted in Guy's *Directory of Cork* as a market town with a head post, money order, telegraph and telephone call office. The town was the middle town on the Cork–Youghal line, with five trains running to and from Cork daily. The main street boasted three banks, the Bank of Ireland, the Munster and Leinster Bank, and the National Bank Ltd. Guy's directory lists thirty-one trades on the main street, with the largest being 8 boot and shoe warehouses, 9 drapers, 25 grocers and provision merchants, 6 hardware merchants, 7 seed and manure merchants, 16 vintners and 10 wine and spirit merchants. The present-day view is taken opposite the town's War of Independence memorial, sculpted by Seamus Murphy and unveiled in 1939.

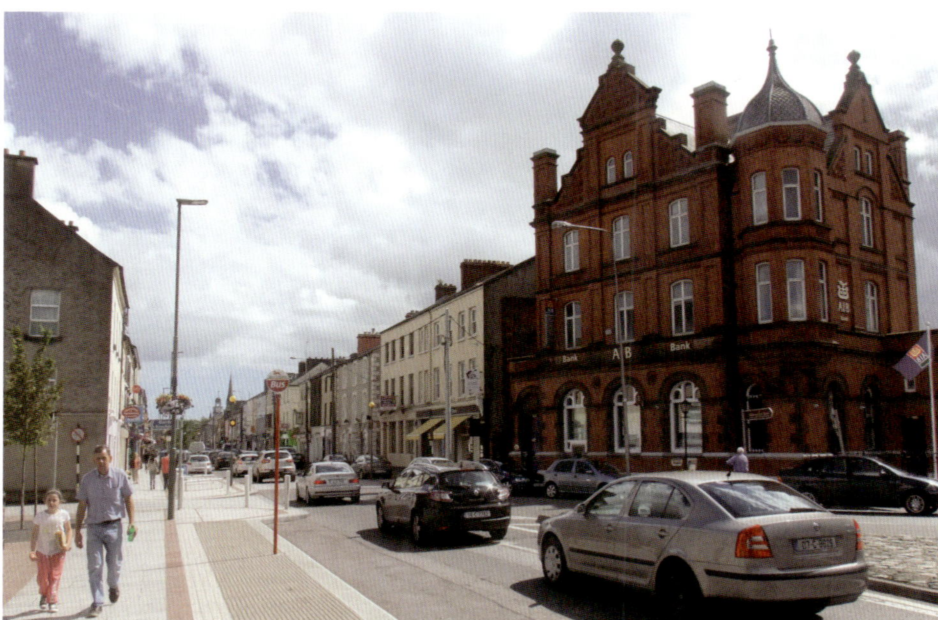

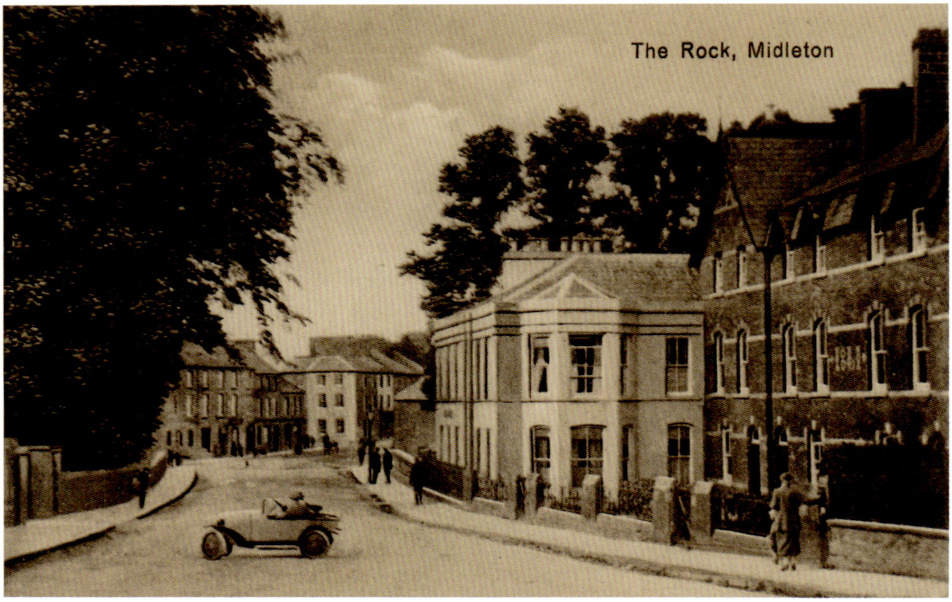

The Bustling Market Town, Midleton

The eastern entrance to Midleton's Main Street boasts colourful Victorian premises. In 1914, the main street, with its thirty-one trades, was a bustling place. The smaller numbers of trades included 5 bakers, 1 blacksmith, 1 car owner, 6 china and glass dealers, 1 clothiers and tailor, 1 coach builder, 1 coal merchant, 2 dressmakers, 6 flour merchants, 1 hairdresser, 4 house furnishers, 4 hotels, 3 insurance agents, Buckley's Watchmaker and Jeweller, Murphy's Undertaker, 1 physican and surgeon, 1 painters and decorators, 3 solicitors, 4 stationers, 4 timber merchants, 5 tobacconists, 5 victuallers, Walsh's Steam, Saw and Corn Mills, and 2 wool merchants.

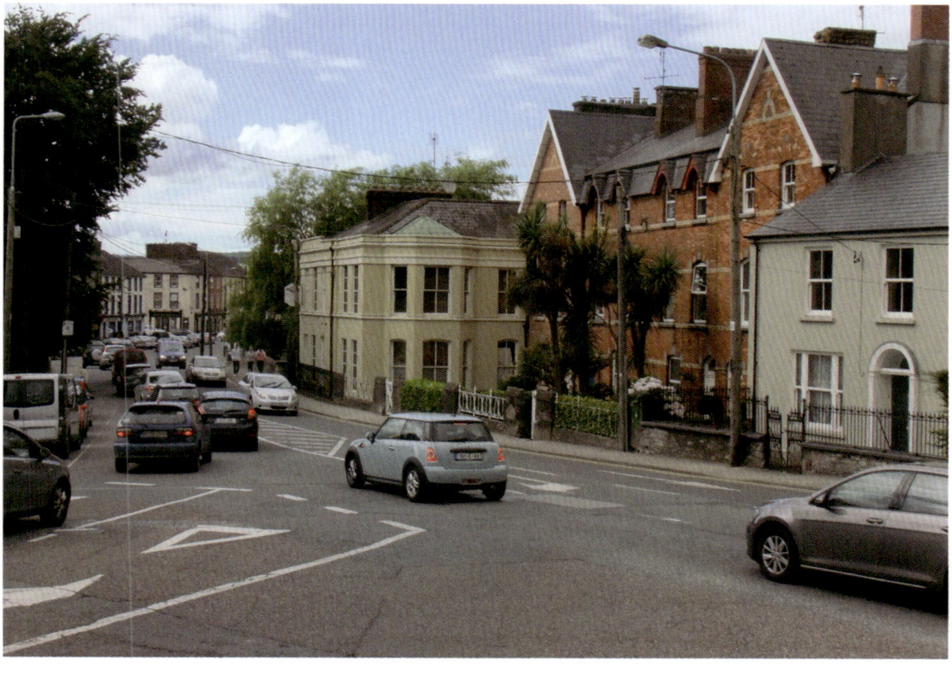

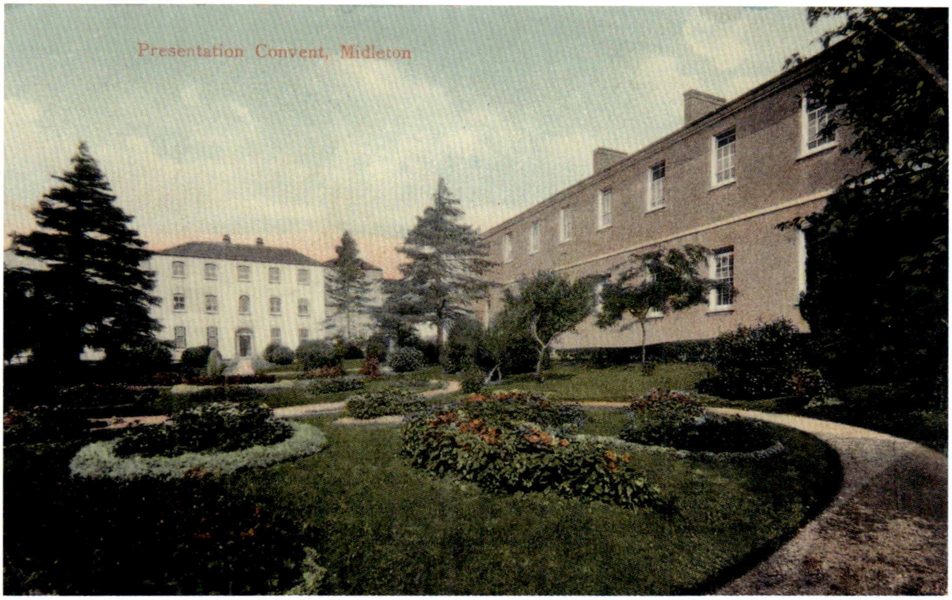

Presentation Convent, Midleton

The Presentation Sisters arrived to Midleton in 1834. The convent was built on a site granted by Lord Midleton and financed by the Coppinger Family and Gould Trust Fund, which had been set up in 1826 for the promotion of Catholic education in the Diocese of Cloyne. The attached primary school was opened in 1834, and St Mary's High School was opened in 1902. In recent years, the old buildings have been demolished and replaced by contemporary convent accomodation. The ornate oratory and the graveyard for the sisters is now a quiet space of reflection.

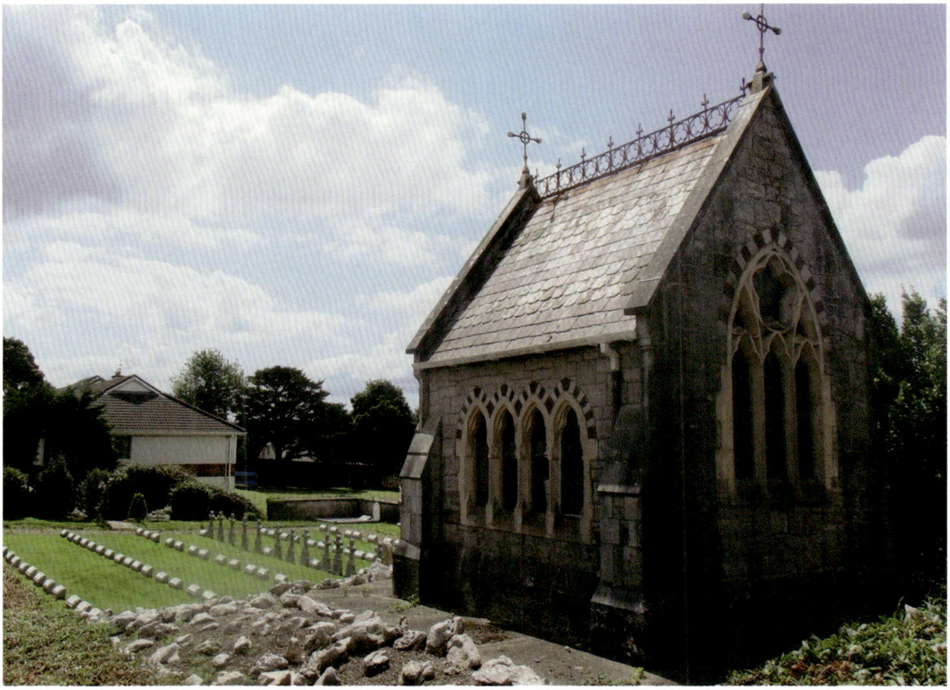

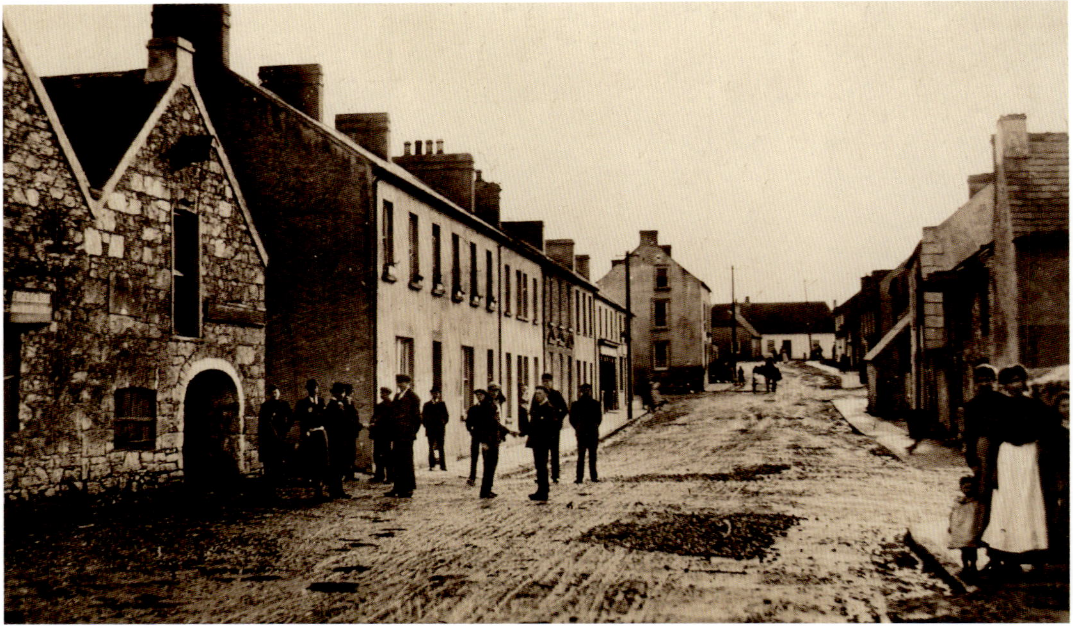

At the Water's Edge, Ballinacurra

Ballincurra has one main street, the centre of which another branches off to the east. In nineteenth-century reports, it contained around 250 houses, most of which were uniform in design. The inhabitants were supplied with water from springs and there are two rivers – the Avannachora (or Midleton river), which bounds the town on the west and falls into the inlet about a mile below it, and the Rocks-borough river, which skirts its southern part and flows into the former. Both rivers at one time were well fished and abundant with salmon and trout, over each river existed stone bridges. In 1824, a new line of road was opened, forming a western entrance. Its location adjacent on a creek leading into Cork harbour meant it possessed all the advantages of a sea port.

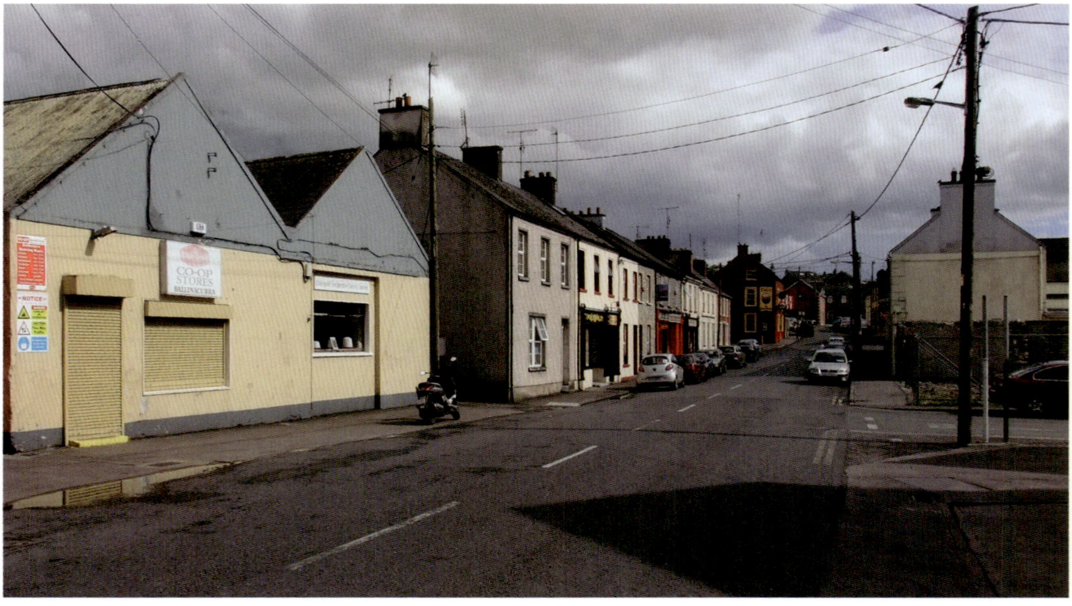

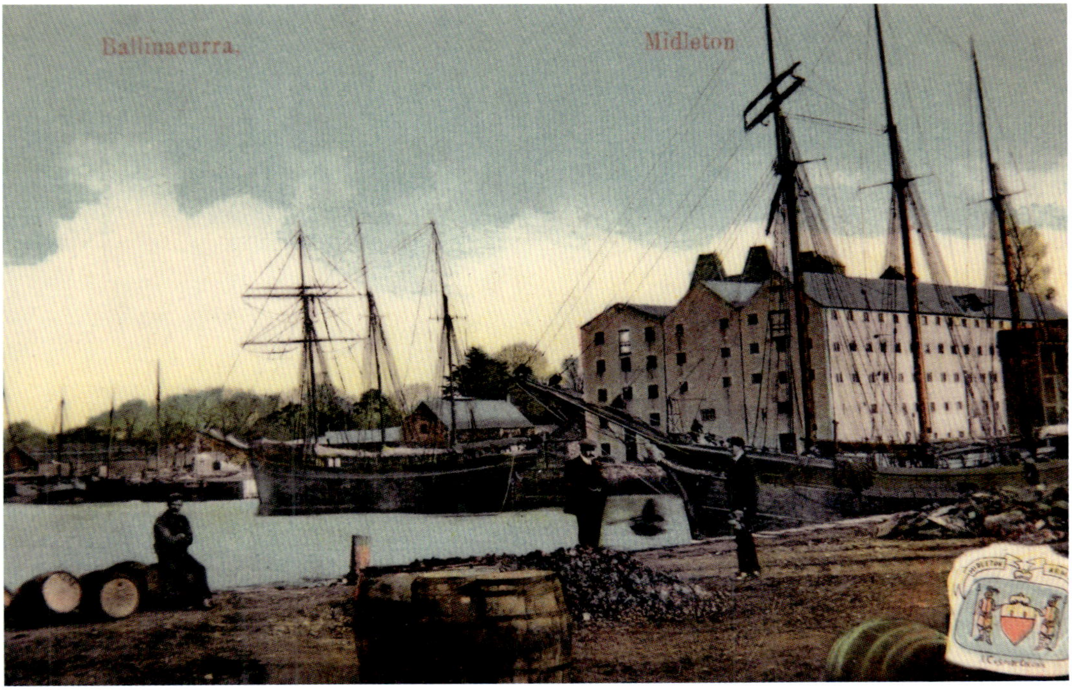

Storehouses of Memories, Ballinacurra

Giving access to Cork harbour, the creek at Ballincurra and Bailick village had 'commodious' quays, accessible to vessels of 300 tons, which could lie alongside and load and both unload safely. There were also some extensive storehouses, where coal, timber, iron, slate, and other heavy goods were landed and warehoused. These are now apartment complexes for modern-day living.

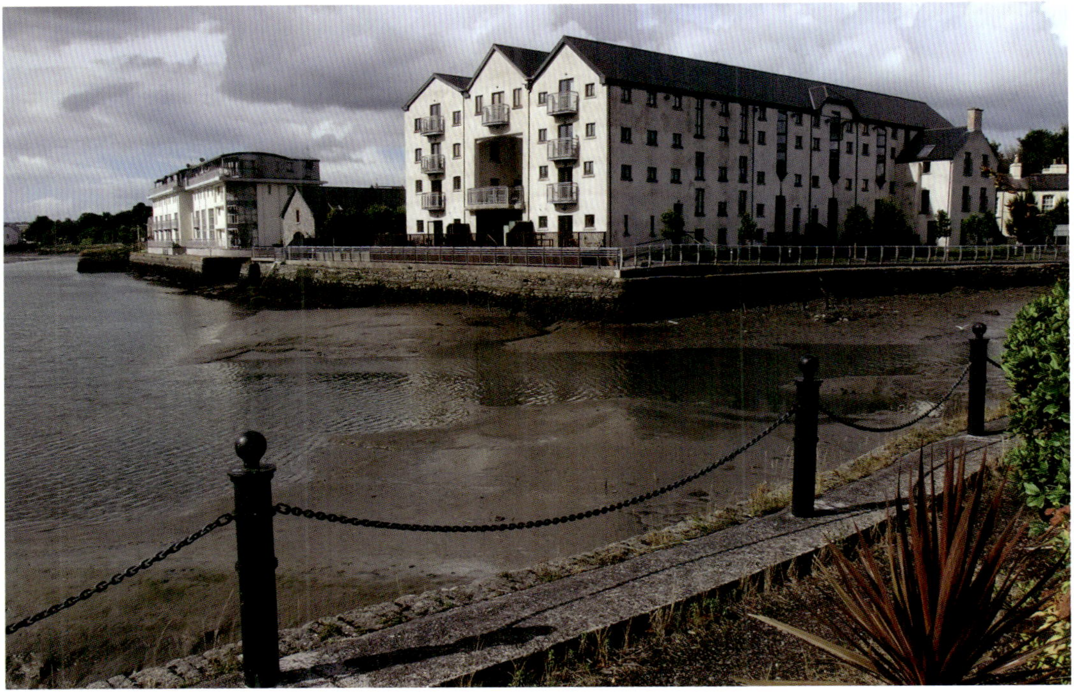

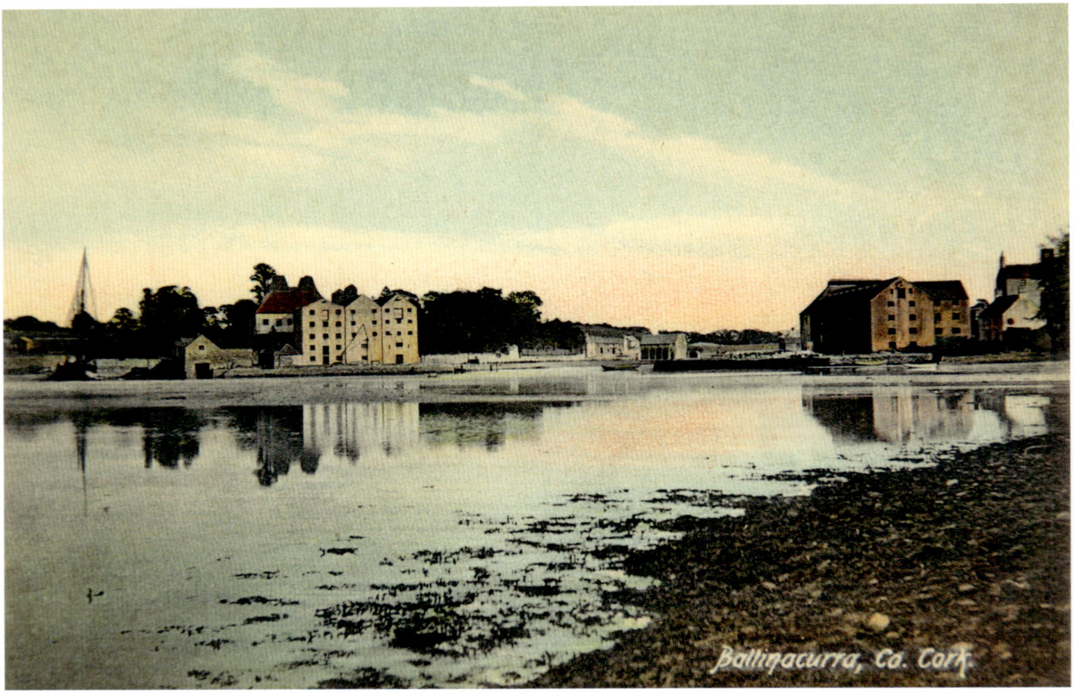

A Sea Port, Ballinacurra

The Ballinacurra warehouses were large spacious stores for the grain, large quantities of wheat and oats which were annually shipped to Liverpool and Bristol markets. A deputy water bailiff was positioned in Ballinacurra to collect the dues claimed by the Cork Harbour Board, and the foundling hospital of the city.

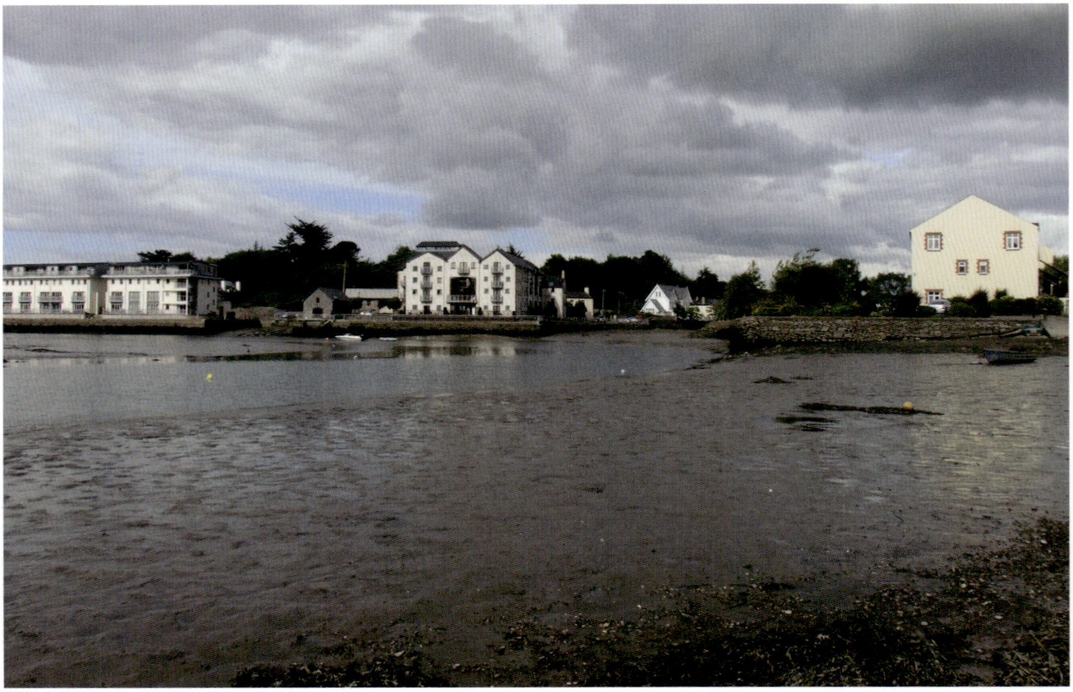

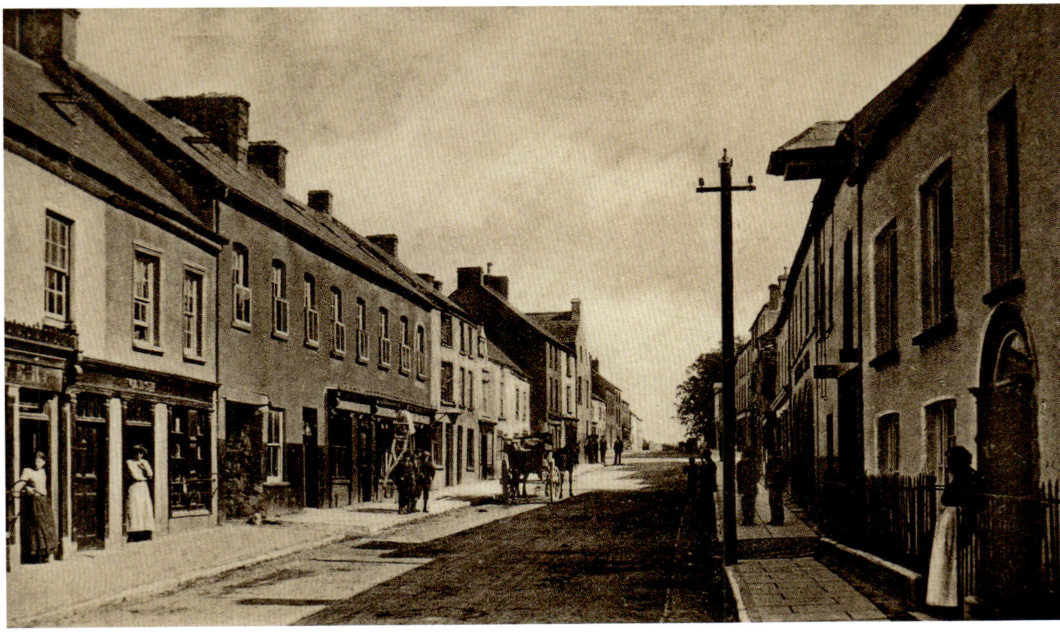

St Colman and Cloyne

Cloyne originated in the foundation of the Sea of Cloyne by St Colman, who died in 604. In 707, an abbey was erected on the west side of the cathedral, which was plundered in 978 by the people of Ossory, and again in 1089 by Dermot, the son of Fiordhealbhach O'Brien. The town comprises two streets intersecting each other at right angles and, in the nineteenth century, contained over 330 houses, most of which were small and irregularly built. The village today still boasts its monastic origins in the shape of a round tower and several well-built Georgian mansions, reminding the visitor of its once market town status. Since 1879, it also possesses a public water supply fountain, given by the Litton family.

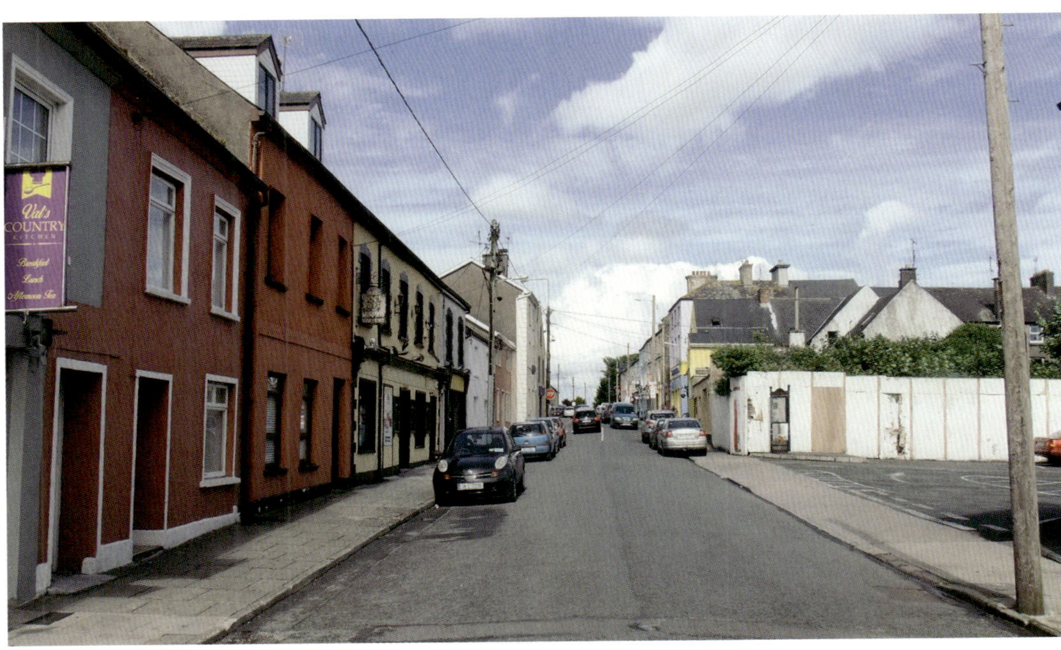

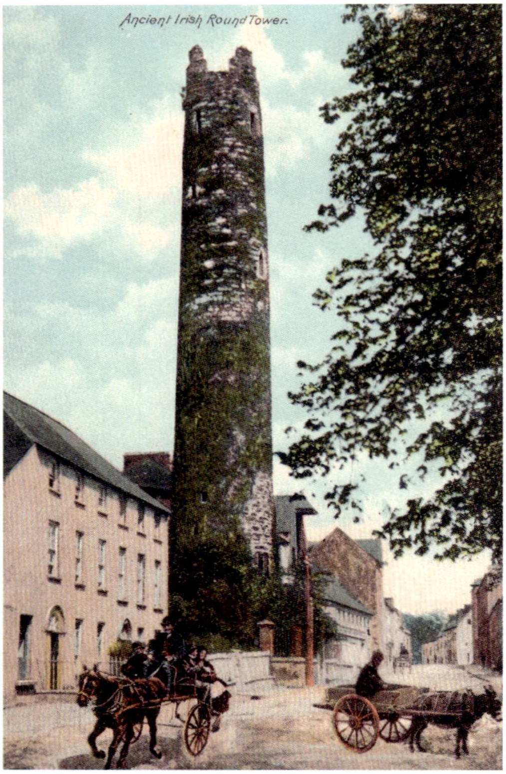

Round Tower, Cloyne

The tower is one of only two round towers in County Cork (the other in Kinneigh near Enniskeane in West Cork), and is one of seventy-three structures in the country. The sandstone tower has a suggested construction date of the tenth to eleventh century, and is over 30 metres high and 5.17 metres in diameter at the base. In the Cloyne tower, internal ladders provided access for a bell-ringer to reach the bell floor of the towers. Its foundations are on a rocky outcrop, which is visible from the west side.

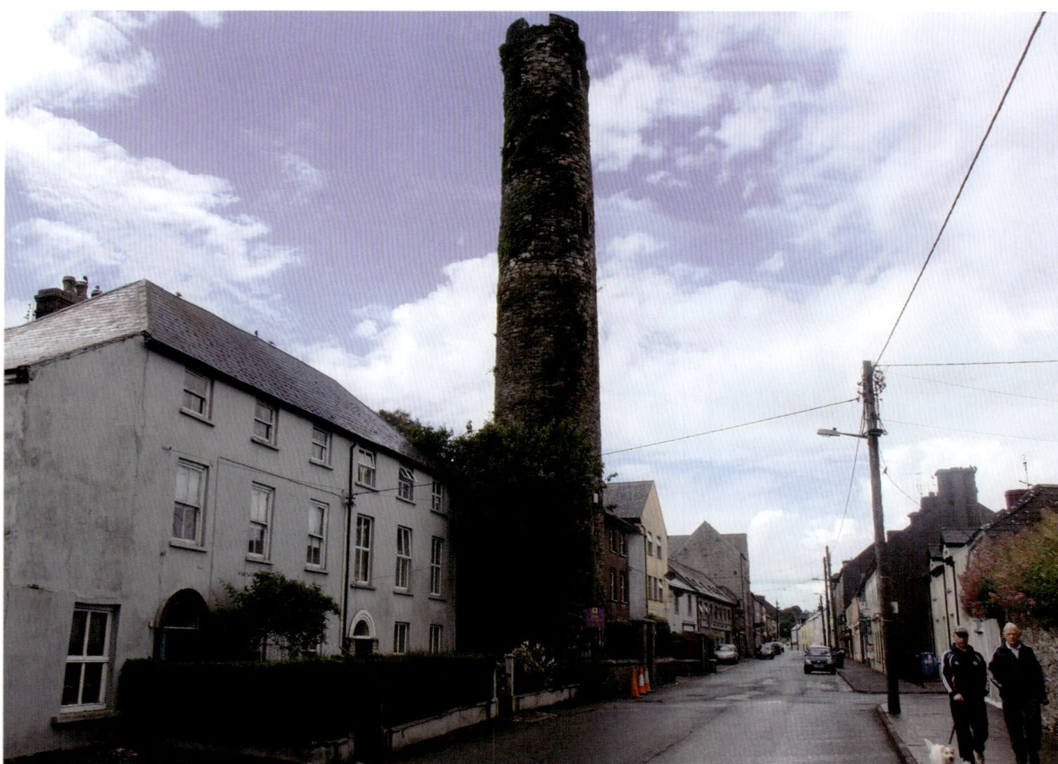

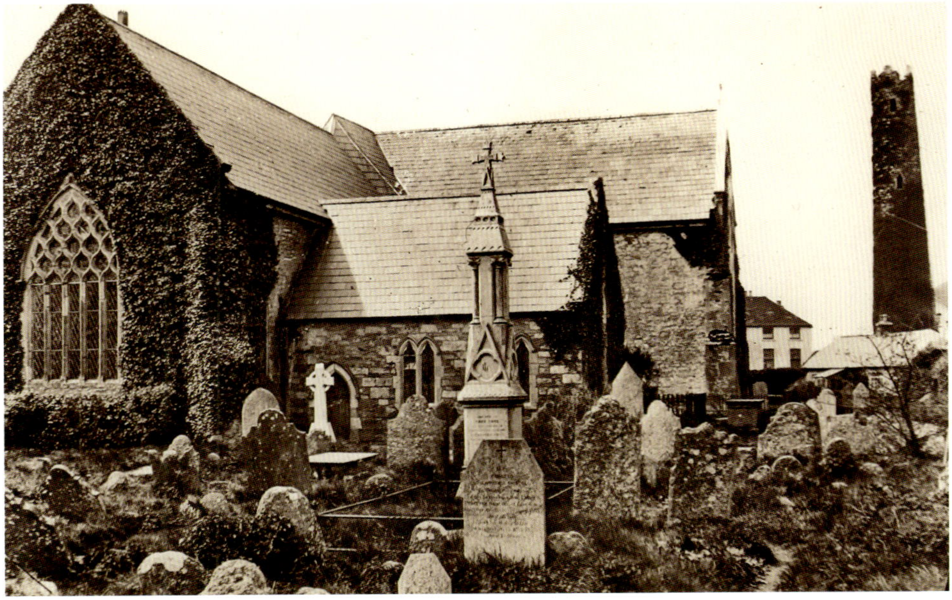

St Colman's Cathedral, Cloyne

The present church dates from the thirteenth century, and was built on the site of older monastic buildings. The Berkeley chapel in the North Transept houses a marble effigy of the distinguished philosopher George Berkeley, who was Bishop of Cloyne from 1734–53. It has undergone many changes through the centuries. Up to the year 1706, there were battlements on the walls of the nave that were thought to be too heavy and thus taken down, depriving the building of its original noble appearance. There is evidence that, at one time, there was a tower at the intersection of the transepts. Previously the Cathedral of the Diocese of Cloyne, it is now one of three cathedrals in the Church of Ireland United Dioceses of Cork, Cloyne and Ross.

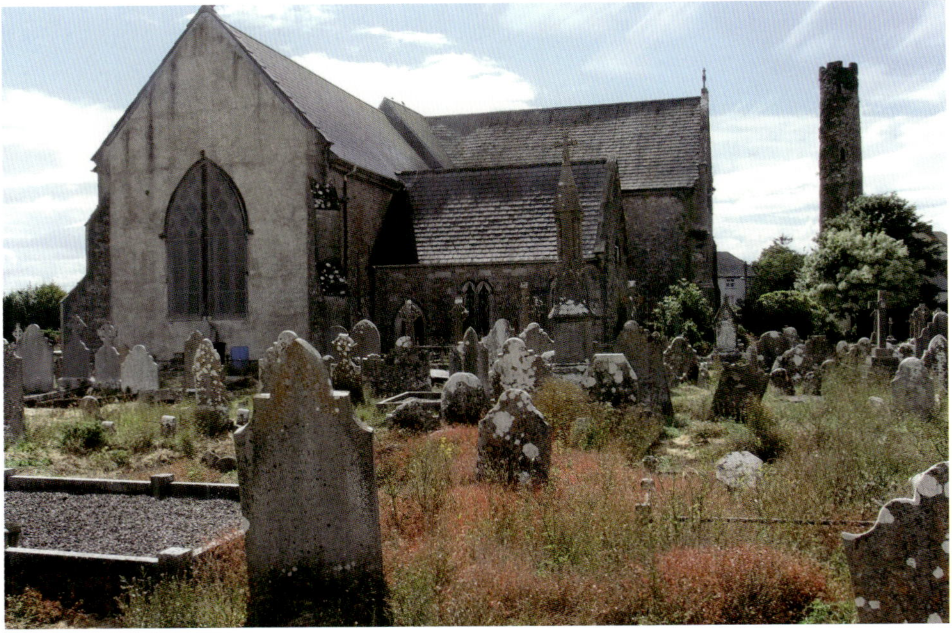

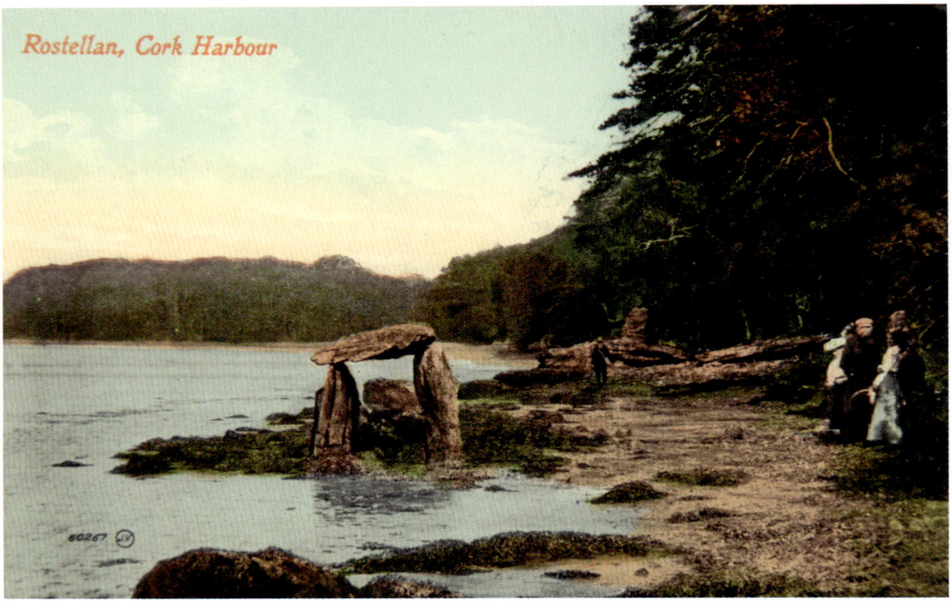

Dolmen, Rostellan

Described as enigmatic by Cork archaeologists, the Dolmen is similar to Neolithic portal tombs, but cannot be confidently identified as such here. Excluded from the Megalithic's survey lists, the monument has three upright stones and a capstone, which, at one time, fell down, but was later repositioned. The site gets flooded at high tides and it is difficult to get to across the local mudflats. It is easier to get to them with a guide through the adjacent Rostellan wood. The wood was created as part of the former estate of Rostellan House. It was built by William O'Brien (1694–1777), the 4th Earl of Inchiquin, in 1721. The Dolmen could be a folly on the estate. There is a folly nearby in the shape of a castle tower, named Siddons Tower, after an actress Sarah Siddons.

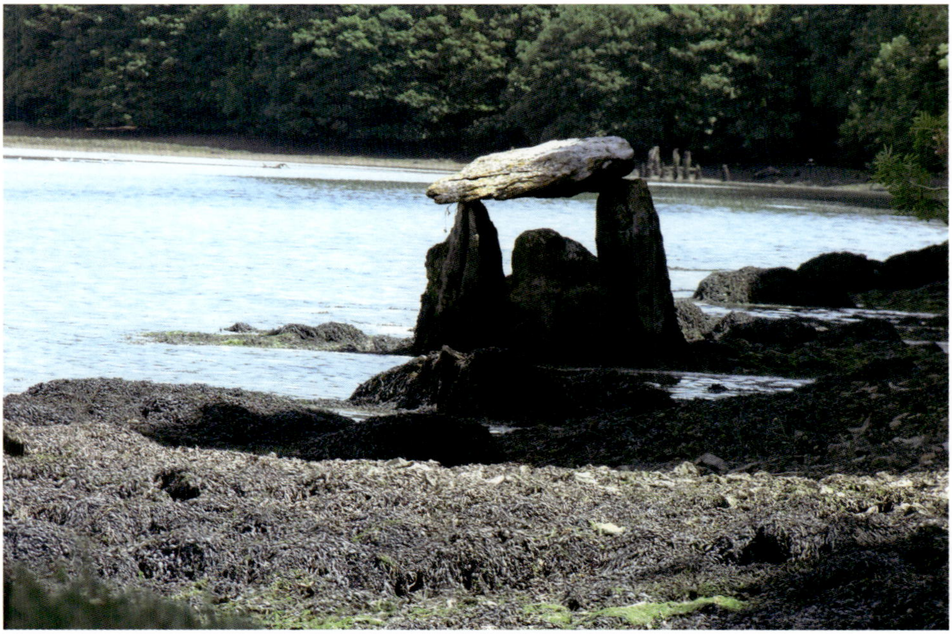

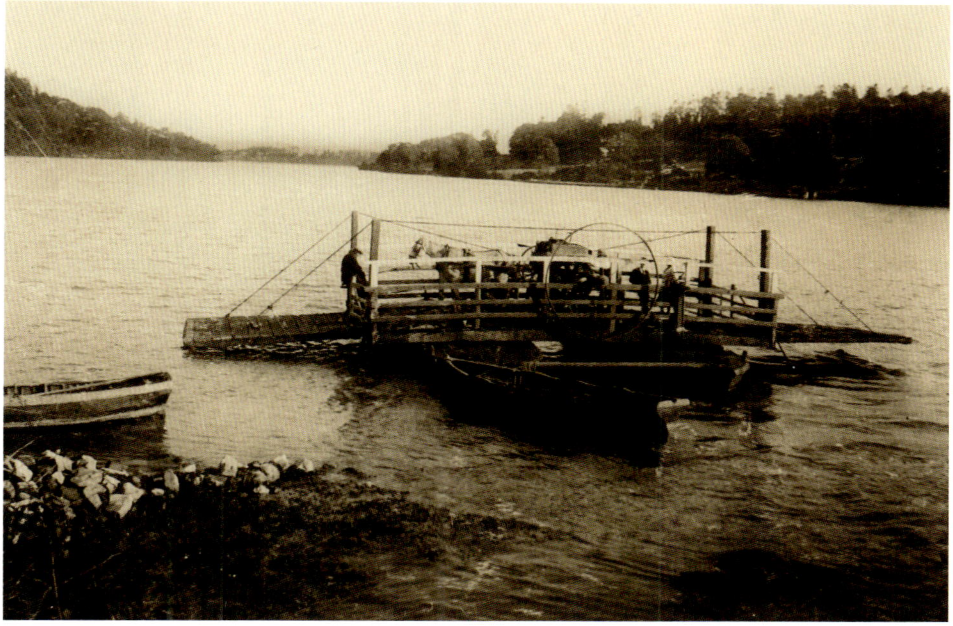

East Ferry

For many decades, up to 1923, a manually operated ferry, popularly described as a 'pontoon bridge', made five or six trips daily across East Ferry, via the eastern channel off Great Island to the general Rostellan area. It transported passengers, carts and cattle from shore to shore. The rare picture shows two pontoons arranged like a catamaran, decked over and fitted at either end with a landing ramp. The pontoon was chained and hauled between its two terminals and served a great social need. Information regarding its final days is conflicting. Some locals say it was wrecked in a westerly gale in 1923, while others say it was rendered inoperative in the Irish Civil War. Local boating still exists in the area.

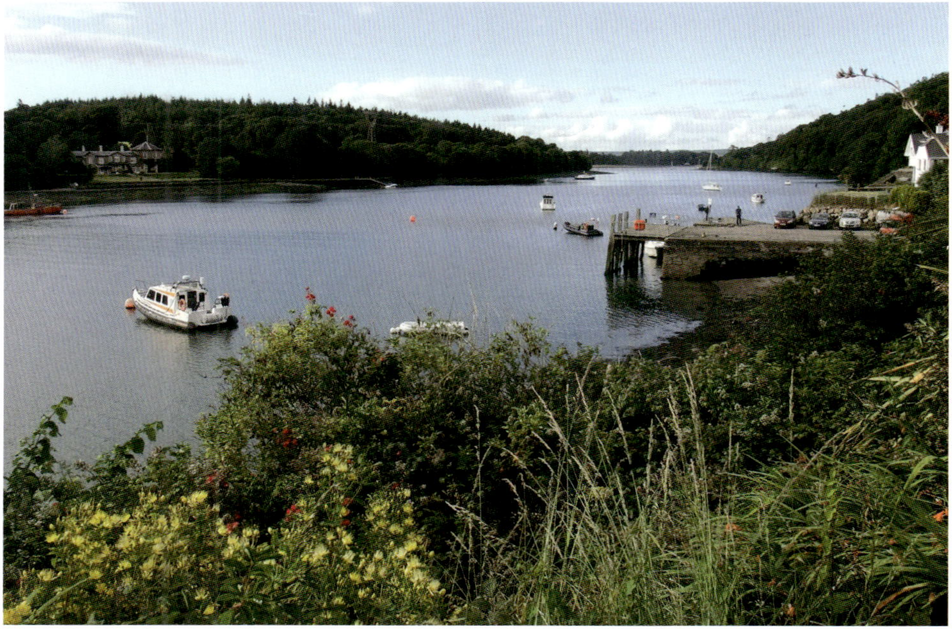

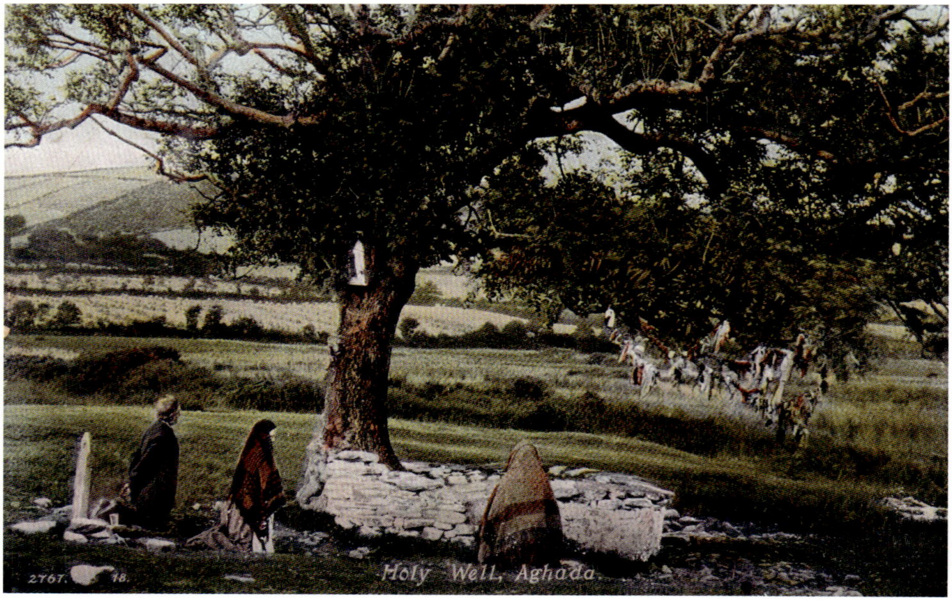

A Pilgrimage of Heart, Our Lady's Well, Aghada

Located at Tileskin townland on the farm of the Russell family, rounds are still performed at this holy well, dedicated to the Virgin Mary, every year. A remarkable stone (*inset*) stands by the well, which dates back to 1731, that gives the pattern formula – seven paters, seven Aves and one Gloria. It is significant that the stone was inscribed in the year 1731, when nearly all the priests of Cloyne were on the run under penal laws. An account of pilgrims recorded 200–300 people drinking water from the well there. Over the well was a tree on which people placed small bits of rags as a symbol of leaving their ailments behind, while several kissed the rude cut figure on the adjacent stone in relief (*inset*).

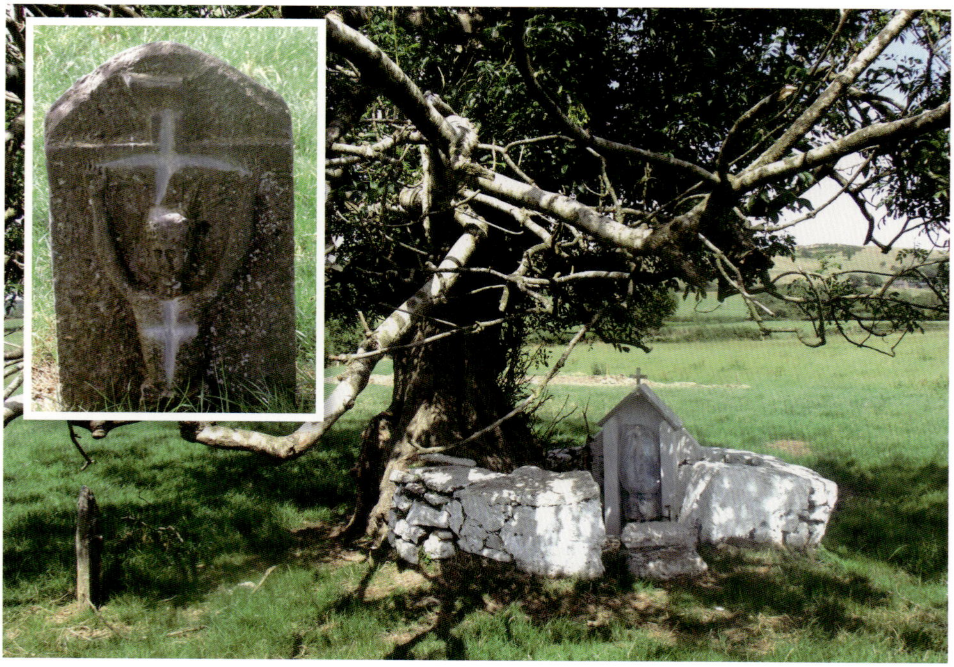

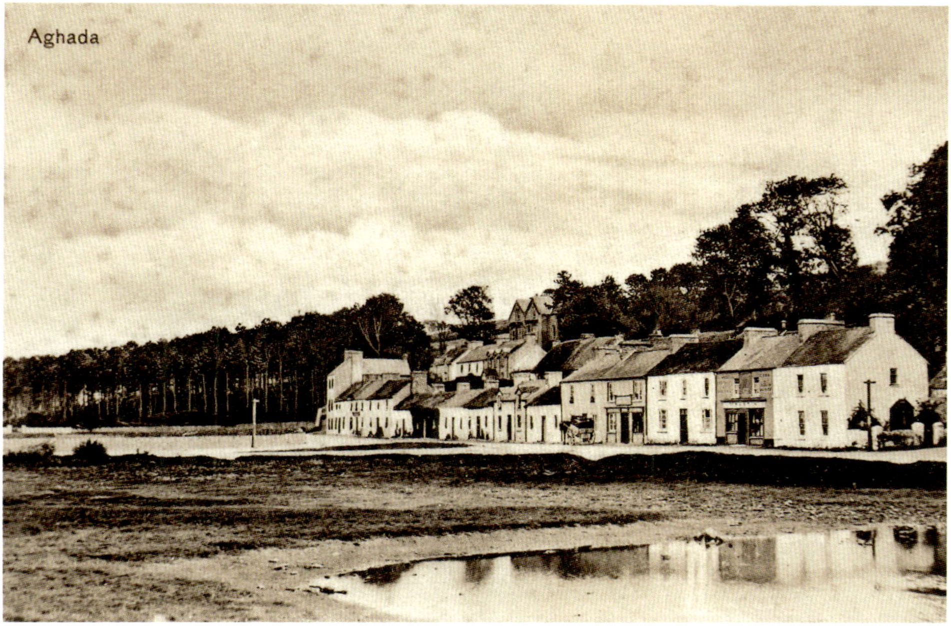

Aghada

Lower Aghada village is described in Guy's *Directory of Cork* 1914 as a seaside village. Its small pier was originally constructed by subscription, where a steamboat from Cork or Queenstown called every Tuesday during the summer, and where coal and sand were occasionally dropped. In the mid-nineteenth century, about fifty local females were employed in plaiting Tuscan straw for exportation, and a few in plaiting the crested dog's tail, or 'traneen' grass. Records from 100 years ago reveal that the parish of Aghada comprised of 2,331 statute acres, as plotted under the Tithe Act – the greater part was under tillage, and nearly the whole of the remainder was pasture.

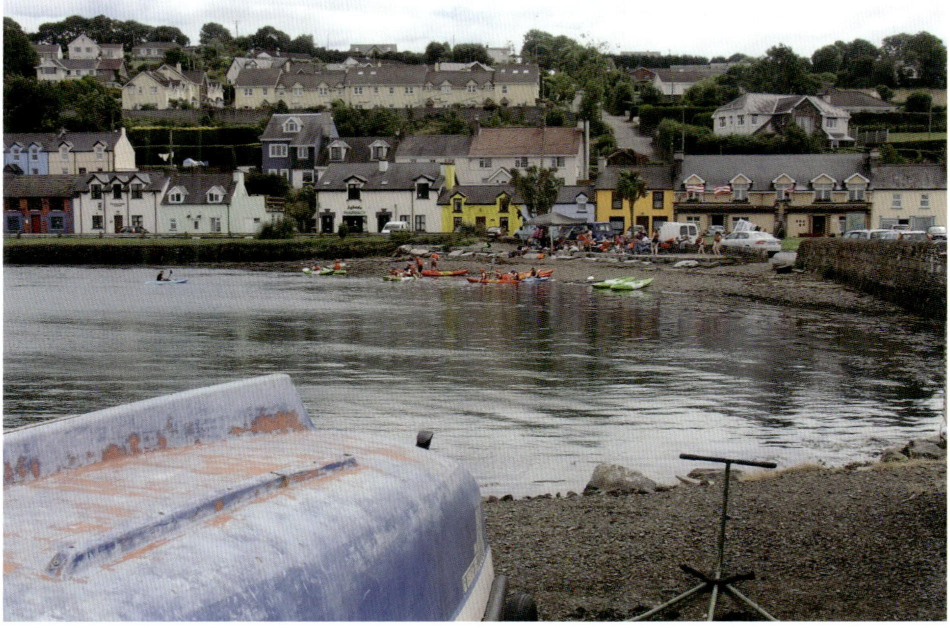

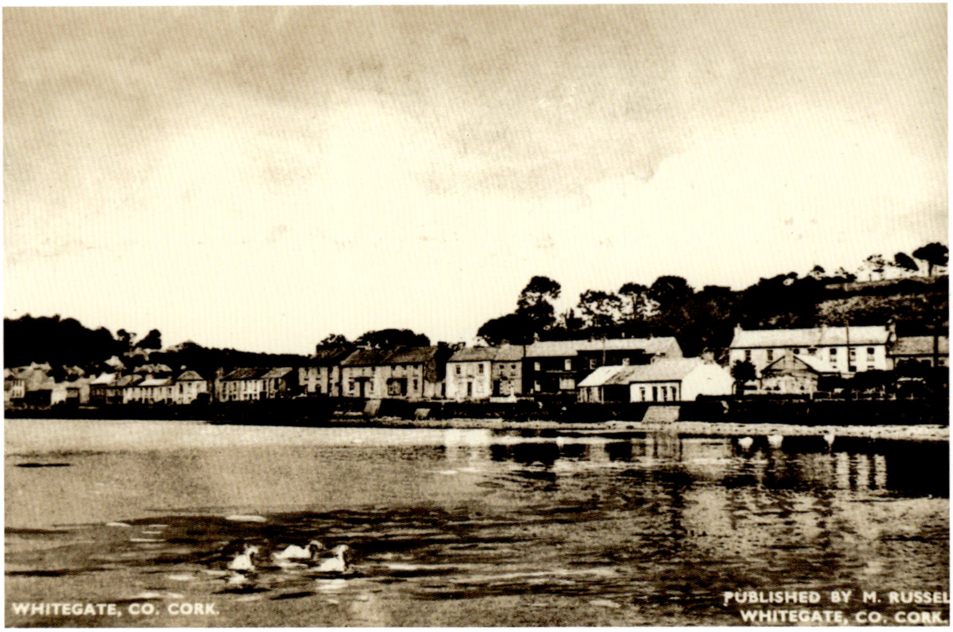

Whitegate

Guy's *Directory of Cork* for 1914 records Whitegate as a village with small, well-built houses, where considerable fishing is carried out. At one time several boats were employed, as well in raising sand from the harbour, used for manure. The surrounding countryside was described as very fertile and embellished by several elegant mansions, the principal of which was Corkbeg House, the residence of the Fitzgerald family. The house and part of the estate were built upon by Whitegate Oil Refinery. The refinery was officially opened on 22 September 1959. Its annual capacity was initially proposed to supply Ireland's total petroleum needs of 262 million gallons.

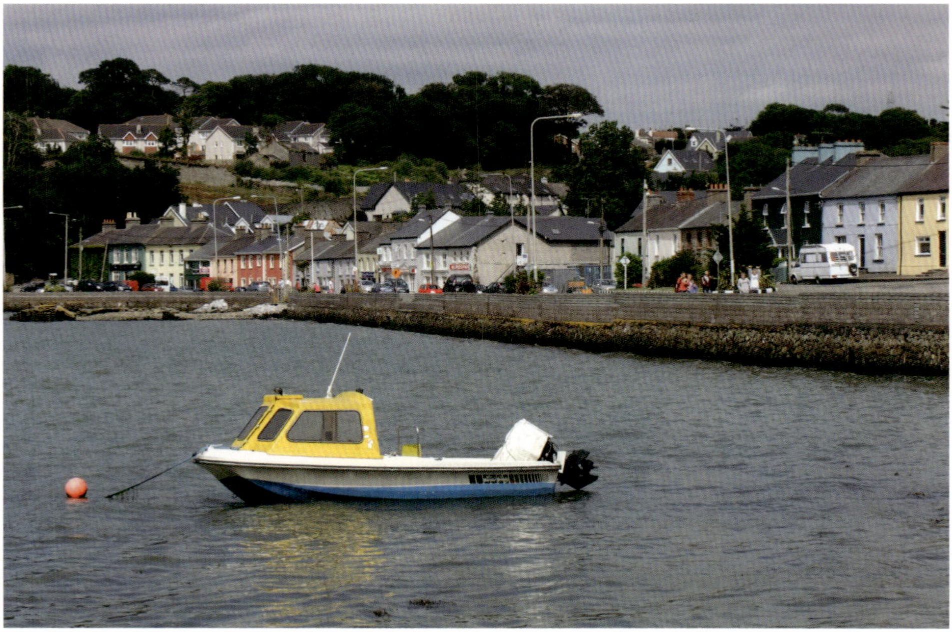

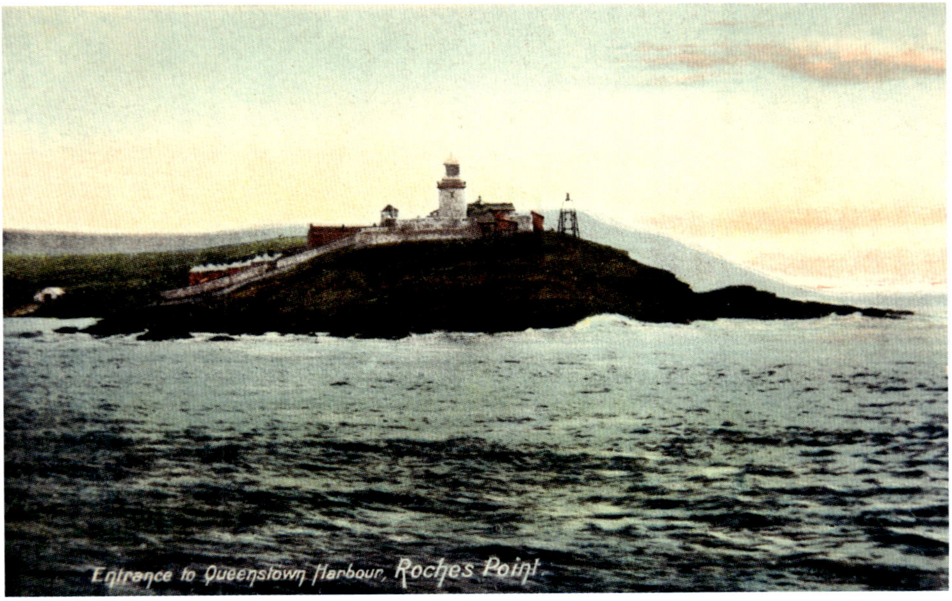

Roches Point

Around AD 1640–50, the Roche family purchased the Fitzgerald estate (around 1,500 acres) from Edmund Fitzgerald of Ballymaloe, and lived for many centuries at Trabolgan. Roches Point, at the mouth of Cork Harbour, is named after this family. A letter from Vice-Adm. Thornborough of Trent, Cork Harbour, dated 28 August 1813, was read to the Ballast Board on 2 September 1813. In this letter, he pointed out the danger vessels frequenting Cork Harbour were put in, as a result of the lack of a lighthouse at the entrance to the harbour. This small lighthouse was working by June 1817, but its tower was not conducive to a major harbour of refuge and port and, in 1835, it was replaced by the present larger tower.

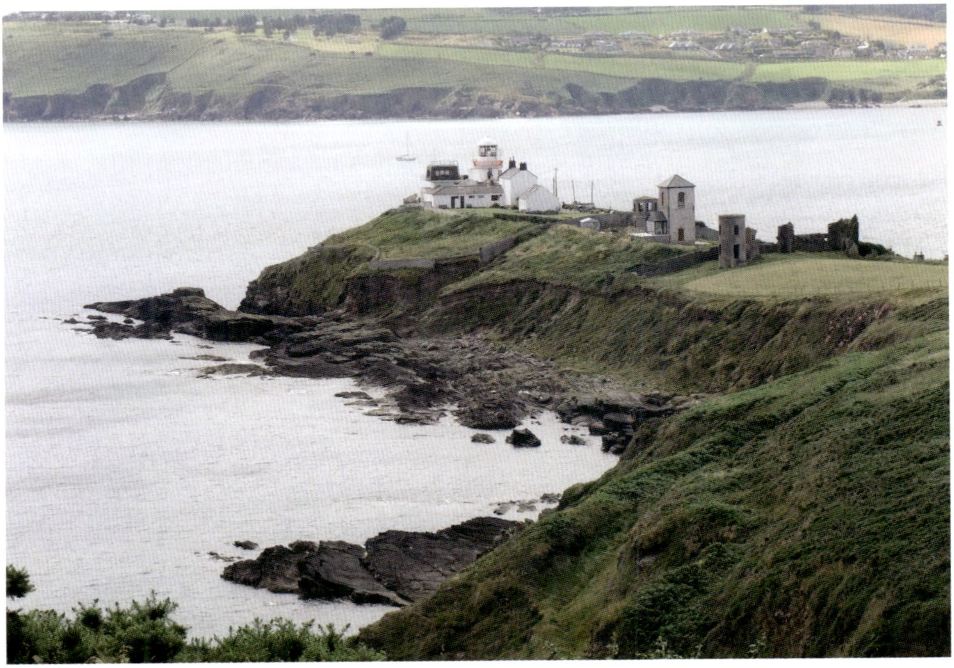

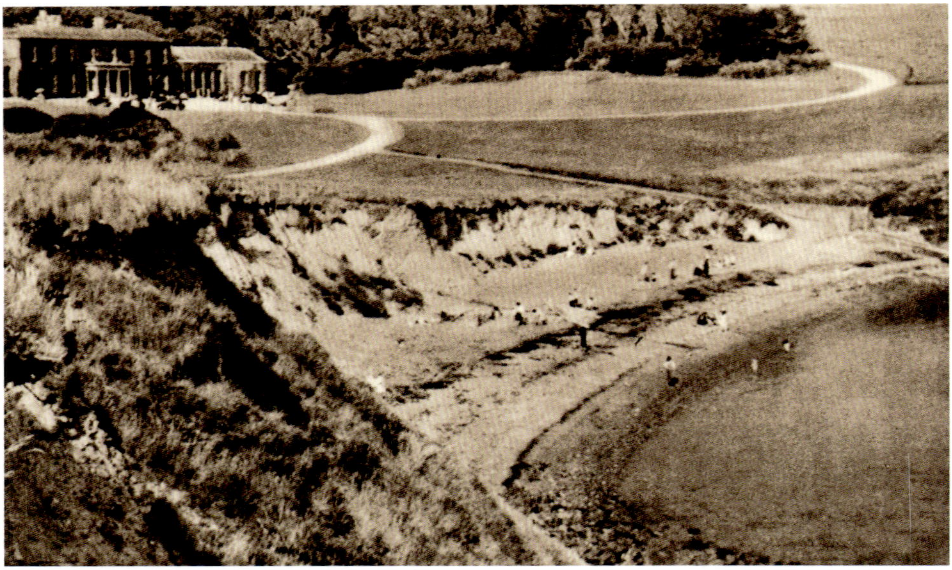

The Strand, Trabolgan

The old Trabolgan house of the Roche family (and later in time owned by the Clarke family) was situated where the swimming pool complex of the holiday centre is today. It was a Georgian house, comprised of two storeys at the front and three storeys at the back, with the front of the house faced out to sea. Halfway up the entrance avenue there is a triumphal arch similar in design to the Arc de Triomphe in Paris. One member of the Roche family is supposedly buried under the arch. Finally, the shape of the bay gave the place its name of *Trá*, meaning 'strand' or 'beach', and Bolgan or Bulgen, meaning 'bulging' or 'big wave'. In 1948, a Mr Bright and Mr White, together with a number of local investors, decided to purchase the remaining estate from the Land Commission and operate the estate as a holiday camp for Pontins. The holiday centre has changed hands several times over the decades and has been redeveloped.

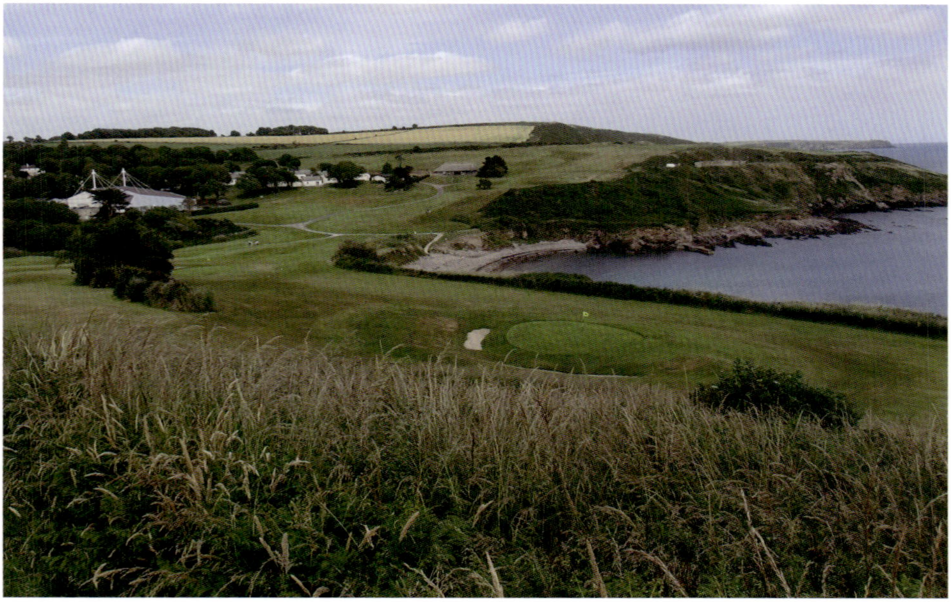

Acknowledgements

We would like to express our gratitude to the curator of Cork Public Museum, Stella Cherry, for her courtesy and encouragement towards this project. The old postcards within the book are archived in the Cork Public Museum. The present-day pictures were taken by the authors. We would like to also thank the staff of Amberley Publishing for their vision with this work.

Biographies

Daniel Breen

Daniel Breen was born in Ballincollig, County Cork, in 1979. Having graduated with a degree in History and Archaeology from University College Cork in 2001, he achieved an MA from Sheffield University in European Historical Archaeology in 2002. While in college, Daniel spent his summer months working on various archaeological sites throughout Ireland. Since graduation, he has worked in Cork Public Museum, where he now holds the position of assistant curator. He co-wrote *Cork City Through Time* with Kieran McCarthy in 2012 and *West Cork Through Time* in 2013. In 2014, he co-authored *The Cork International Exhibition 1902–1903: Snapshot of Edwardian Cork* with Tom Spalding, published by Irish Academic Press.

Kieran McCarthy

For over twenty years, Kieran has actively promoted Cork's heritage with its various communities and people. He has led, and continues to lead, successful heritage initiatives through his community talks, City and County school heritage programmes, walking tours, newspaper articles, books, and his work through his heritage consultancy business. For the past fifteen years, Kieran has written a local heritage column in the *Cork Independent* on the history, geography and its intersection of modern-day life in communities in Cork City and County. He is the author of thirteen books; *Pathways Through Time, Historical Walking Trails of Cork City* (2001), *Cork: A Pictorial Journey* (co-written 2001), *Discover Cork* (2003), *A Dream Unfolding, Portrait of St Patrick's Hospital* (2004), *Voices of Cork: The Knitting Map Speaks* (2005), *In the Steps of St Finbarre, Voices and Memories of the Lee Valley* (2006), *Generations: Memories of the Lee Hydroelectric Scheme* (co-written, 2008), *Inheritance, Heritage and Memory in the Lee Valley, Co. Cork* (2010), *Royal Cork Institution, Pioneer of Education* (2010), and *Munster Agricultural Society, The Story of the Cork Showgrounds* (2010), *Cork City Through Time* (co-written, 2012), *Journeys of Faith, Our Lady of Lourdes Church Ballinlough, Celebrating 75 Years* (2013) and *West Cork Through Time* (co-written, 2013). In June 2009 and May 2014, Kieran was elected as a local government councillor (Independent) to Cork City Council. More on Kieran's work can be seen at www.corkheritage.ie and www.kieranmccarthy.ie.

Cork Public Museum

The postcards shown in this book come from the archives of Cork Public Museum, which was first opened in 1910 and is the longest established local authority museum in Ireland. It is housed in a beautiful Georgian building, set in the wonderfully landscaped Fitzgerald Park. During the turbulent period before the Second World War, the building was utilised for a variety of civic and municipal functions that distracted from its museum role. Finally, in 1945, the present incarnation of the Cork Public Museum was officially opened to the public, and it has remained a museum ever since. In 2005, a contemporary and modern extension was added to the existing building, making Cork Public Museum one of the most celebrated public buildings in Cork City. The collections of Cork Public Museum are as rich and as diverse as the history of the city itself. The ground floor of the museum has two permanent galleries, each dealing with the historical and archaeological heritage of Cork City and County. A visitor can trace the record from our earliest Mesolithic ancestors, to the civic leaders that brought the city into the twentieth century and beyond.

The museum displays some of the most important archaeological pieces known to be from Cork, including Ireland's oldest pick and shovel from a Bronze Age copper mine, the Iron Age Cork Helmet Horns, and the Garryduff Gold Bird, a marvel in early medieval craftsmanship. The archaeological section also takes the visitor into what life was like in medieval Cork. The finds from many recent excavations are exhibited, highlighting the importance of Cork as a trading and economic centre during medieval times. The historic displays focus on many important industrial, social and political aspects of Cork City's development since the eighteenth century.

The visitor will see the ebb and flow of Cork's industrial past, where butter making, glass manufacture and silver working were once dominant, but are now nonexistent in modern Cork's industrial landscape. The civic exhibition enlivens us to the history of past Cork mayors, and the legendary Lord Mayors like Tomás MacCurtain and Terence MacSwiney, who both died in 1920 during the Irish War of Independence. The road to Irish independence is long and detailed, and Cork Public Museum traces the roles played by many Cork people in achieving this aim, from the eighteenth to the early twentieth century.

From amateur genealogists to university academics, Cork Public Museum proves invaluable to researchers and students alike. The museum houses a vast amount of artefacts and documents in its reserve collection. Though they may never be publically exhibited, they need to be protected and preserved, so that future generations can have access to this material to aid further research and education in the future. Cork Public Museum has served people from Cork and further afield since 1910, and its intent and desire is to continue as custodians of Cork's historical and archaeological legacy for the foreseeable future.